D1127059

*The Beginnings of Rhetorical Theory
in Classical Greece*

EDWARD SCHIAPPA

The Beginnings of Rhetorical Theory in Classical Greece

Yale University Press
New Haven &
London

In memoriam matris

Set in Sabon type by Keystone Typesetting, Inc.
Printed in the United States of America.

Library of Congress Cataloging-in-Publication Data

Schiappa, Edward, 1954–
    The beginnings of rhetorical theory in classical Greece / Edward
Schiappa.
        p.   cm.
    Includes bibliographical references and index.
    ISBN 0-300-07590-1 (cl. : alk. paper)
    1. Greek literature — History and criticism — Theory, etc.
2. Criticism — Greece — History.   3. Rhetoric, Ancient.   I. Title.
PA401.S24   1999
808'.00938 — dc21   98-42659
                                                                CIP

A catalogue record for this book is available from the British Library.

The paper in this book meets the guidelines for permanence and durability of the
Committee on Production Guidelines for Book Longevity of the Council on Library Resources.

10   9   8   7   6   5   4   3   2   1

Contents

Preface

In 1998 I became convinced that the Greek word for rhetoric was a later linguistic innovation than has been assumed in almost all historical accounts of early Greek rhetorical theory. Over the past decade I have been relieved to learn that I am not alone in this belief. Nonetheless, there is still considerable skepticism about the importance of the coining of this term, *Rhētorikē,* both for the work of ancient Greeks theorizing about discourse education and for contemporary historical accounts of rhetoric and philosophy. This book is intended to contribute to a scholarly conversation about the origins of rhetorical theory that is taking place in four disciplines: classics, philosophy, communication studies, and English. It has been an invigorating discussion involving issues of philology, methodology, historiography, and philosophy of language. I am appreciative of all those who have joined in, perhaps especially those who have challenged my work and thus encouraged me to refine my thinking and my arguments.

The debts I have accumulated while completing this project are too numerous to list, so I must be satisfied with hitting the highlights. John T. Kirby, Wilfred E. Major, and Steven Mailloux read the entire manuscript and did their best to keep my mistakes to a minimum. I am particularly grateful for John Kirby's patience, counsel, and friendship. David Timmerman, Stacey Hoffman, and Wilfred E. Major co-wrote specific portions that are identified accordingly. For the past two years Michael Tiffany has worked as my tireless research assistant and has been enormously helpful. André Lardinois and Elizabeth Belfiore have provided valuable feedback to my many queries since my arrival at the University of Minnesota in 1995. I know I have been very lucky, indeed. I cannot imagine a more supportive group of friends and colleagues than the scholars I have benefited from over the past eight years.

Portions of this book have appeared previously in assorted venues. I am grateful for the opportunity to bring it all together in one place where I hope the whole of the argument is greater than the sum of its parts. My thanks to the National Communication Association, Northwestern University Press, the *Rhetoric Review* Association of America, Pennsylvania State University Press, Cambridge University Press, and Victor J. Vitanza for permission to reprint the portions that they previously published.

A special debt of thanks is owed to George A. Kennedy, who published my first essay on classical rhetoric and to this day is wonderfully supportive of my work. His graciousness as a scholar and a gentleman is no longer a surprise to me, but is always pleasant to experience.

Note on Translations and Abbreviations

To keep the book accessible to scholars in a variety of disciplines, all Greek and Latin passages are translated into English. Quotations from most ancient authors are cited by the name of the text and the standard section number. For example, "*Funeral Oration* Lysias, 67" refers to the text of Lysias commonly referred to as the "Funeral Oration" at section 67. For Plato's texts the Oxford Classical Texts series by John Burnet was consulted, along with the translations of Edith Hamilton and Huntington Cairns (1961) and Reginald Allen (1984–1991). For Aristotle, I relied most often on the collection of translations by Jonathan Barnes (1984), except with respect to translating Aristotle *Rhetoric,* in which case the obvious choice is George A. Kennedy (1991). Unless indicated otherwise, the remaining Greek text and English translations are from the relevant Loeb Classical Library editions published by Harvard University Press.

The standard collection of surviving fragments concerning the Older Sophists is that of Herman Diels and Walther Kranz (1951–52); traditionally abbreviated DK. Fragments are divided into sections A and B, the first of which consists of statements by later writers concerning the life, writings, and doctrines of the person in question. The second records fragments which Diels and Kranz believe are quotations from the person's writings. Hence, Protagoras' "human-measure" fragment is cited as DK 80 B1. English translations of fragments of or about the Older Sophists (DK 79 through DK 90) are generally from Rosamond Kent Sprague (1972). For Gorgias' texts see also Thomas Buchheim (1989).

*Reconstructing the Origins
of Rhetorical Theory*

I

The Standard Account of Rhetoric's Beginnings

This book is an effort to revise the traditional accounts of the Older Sophists and early Greek theorizing about rhetorical theory. Before revising the standard account, I need first to describe it. The purpose of this chapter is to provide a summary of the claims that embody the standard account and to identify its key "facts" and assumptions. These claims are the focus of the remaining chapters in Part I of this book.

By "standard account" I mean the historical description of the origins of rhetorical theory that is found in the most prevalent sources on the subject, and that is so widely held as to turn up in the majority of secondary discussions of Greek rhetoric. I have no doubt that I have overgeneralized and over-simplified various scholars' positions in the account that follows. It would be difficult to find a single scholar who would agree with every single claim identified. Nonetheless, I believe that the following is sufficiently grounded in the literature to be considered a fair approximation of the standard account.

One study reports that George A. Kennedy's *Classical Rhetoric and Its Christian and Secular Tradition from Ancient to Modern Times* (1980) is the most commonly used secondary source in graduate courses on classical rhetorical theory (Enos 1989, 45–48). Combined with his earlier work, *The Art of Persuasion in Greece* (1963), and his more recent *A New History of Classical Rhetoric* (1994), Kennedy's texts have become the standard reference works in English on early Greek rhetoric for classical scholarship and pedagogy from which other standard reference works differ only marginally. Accordingly, my analysis of the standard account focuses primarily — though not exclusively — on Kennedy's texts.[1]

The "Invention" of Rhetoric and the Handbook Tradition

The basic facts of the standard account of the "invention" of the Art of Rhetoric are as follows: The overthrow of tyranny in Sicily around 467 B.C.E. and the resulting establishment of a democracy created a sudden demand for the teaching of rhetoric for citizens' use in the law-courts and in the assembly. Two Sicilians, Corax and Tisias, responded to this demand by "inventing" rhetorical theory through the introduction of the first written *Art of Rhetoric*. The primary theoretical contributions of Corax and Tisias were the identification of the parts of forensic speeches and the theory of the "argument from probability."

The story that credits Corax with the "invention" of rhetoric is widely accepted by historians of early rhetoric. Kennedy's version of the story is as follows:

> In Syracuse in Sicily . . . democracy on the Athenian pattern was introduced suddenly in 467 B.C. Citizens found themselves involved in litigation over the ownership of property or other matters and forced to take up their own cases before the courts. Nowhere in Greece did the profession of lawyer, advocate, or patron at the bar exist. Need to speak in the democratic Syracusan assembly was less pressing, but opportunities for political leadership came to involve the skill of public speaking in a way not previously evident. A few clever Sicilians developed simple techniques (Greek *technē* means "art") for effective presentation and argumentation in the law courts and taught these to others for a price. (Kennedy 1980, 18–19)

Most modern scholarship tends to regard the story of Corax and Tisias inventing the art of rhetoric as questionable only with regard to details. Though in doubt about the cause and effect relationship between the rise of democracy and the teaching of rhetoric, M. I. Finley declares that "it is a fact that Corax of Syracuse and his pupil Tisias were the founders of the Greek art of rhetoric" (1968, 61). Friedrich Blass (1887, 1: 17–23), D. A. G. Hinks (1940), M. L. Clark (1957), D. C. Bryant (1968), W. K. C. Guthrie (1971), and James J.

---

1. As Michael Gagarin notes, Kennedy is "the most important contemporary scholar of Greek rhetoric writing in English" (1990, 23n).

Murphy (1972) have all written standard reference works or textbooks that accept the general validity of the Corax and Tisias legend.[2]

Kennedy categorizes the teachings of Corax and Tisias as part of a tradition he describes as "technical rhetoric." The most commonly held beliefs concerning fifth-century technical rhetoric can be distilled into a series of specific claims:

> 1. The Art of Rhetoric originates with Corax of Sicily around 467 B.C.E.
>
> 2. Corax was probably the teacher of Tisias, a fellow Sicilian.
>
> 3. Corax and/or Tisias authored the first *technē,* or book designated as an Art of Rhetoric.
>
> 4. Corax/Tisias may have been the first to define rhetoric, specifically as "the artificer of persuasion."[3]
>
> 5. An important contribution of Corax's and/or Tisias' handbook was the identification of the parts of forensic speeches. Though the specific number of parts differs from account to account (3, 4, 5, or 7), few scholars doubt that some practical system of division was introduced by Corax, Tisias, or both.
>
> 6. The primary theoretical contribution was their identification of the "argument from probability."
>
> 7. By the end of the fifth century B.C.E., written technical handbooks (*technai*) were commonly available to which people could turn to learn rhetoric (Kennedy 1980, 19).
>
> 8. Most early teaching of the Art of Rhetoric, including that of Corax and/or Tisias, concentrated on forensic rhetoric; that is, the successful pleading of one's case in a law-court. Since the Greek judicial system required individuals to defend themselves, rhetoric quickly became an attractive subject of study (Kennedy 1980, 19).

Though most scholars agree that the story is probably apocryphal, the following anecdote is often repeated in connection with early accounts of Corax and Tisias:

> Tisias was a pupil of Corax who refused to pay for his instruction. Upon being dragged into court he argued that if he won the dispute he need not pay by that decision, if he lost, however, payment would be unjust since the art would be proved worthless. Corax replied by reversing the argument. The

2. For other textbooks that set forth the basic story as probably true, see Foss, Foss, and Trapp (1991, 1–2), Enos (1993), and Golden, Berquist, and Coleman (1993, 5). The influence of the Corax/Tisias legend is further illustrated by recent writings that retell the standard account, usually but not always taking it at face value: Jamieson (1988, 47); Billig (1987, 35); Vickers (1988, 6); Eagleton (1981); Stone (1988, 90); Welch (1990, 113–19).

3. See Kennedy (1963, 61); Cope (1855, 11–12); Vickers (1988, 6); Marrou (1956, 53).

> court turned them both out with the epigram "a bad egg from a bad crow" (*korax*). (Kennedy 1963, 59)

Fiction or not, the very existence of the story is often cited as evidence that rhetoric and its early teachers often were not held in high esteem. The story also tends to reinforce the belief that Tisias was once a student of Corax, a point to which I return in chapter 3.

According to Kennedy, the defining characteristic of technical rhetoric was its emphasis on rhetorical handbooks. In addition to noting the emphasis on forensic rhetoric, argument from probability, and the proper organization of speeches (all noted above), Kennedy's account identifies several other facets of the handbook tradition that can be rendered into specific claims.

> 9. At least some of the handbooks "included discussions of *style,* specifically of the various kinds of diction available to the orator and the forms of linguistic ornamentation which he could use" (Kennedy 1980, 20).

Aristotle's lost work *Synagōgē Technōn,* or *Collection of the Arts,* was a summary of the rhetorical handbooks still extant in the mid-fourth century that "seems to have rendered the survival of the original [including fifth-century] handbooks superfluous. They ceased to be copied and preserved" (Kennedy 1980, 19). Accordingly, some scholars believe that:

> 10. No fifth-century rhetorical handbooks exist because Aristotle's writings made them obsolete.

Sophistic and Philosophical Rhetoric

During the mid- to late fifth century, a competing approach to the purely technical teaching of rhetoric appeared through the teaching practices of the Older Sophists: Students learned rhetoric primarily through imitating exemplary speeches. Kennedy describes this method as the tradition of "Sophistic" rhetoric. The Sophists were mostly non-Athenian Greeks who could not participate directly in Athens' politics, but who earned substantial amounts of money as itinerant orators and teachers of rhetoric. Because their teaching was theoretically modest and philosophically relativistic, and emphasized political success above all else, the Sophists motivated Plato and Aristotle to develop more *philosophical* treatments of rhetoric. Hence, according to Kennedy, three traditions of rhetorical theory are identifiable in the fifth and fourth centuries B.C.E.: technical, Sophistic, and philosophical.

Though there is no overwhelming consensus regarding the Sophists, a number of claims can be identified as accepted in most historical accounts of the Sophists and "Sophistic" rhetoric.

11. Though specifically held doctrines may have varied, there was a commonly identified group of individuals in the fifth century known as the Sophists. The group included Protagoras, Gorgias, Hippias, Prodicus, Thrasymachus, Critias, and Antiphon.

12. The most important shared characteristic of the Sophists was that they all taught an Art of Rhetoric.

Eric A. Havelock claims that "of course they [the Sophists] taught rhetoric" (1957, 230). John Poulakos agrees: the Sophists "all taught rhetoric" (1995, 18). Rhetoric is one subject that all fifth-century Sophists "taught in common," declares Guthrie in his acclaimed *History of Greek Philosophy* (1971, 44). Heinrich Gomperz virtually equates the Sophists with rhetoric in *Sophistik und Rhetorik,* suggesting, for example, that all of Protagoras' teachings radiated from what he calls the "rhetorical center" (1912, 282). The teaching of rhetoric ran through the entire Sophistic movement "like a red thread," according to Wilhelm Kroll (1940, 1043). These examples can be multiplied. Not only do almost all treatments of the early Sophists take for granted that rhetoric represented a distinct subject or discipline that the Sophists taught; many conclude that *all* aspects of Sophistic teaching had to do with rhetoric.

Believing that rhetoric must be concerned chiefly with the speaker's ability to adapt to an audience's beliefs, Sophistic teaching allegedly promoted a certain amount of catering to the appetites of different listeners. The result was an approach to rhetoric that favored a kind of situational ethics. Based on the perceived link between rhetorical instruction and relativism, a number of scholars contrast "rhetorical" pursuits with non-relativistic "philosophical" teachings. Douglas J. Stewart's introduction to the fragments of Prodicus endorses the "prevailing opinion" that the "real interests" of all the Sophists were rhetorical and hence "their reported views and writings on special questions in science, history, or politics are normally taken as mere methodological devices and stances bound up with their prime goal of teaching their pupils cultural and political adroitness" (in Sprague 1972, 70–71). Kennedy once asserted that in the tracts of Sophists such as Gorgias, "the subject matter was apparently of only incidental importance — a fact which awakened the opposition of Socrates. The technique was the thing: the Sophist is purely rhetorician" (1959, 170). Bruce A. Kimball's *Orators and Philosophers: A History of the Idea of Liberal Education* exemplifies this tendency: "The Sophists thus attended more to devising persuasive techniques than to finding true arguments, and this amoralism exacerbated the disintegration of the ethical tradition and led to their condemnation" (1986, 17).

Three specific claims can be adduced from such comments:

13. The rhetorical teachings of the Sophists were amoral: "Writers of such handbooks usually do not regard it as part of their task to tell an orator what cases he should or should not undertake or what should be the limits of his appeal to an audience; they do undertake to tell him how to present any case as effectively as possible" (Kennedy 1980, 22).

14. The Sophists were relativists who eschewed any positive notion of "truth" in favor of subjectivism. This claim is closely related to the next.

15. The Sophists were more concerned with teaching political success than pursuing "truth," per se.

Most of the specific contributions of individual Sophists have been interpreted through the "rhetorical" framework described above. So, for example, Protagoras has been described as the "father of debate" since he is credited with claiming that there are "two sides to every argument." He is also often considered a subjective relativist because he claimed that "Man is the measure of all things: of the things that are, that they are; and of the things that are not, that they are not." Prodicus' interest in distinguishing the meaning of apparent synonyms is viewed as an early effort to correct language used by orators. Gorgias is most often remembered for his highly poetic style and his heavy use of what have come to be called "Gorgianic figures." In short, once the general premise is accepted that the Sophists were occupied chiefly with the teaching of rhetoric, the specific fragments and doctrines attributed to them are often understood as part and parcel of such rhetorical training. The "verdict" of much of posterity has wavered between Plato's outright condemnation of Sophistic rhetoric to Hegel's assignment of the Sophists to the status of a necessary foil for Plato's and Aristotle's reformed view of rhetoric — necessary because their views were excessively subjective and relativistic.

A relatively recent line of thought concerning Sophistic rhetoric requires mention at this point. One can find in the writings of Hegel (1914) and Friedrich Nietzsche (see Consigny 1994) the beginnings of a more positive assessment of the Sophists' contribution to the intellectual milieu of ancient Greece. Due, I think, to the efforts of George Grote (1851) more than Hegel or Nietzsche, a number of scholars in the past century have returned to the evidence concerning the Sophists and have provided a far more balanced and productive picture of their achievements than one finds in the dialogues of Plato — the primary source for the "traditional" pejorative account of the Sophists.[4] The rehabilitating work of such scholars as Eugène Dupréel (1948), Mario Untersteiner (1954), George Kerferd (1981a, 1981b), and Jacqueline de Romilly

---

4. On Grote's importance to the positive recovery of the Sophists, see Kerferd (1981b, 8–9) and Schiappa (1991, 9–11).

(1988) has done much to restore the reputation of the Sophists to respectability and to challenge aspects of the standard account. Typically these scholars interpret the philosophy of the Sophists as part of Sophistic rhetorical theory, or vice versa. In most cases, though not all, contributions to Sophistic rhetoric and to Sophistic philosophy are understood as discrete; for example, William M. A. Grimaldi refers to "Sophists who engaged in philosophy and other disciplines as well as those who devoted themselves mostly to rhetoric" (1996, 27).

Consistent with such efforts to reassess the philosophical content of individual Sophists' surviving texts and fragments, a number of scholars have sought to reevaluate our understanding of Sophistic rhetoric. For the most part, these accounts accept the basic thrust of claims 11–15 above, but reverse the traditional normative evaluation. The scholars I will refer to as Neosophistic rhetorical theorists accept the traditional account that a specific group of Sophists taught a relativistic rhetorical theory, but suggest that such a theory was and is justified and appropriate.

A number of scholars — primarily within English and communication departments — have encouraged a return to the study of Sophistic rhetorical theory as a valuable source of insight into contemporary rhetorical theory and practice.[5] Neosophistic scholars obviously do not accept the wildest claims of the Sophists' critics, such as Hegel's assertion that the Sophists led to the moral decay and downfall of ancient Greece. But for the most part the claims identified above are only modified or recontextualized.

John Poulakos may be the most prolific contemporary scholar writing about Sophistic rhetoric. In an important essay, "Toward a Sophistic Definition of Rhetoric" (1983c), Poulakos specifically embraces the traditional list of seven "Older Sophists" and attempts to describe a definition of rhetoric common to the group. I therefore think it is fair to assume that he would subscribe to claims 11 and 12 above. In a series of essays, Poulakos has described Sophistic theory and practice in terms that resonate with certain tenets of existentialism and postmodernism. Accordingly, if claims 13–15 above were translated into such a vocabulary, I believe that he and other Neosophists would assent to them.

Plato and Rhetoric

In virtually all historical accounts of Greek rhetorical theory, Sophistic rhetoric is viewed as leading to Plato's philosophical critique. The standard

5. In English see Consigny (1996), Crowley (1989), Jarratt (1991), McComiskey (1993, 1994), Moss (1982), Neel (1988), and Vitanza (1997); in comparative literature see Mailloux (1995); in communication see John Poulakos (1983c, 1984, 1987, 1995).

account generally paints Sophistic rhetoric as in need of correction: "Because of its newness, it [rhetoric] tended to overdo experiments in argument and style. Not only did it easily seem vulgar or tasteless, it could seem to treat the truth with indifference and to make the worse seem the better cause. Reaction was predictable, and that reaction produced what may conveniently be termed 'philosophical' rhetoric" (Kennedy 1980, 41).[6]

Neosophistic scholars would generally agree that Plato attacked Sophistic rhetoric in order to constrain its influence; they differ from tradition both in their assessments of the value of the Sophistic rhetoric that Plato condemned and in the evaluation of Plato's account of rhetoric. Despite the Neosophists' alternative normative assessments, I believe that the claims identified below are shared by traditionalists and revisionists.

Plato's most thorough discussion of rhetoric is found in two dialogues. The *Gorgias* dates to the 380s B.C.E. and is considered an early dialogue, while the *Phaedrus* dates some decades later and is commonly regarded as representing a more balanced and mature view of rhetoric. The details concerning Plato's treatments of rhetoric are best dealt with elsewhere. For the moment, the following two claims are sufficient to note as those commonly shared by most accounts of early Greek rhetoric:

> 16. Plato's philosophical rhetorical theory was formulated primarily in response to fifth-century Sophistic rhetorical theory.
> 17. Plato's philosophical rhetorical theory can be distinguished from Sophistic rhetorical theory by its commitment to truth — even when truth conflicts with political success.

The above set of seventeen claims provides a useful starting point for providing an alternative account of the origins of Greek rhetorical theory. Despite the popularity of the standard account, I believe that it is flawed on every point.

Method and Organization

This book is informed by several theoretical beliefs that may be usefully identified at the outset. The first is that the original words of ancient theorists, the *ipsissima verba*, should be given priority over accounts of those theorists by later writers. The most important practical implication of such a belief is that Plato and Aristotle, in particular, are not considered wholly reliable guides to the status of the Greek theorizing about discourse that took place prior to them. The second belief is that one important and useful way to

---

6. More recent work suggesting Plato was reacting appropriately to the Sophists' rhetorical excesses includes Golden, Berquist, and Coleman (1993, 13–28).

approach intellectual history is by attending to the key terms — in some instances the technical vocabulary — found in various theorists' texts. The most telling example of the importance of this belief (in fact, the example that motivated this whole book) is the philological evidence supporting the claim that the Greek word for rhetoric (*rhētorikē*) originates in the early *fourth* century B.C.E., and thus it is somewhat anachronistic to talk of "theories of rhetoric" prior to that time. A more careful charting of the development of the technical vocabulary of Greek rhetorical theory provides, I believe, a very different picture of that theorizing — and especially the role of the Older Sophists in that theorizing — than the portrait that has been dominant for many years.

My interest in the precise vocabulary used in the fifth and fourth centuries follows the traditions of classical philology spiced with the insights of two twentieth-century writers: Thomas S. Kuhn and Michel Foucault. Historian and philosopher of science Kuhn argues that to comprehend the history of past theories one must understand the technical vocabulary of such theories: "To understand some body of past scientific belief, the historian must acquire a lexicon that here and there differs systematically from the one current in his [or her] own day. Only by using that older lexicon can he or she accurately render certain of the statements that are basic to the science under scrutiny" (1989, 9). Influenced by such philosophers of language as Ludwig Wittgenstein and Willard V. O. Quine, Kuhn contends that "To possess a lexicon, a structured vocabulary, is to have access to the varied set of worlds which that lexicon can be used to describe. Different lexicons — those of different cultures or different historical periods, for example — give access to different sets of possible worlds, largely but never entirely overlapping" (1989, 11). Kuhn suggests that one of the defining characteristics of a scientific revolution is that "the set of objects or situations" that scientists produce discourse *about* — that to which their terminology refers or "attaches" — changes (1987, 19). In short, in a paradigm shift, one "terministic screen" is replaced with another: "What characterizes revolutions is, thus, change in several of the taxonomic categories *prerequisite* to scientific descriptions and generalizations" (1987, 20, emphasis added). My argument is that the introduction of the term *rhētorikē* signals a revolution of sorts in the way discourse education was thought about. Although Kuhn is talking about the history of the physical sciences, the applicability of his insights is illustrated by classicist Eric A. Havelock's work. Havelock contends that when we superimpose a later-developed conceptual vocabulary upon the texts of the fifth century, we distort "the story of early Greek thought by presenting it as an intellectual game dealing with problems already given and present to the mind, rather than as a groping after a new language in which the existence of such problems will slowly emerge" (1983,

57). Thomas Cole applies this insight to the study of Greek rhetorical theory when he argues that the origin of rhetorical theory is when a metalanguage is introduced for the study of discourse — including the introduction of the term *rhētorikē* (1991a). Foucault brings to the table a concern for the ideological work to which specialized vocabularies are put (1972). As I argue in chapter 2, the act of naming matters because we never describe phenomena neutrally. Our thoughts, attitudes, and behaviors are influenced by the language we have to make sense of the world. When that language changes, so do we.

The third key belief is that classical Greece underwent a transition from a predominantly oral culture to a culture in which literacy became increasingly widespread and, consequently, became an important social and intellectual resource. Both the form and the content of the texts we now regard as pertinent to the history of theorizing about discourse contributed to and were a product of a changing intellectual milieu (Cole 1991a; Robb 1994; Thomas and Webb 1994). I argue in several chapters that follow that recognition of greater "book-oriented" literacy during the fifth and fourth century and of attendant changes in modes of expression is helpful to understanding certain aspects of classical Greek rhetorical theory and practice.

The usefulness of these theoretical beliefs cannot be proven in advance, but can be demonstrated only through their use. In an earlier book, *Protagoras and Logos: A Study in Greek Philosophy and Rhetoric,* I utilized these beliefs to provide an improved understanding of Protagoras' contributions to early Greek theorizing. In the chapters that follow, I turn to the status of the distinct discipline of rhetoric and to the contributions of such figures as Gorgias, Isocrates, and Aristotle.

Part I of this book is an effort to justify revisiting the question of the origins of Greek rhetorical theory and calling into question the seventeen points summarized above. The next chapter is a sustained argument for why the issue of the dating of the Greek word *rhētorikē* should matter to historians interested in the origins of rhetorical theory. Chapter 3 calls into doubt the standard story of the origins of rhetoric; namely, that the discipline began when two Sicilians initiated "technical rhetoric" by publishing a technical handbook of rhetoric to assist participants in a new democracy. Chapter 4 calls into question the usefulness of the construct "Sophistic rhetoric." Chapter 5 identifies the problems with the belief that Plato and Aristotle formulated a "philosophical rhetoric" and that their predecessors did not.

An alternative approach to the relevant texts of the fifth and fourth century is illustrated in Parts II and III. A recurring theme developed here is that fifth-century texts ought to be considered "predisciplinary." That is, such texts were produced at a time when categories that we take for granted — most significantly, "Rhetoric" and "Philosophy"—were far from clearly recognized, accepted, or influential to the theorizing of the period. Part II consists of studies of three texts by Gorgias of Leontini. Chapter 6, "Gorgias' Composition Style," challenges the long-held negative verdict on the merits of Gorgias' style and argues that a more positive assessment is warranted. Chapter 7, "Reconsidering Gorgias' *Helen*," contends that most previous studies of Gorgias' text impose inappropriate disciplinary expectations on the text. Chapter 8, "Rhetoric and Philosophy in *On Not Being*," offers a critical assessment of how "being" ought to be understood in Gorgias' infamous argument.

Part III consists of three case studies of fourth-century efforts to "disciplinize" discourse through, in part, the introduction and development of a technical vocabulary. Chapter 9, "Early Use of the Terms *Rhētoreia* and *Rhētoreuein*," examines the use of the precise terms for "oratory" and "to orate" and concludes that the terms emerged much later than is typically assumed and have a wide range of meanings that are underappreciated. Chapter 10 explores Isocrates' *philosophia* and challenges the way in which Isocrates is traditionally placed as a pivotal figure in the history of rhetoric while being all but ignored by historians of philosophy. Chapter 11 provides Aristotle's descriptions of the genre of epideictic as a prototypical example of what is meant in this book as the disciplining of discourse.

It is my hope that this book will provide encouragement to other scholars to explore these very old texts in new ways.[7] The arguments offered here are intended to suggest a new direction for the historical study of early Greek rhetorical theory. By taking seriously the changing technical vocabulary of fifth and fourth-century thinkers, the resulting picture of the development of rhetorical theory will vary considerably from the standard account.

In some of the chapters I discuss historiographical issues of ideology and social construction. It is my belief that a more self-reflexive stance than is usually found in classics research not only produces better scholarship and more interesting reading; it is also more intellectually honest. But I leave it to the reader to decide the merits of this belief—a belief I regard as the single most important claim advanced in this book.

7. See, for example, such work as Arthurs (1994), Cassin (1995, 411–13), Jacob (1996), Lu (1998), Major (1996), Papillon (1995, 1996), and Timmerman (1993, 1998).

2

The Origins of the Word Rhētorikē
What Does It Matter?

The starting point for many of the claims of this project concerns the dating and subsequent use of the Greek word for rhetoric, *rhētorikē*. My claim is that the word does not enter widespread usage among the writers we traditionally associate with the history of rhetorical theory until the early decades of the fourth century B.C.E. I also claim that the use of the word matters to how we interpret the texts of the fifth and fourth centuries B.C.E. For ease of reference I will refer to these two claims as the "origins-of-*rhētorikē* thesis." In this chapter I review the arguments in support of the origins-of-*rhētorikē* thesis and the arguments of those scholars who have challenged it. I should note that most of the claims advanced concerning the specific texts discussed in subsequent chapters can be judged independently of how viable readers may ultimately find the origins-of-*rhētorikē* thesis. Nonetheless, the thesis is of sufficient importance to require explicit restatement and defense.

The philological evidence for the origins-of-*rhētorikē* thesis is straightforward: The word *rhētorikē* simply cannot be found in any text that has been dated prior to Plato's *Gorgias*, usually dated to the 380s B.C.E.[1] I am far from the first to call attention to the surprisingly late appearance of the term. In

---

1. Even Debra Nails, despite her challenge to traditional chronologies of Plato's dialogues, acknowledges that Plato's Academy began about 387 and that the *Gorgias* would have been an ideal "college brochure" to advertise its opening (1995, 213–15).

1934 Werner Pilz noted in passing that the word "*rhētorikē* is not found prior to Plato."[2] The same observation can be found in Wilhelm Kroll's influential essay on rhetoric in the German classical encyclopedia *Paulys Realencyclopädie der classischen Altertumswissenschaft* (1940, 1039), J. W. H. Atkins' article on Greek rhetoric in the first edition of the *Oxford Classical Dictionary* (1949, 766), the *Greek-English Lexicon* by Henry George Liddell and Robert Scott (1940, 1569), and, subsequently, H. Hommel's note on rhetoric in *Der Kleine Pauly* (1972, 4: 1396) and Josef Martin's *Antike Rhetorik* (1974, 2). A search of the entire database of Greek texts in the *Thesaurus Linguae Graecae* supports the claim that the earliest surviving use of the Greek word for rhetoric is in the dialogues of Plato.[3] Only one scholar has disagreed in print with the claim that there are no extant pre-fourth-century B.C.E. texts that contain *rhētorikē* (Poulakos 1990), but his examples have been adequately addressed elsewhere and I know of no other scholar who shares his views (see Schiappa 1990b).

I have hypothesized previously that Plato may have coined the word to portray and define the teachings of his rival Isocrates (Schiappa 1990a). Plato's penchant for coining technical jargon is well documented, particular with respect to terms denoting verbal arts. He coined a wide assortment of words ending with *-ikē* ("art of") and *-ikos* (which, depending on context, denotes a person with a particular skill). One study documents that of the more than 350 *-ikos* words in Plato, more than 250 are not found earlier (Chantraine 1956, 97–171). A computer search of the entire database of the *Thesaurus Linguae Graecae* project suggests that the Greek words for eristic (*eristikē*), dialectic (*dialektikē*), and antilogic (*antilogikē*), like rhetoric, all originate in Plato's works (Schiappa 1990a, 464).[4] As Thomas Cole concludes, there is "no trace" of *rhētorikē* before Plato's *Gorgias,* and the word itself "bears every indication of being a Platonic invention" (Cole 1991a, 2). Egil A. Wyller agrees that *rhētorikē* is "a term which he [Plato] himself coined . . . in the Syracusan-inspired dialogue *Gorgias*" (1991, 52).

The claim that Plato may have been the person who coined the term *rhētor-*

---

2. "'Ρητορικ- findet sich nicht vor Plato" (Pilz 1934, 15).

3. See Schiappa (1991, app. B). The *Thesaurus Linguae Graecae* project provides a comprehensive computer-based data bank of all available ancient Greek texts. Its database can be searched for specific words, stems, or collections of words. For an overview of the *Thesaurus Linguae Graecae* project, see Luci Berkowitz and Karl A. Squitier (1990, xi–xlix).

4. A search for the stems *eristik-, antilogik-,* and *dialektik-* in all corrected and uncorrected *Thesaurus Linguae Graecae* texts was conducted by *Thesaurus Linguae Graecae* director Theodore Brunner in March 1990 at the request of the author. See also A. N. Ammann (1953, 25–26, 55–57, 80, 176–77).

ikē is not a necessary part of the origins-of-*rhētorikē* thesis. Though Plato is the likeliest suspect, the thesis does not stand or fall on such a belief. The origins-of-*rhētorikē* thesis simply states that the term is novel in the early fourth century B.C.E. — nothing more and nothing less.

Two objections to the origins-of-*rhētorikē* thesis deserve consideration. First, the argument has been made that the term *rhētorikē* was in use but simply does not survive in any extant text. In the case of *rhētorikē*, however, the argument "from silence" gains strength when one surveys the wide variety of materials that survives and that can be reasonably expected to employ the word. A wealth of material reflecting the intellectual climate of fifth-century Greece appears in the extensive histories of Herodotus and Thucydides, the philosophical texts and fragments of the Presocratics, the extant plays of Euripides, Aristophanes, and Sophocles, and the surviving speeches and sayings of the early Sophists. Moreover, as illustrated in subsequent chapters, a number of surviving texts explicitly are concerned with what we now would classify as persuasive speaking, such as Aristophanes' *Clouds* and *Wasps,* the text known as *Dialexeis* or *Dissoi Logoi,* and the preserved texts of the so-called Older Sophists (including the noteworthy *Encomium to Helen* of Gorgias). I discuss these texts throughout this book in order to show that what they "mean" is nontrivially different than what they would have meant had they used the term *rhētorikē.* For the moment, I would reassert the belief that the fact that *rhētorikē* fails to appear in any of these documents, even in passages explicitly concerned with persuasive speaking or education, is compelling evidence for a later date for the coining of *rhētorikē.*

Several scholars have argued that even though no texts using *rhētorikē* prior to Plato's *Gorgias* are extant, the term must have been in use significantly prior to its writing. The most developed argument of this sort has been made by Neil O'Sullivan, who posits that the manner in which the term *rhētorikē* is introduced in Plato's *Gorgias* proves that the term was already well known. Other scholars, including George A. Kennedy, Michael Gagarin, Stephen Halliwell, and Robert Wardy, make the same argument in passing comments that attempt to dismiss the origins-of-*rhētorikē* thesis.

My original argument was twofold; first, I noted that surviving instances of the word indicate that its use in Plato's *Gorgias* is novel. As O'Sullivan observes, most writings of the Older Sophists have disappeared. But as I have just noted, the *argumentum ex silentio* gains credence given the absence of *rhētorikē* in the wide variety of extant materials can be expected to employ the word. Even in the fourth century the word *rhētorikē* scarcely can be found outside of Plato and Aristotle. Isocrates, for example, never once uses *rhētorikē.* O'Sullivan et al. offer no explanation whatsoever for the fact that *rhētorikē* does not appear in any of these documents, even in passages explicitly concerned with persuasive speaking or education.

O'Sullivan pokes fun at my idea that *rhētorikē* should have appeared in Aristophanes' *Clouds* had it been a word in common use: "The implicit assumption here is that every term — at best every important term — used by the Sophists was included in Aristophanes' play, a fantasy worthy of the playwright himself" (1993, 87). But here we are not talking about *an* important term — such as *epideiktikē* or *orthoepeia* — we are talking about *the* word that is often used to sum up the entire teachings of the Sophists; a term that both Plato (*Gorgias* 465c, 520b) and Aristotle (*Rhetoric* 1355b17–21) treat on par with the art of *sophistikē* itself (Striker 1997, 9). J. D. Denniston has amply documented Aristophanes' habit of using and making fun of Sophistic terminology (1927). Examinations of *logos, technē,* and *physis* abound in Aristophanes, and he had great fun with these words in numerous substantive, verbal, adjectival, and adverbial forms. He similarly had sport with *dialexis, dialegesthai,* and *agoreuō.* Given such activity, one could expect the playwright to allude to the Art of Rhetoric by means of puns or metaphors related to *rhēnai* ("to flow") or the stem *rhētorik.* It is difficult *not* to find in Aristophanes most terms pertaining to the verbal arts except, of course, *rhētorikē.* Accordingly, it is hard to imagine that he would omit *rhētorikē* from plays such as *Wasps* and *Clouds* had it been used by the Sophists to describe their teachings.[5]

Consider also the following passage from *Dialexeis,* or *Dissoi Logoi,* a text traditionally dated about 400 B.C.E.: "I believe it belongs to the same man and to the same skill to be able to hold dialogue succinctly, to understand the truth of things, to plead one's court-cases correctly, to be able to make popular speeches, to understand argument-skills, and to teach about the nature of all things — how they are [their condition] and how they came to be" (*Dialexeis* 8.1).[6] *Dialexeis* 8 virtually cries out for the use of such simple terms as *rhētorikē* and *dialektikē.* Yet they do not appear. Why not? Perhaps because, as Cole and I surmise, such Platonic terms had not yet entered into common usage.

My second argument was that Plato has a documented penchant for coining terms ending in *ikē,* particularly for terms designating verbal arts. O'Sullivan's sole counterargument is that Plato's use of the phrase *tēn kaloumenēn rhētor-*

---

5. My thanks to Michael Tiffany for contributing to this analysis of Aristophanes.

6. ⟨τῷ αὐτῷ⟩ ἀνδρὸς καὶ τᾶς αὐτᾶς τέχνας νομίζω κατὰ βραχύ τε δύνασθαι διαλέγεσθαι, καὶ ⟨τὰν⟩ ἀλάθειαν τῶν πραγμάτων ἐπίστασθαι, καὶ δικάζεν ἐπίστασθαι ὀρθῶς, καὶ δ ἀμαγοῖρεῖν οἷόν τ' ἦμεν, καὶ λόγων τέχνας ἐπίσταθαι, καὶ περὶ φύσιος τῶν ἁπάντων ὥς τε ἔχει καὶ ὡς ἐγένετο, διδάσκεν (DK 90.8.1) For text and translation see Robinson (1979).

ikēn (*Gorgias* 448d9) is "really fatal" to my case, for "it must mean 'that which is called' " and cannot refer to a neologism or a new significance (1993, 87). Similarly, Kennedy argues that "the dramatic date of the dialogue is in the late fifth century, and both Gorgias and Polus are represented there as accepting the term without objection" (1994, 7n). Gagarin points to the phrase *tēn kaloumenēn rhētorikēn* as suggesting "that this was not its [*rhētorikē*] first use" (1994, 65n), Halliwell declares that Socrates' reference to "so-called *rhētorikē*" indicates "unambiguously that the word already had some currency" (1994, 224), and Wardy claims the phrase "strongly implies that the word 'rhetoric' was current outside, and predated, the Platonic writings" (1996, 167n).

For the moment, let us give these doubters all that they ask. What follows is only that the character of Socrates implies that the word was in use at the time. Such use could have been limited to the Socratic/Platonic circle. The more likely scenario is that Plato's attribution was simply anachronistic. The objection by O'Sullivan, Kennedy, Gagarin, Halliwell, and Wardy requires the following assumption to be true: Plato does not deliberately portray the dramatic Socrates as using language in a way counter to that of the historical Socrates. I know of few if any Plato scholars who would agree to such an assumption. Plato commonly introduces new terms or constructions into dialogues where the vocabulary could not have been used in the dramatic setting portrayed. As mentioned previously, Pierre Chantraine documents that of the more than 350 *-ikos* words in Plato, more than 250 are not found earlier (1956, 97–171), and the words for such verbal arts as eristic, dialectic, and antilogic all first appear in Plato's works (Schiappa 1990a, 464; see also Ammann 1953). Given the absence of such terms prior to Plato and the clear evidence of Plato's neologistic tendencies with respect to verbal arts in particular, it would be odd, indeed, if Plato did not coin *rhētorikē*.

There is no reason to treat this one odd phrase in *Gorgias*, *tēn kaloumenēn rhētorikēn*, as a sort of linguist's field guide to fifth-century usage, especially in the context of a fictional dialogue brimming with neologisms that is described as so deliberately "riddled with anachronism" that "tense distinctions lose their relevance" (Allen 1984, 189). At best, O'Sullivan et al. have succeeded in demonstrating only that Plato can conceal his neologisms by presenting Socrates as just happening upon them. I simply do not understand why Plato should be treated as a lexicographer (rather than as a creative author) when all other evidence points to the contrary.

Furthermore, Plato certainly was capable of taking a word and transforming completely its meaning and implications. Thus even if he did not coin the word *rhētorikē,* acknowledging the evidence that it is a younger term than typically assumed may help us to understand the ways in which traditional accounts of fifth-century rhetorical theory need to be revised. I argue below that there is a significant difference in the theoretical treatises concerned with *logos* in the fifth century and those in the fourth century concerning *rhētorikē.* Even if Plato did not coin *rhētorikē,* he may as well have, given the subsequent history of the word.

But must we give O'Sullivan and company all that they ask for? O'Sullivan argues that there is no other precedent for Plato using *kaloumenos* to introduce a new word or meaning. Of course, even if he is correct, it does not necessarily follow that Plato is not using *kaloumenos* in just such a way in this particular passage. In fact, here O'Sullivan is relying on precisely the sort of *argumentum ex silentio* to which he objected earlier. Despite his protest, the clearest example of such usage is in *Laws* 894c where Plato uses *kaloumenos* to distinguish what is truly (*ontōs*) called universal motion. Plato must use the adverb *ontōs* here to distinguish his novel use of *metabolē* and *kinēsis* from earlier usage. If Cole and I are correct that Plato's use of *rhētorikē* in *Gorgias* is novel, no such adverb is necessary. Otherwise, the two passages are reasonably similar. The verb *kaleō* is Plato's verb of choice when giving a name to something, and careful analysis of those places where he deliberately endeavors to define a *technē,* in particular, suggests that he often does so by using the verb *kaleō.* Consider, for example, Socrates' naming of the four arts in *Gorgias* (463b). Socrates' use of *kaleō* at *Gorgias* (448d) perhaps is best understood as saying "what is being called 'rhetoric'."

Though O'Sullivan criticizes the examples offered of a specialized use of *kaloumenos* to introduce new words or meanings, none of the critics of the origins-of-rhētorikē thesis deny my more general claim (Schiappa 1990a, 468) that *kaloumenos* is used by Plato as a way of making clear that the use of a word is self-conscious. If *rhētorikē* was a common word, at *Gorgias* 448d Socrates would not need to call our attention explicitly to the nomenclature at use; he would have said simply that Polus is more accomplished at rhetoric than at philosophical discussion (*dialegesthai*). Thus, the construction "that which is called rhetoric" hints that something unusual is going on. Since we can only guess what that something is, we must look outside of the text in order to form our judgments as to what sense of *kaloumenos* is being used. Once we do so, there is reason to believe that the use of the word *rhētorikē* in Plato's *Gorgias* is novel and perhaps even original.

Gagarin and Halliwell both suggest that Alcidamas' *On the Sophists* might predate Plato's *Gorgias* as the earliest extant use of the term *rhētorikē.* I have argued previously on behalf of those scholars who contend that Alcidamas' text is significantly later than Plato's *Gorgias*.[7] As O'Sullivan notes, however, establishing the chronological relationship between Alcidamas' tract and other fourth-century texts has proved to be extremely difficult (1992, 24–31). Though I remain convinced that a later date for Alcidamas' *On the Sophists* is the most plausible conjecture, not much rides on the question.

Again, it is worth stressing that the origins-of-*rhētorikē* thesis does not depend on the precise identification of the originator of the word *rhētorikē*. It does not matter if it was Plato, or Socrates, or Alcidamas, or whoever. The key questions concern when the term began to be used and, more important, how texts that use the term differ from those that do not. As stated earlier, there are no extant texts from prior to 400 B.C.E. that use the term. Just how texts discussing such topics as discourse and education change once the term *rhētorikē* is introduced is the subject of the remaining chapters of this book. The utility of the origins-of-*rhētorikē* thesis cannot be determined once and for all

---

7. I repeat my case here for the simple reason that it has not yet been answered by the critics of the origins-of-*rhētorikē* thesis: "Though the pamphlet has been dated by Larue van Hook as written between 391 and 380 B.C.E., a closer textual analysis would date it well *after* 380, and hence well after the *Gorgias*. Hook's argument is that Alcidamas' pamphlet was in response to Isocrates' *Against The Sophists* (392 B.C.E.) and that Isocrates' reply appeared in the *Panegyricus* (380 B.C.E.). The basis for Hook's chronology is a passage in the *Panegyricus* (11) which seems to respond to Alcidamas' attacks (*On the Sophists* 6, 12–13), but the link is tenuous at best. Alcidamas' pamphlet attacks those who teach the writing of speeches rather than extemporaneous speaking. In 6, Alcidamas argues that extemporaneous speaking is more difficult than writing speeches, hence by mastering his art a student will be trained to both speak *and* write, but that writing does not train one to speak. The *Panegyricus* (11) does *not* respond to the difference between speaking and writing, but rather to the difference between plain and elegant styles. Isocrates *does* respond more directly to Alcidamas' argument at 6 in the *Antidosis* (49) circa 354/3 B.C.E. In 12–13, Alcidamas says extemporaneous speaking is perceived as more spontaneous and hence more sincere by the audience. If Isocrates is responding to this charge in the *Panegyricus* (11) as suggested by Reinhardt (cited by Hook, 92, note 46), his defense is not particularly direct — but there *does* seem to be a direct reference to Alcidamas' description of Isocrates' style as akin to poetry (2, 12) in Isocrates' *Antidosis* (46–47). Hence I believe a chronology that does more justice to Isocrates' argumentative skills would have him answering Alcidamas' charges in the *Antidosis*, around 354/3, not in the *Panegyricus*.

Furthermore, there is good evidence in Alcidamas' text to suggest that it is in response to the *Panegyricus* rather than the other way around (as argued by Hook). The evidence includes: 1) Alcidamas' reference to Isocrates' vanity. Hook's own examples of Isocrates' vanity are from the *Panegyricus* (4–14) or even later works. 2) References that apparently refer to a whole career of writing, not the beginning of a school (*On the Sophists* 1–2). 3)

through further theoretical debate. Instead, it must be tested through its use as a hermeneutic guide. Can we learn something new from the texts of the fifth and fourth centuries B.C.E. that concern discourse and education by looking at them without the traditional disciplinary expectations associated with such terms as "philosophy" and "rhetoric"? That is the question this book attempts to answer in the affirmative.

The last objection I want to address is the claim that it does not matter precisely when *rhētorikē* entered popular usage because "rhetoric" obviously existed prior to the word. Claiming that "rhetoric" did not exist amounts to saying that things do not exist if we do not have words for them. So, as one scholar argued at a convention I attended, just because the Greek texts of a period do not use a word for urination does not mean that no one was urinating at the time.

Two points will make my position clear. First, a distinction needs to be made between the use of the word *rhetoric* to denote the practice of oratory and the use of the word to denote a specific domain of theorizing. The first sense, rhetoric as persuasive speaking or oratory (what Kennedy calls "traditional" rhetoric), obviously occured long before Plato, but is distinct from the second sense, the history of rhetorical theory. Since traditional rhetoric is as old as civilization, rhetoric as a practice is coextensive with the history of society (Kennedy 1980, 8). What this book addresses is the emerging status of rhetoric as a distinct subject or discipline — the status of rhetorical theory qua rhetori-

---

Alcidamas' complaint (4) that written works are the product of long premeditation and revision seems to be a direct reference to the *Panegyricus* which took Isocrates ten years to complete (Quintilian, 10.4.4). 4) Alcidamas' complaint (4) that written works have the luxury of assembling thoughts from many sources seems to be a direct response to Isocrates' *Panegyricus* (see 4, 7–10, 74; and Hook, 91 note 41). 5) Alcidamas' complaint (4) that Isocrates revised his texts based on the advice of others *could* be the result of information in Alcidamas' possession early in Isocrates' career, but the practice is not mentioned by Isocrates until *To Philip* (17), *circa* 346 B.C.E. (see also *Panathenaicus* 200, 233).

My suggested revised chronology thus has Alcidamas' *On the Sophists* coming some time after the *Panegyricus* (380 B.C.E.) and before Isocrates' *Antidosis* (354/3 B.C.E.). Such a chronology makes better sense of both authors' arguments. This dating also preserves the possibility that Alcidamas' criticism of written texts in 27–28 is, in fact, based on Plato's *Phaedrus* 275d. This possibility is acknowledged by Hook, but must be rejected if one accepts a pre-380 B.C.E. date for *On the Sophists*. Finally, it should be noted that Alcidamas' passing reference to classifications of public speaking (9) seems more appropriate to mid-fourth-century rhetorical theory than that circa 385 B.C.E." (Schiappa 1990a, 461–63). On the dates of Alcidamas see also Guthrie (1971, 311–13, esp. 311 n 5).

cal theory in Greece in the fifth and fourth centuries B.C.E. Put another way, this book is concerned with the status of conceptual or metarhetoric that attempts to theorize about oratory (cf. Kennedy 1994, 3). For clarity I will capitalize Rhetoric when I refer to the concept or discipline.

Cole's important book, *The Origins of Rhetoric in Ancient Greece,* deliberately conflates these two senses of the word *rhetoric.* While I agree with much in Cole's book, I believe that this conflation is unnecessary and underestimates the self-conscious artistry of persuasive efforts prior to Plato. It is difficult to maintain that such speeches as Pericles' Funeral Oration or the speeches found in Homer are not rhetorical in the usual sense of the term (Johnstone 1996). Accordingly, I am more than willing to concede that discursive practices existed in ancient Greece that are properly categorized as "rhetoric" (or, more precisely, as "oratory") in both classical and contemporary senses of the term. However, what about what we would now call Rhetoric as a discipline or rhetorical theory?

Here I want to return to the presumably facetious example of ancient Greek urination. Given our beliefs concerning human biology, it is fairly safe to believe that the ancient Greeks urinated on a regular basis. However, what claims can be made concerning the status of Greek theorizing about urination? Were there Greek theories of urination? Was the activity of urinating philosophized about, defined, and described with a technical vocabulary? When did urination become an object of systematic study and education? Did the practice of urination change in light of competing popular theories of urination? Answers to these sorts of questions, which obviously (if facetiously) parallel my concerns about the emergence of Rhetorical Theory, cannot be provided without some sort of textual evidence.[8] The presence or absence of Greek words concerned with urination becomes central to the debate. Similarly, the presence or absence of *rhētorikē* ought to be considered central to debates about the origin of Greek theorizing, defining, and education in Rhetoric.

At this point, readers familiar with ancient Greek texts may point out that other terms, such as *logos, peithō,* or even *logōn technē,* may have performed related semantic functions of the word *rhētorikē.* Would not the use of such terms render the usage of the word *rhētorikē* superfluous? That question is precisely the matter that will occupy the remainder of this book. I do not believe that the significance of the origins-of-rhētorikē thesis can be denied — or established — a priori. Rather, nothing short of a close examination of the

8. Some time after this conference Ms. Ingrid C. Barnes-Pietsch brought Hesiod's *Works and Days* 727–32 to my attention. Not wanting to get involved in another controversy, I leave it to historians of biology to hash out who the first urinary theorists were.

relevant texts, their key terms, and the work such terms perform can provide a full answer to the question "Does the dating of the word *rhētorikē* matter?"

My belief is that the semantic field constituted through the Greek theoretical vocabulary changed in nontrivial ways with the introduction and use of the word *rhtorikē*. Prior to the coining of *rhētorikē, logos* was the key term thematized in the texts and fragments generally assigned to the fifth-century history of rhetorical theory. The texts and fragments concerning *logos* suggest important differences between the way the art of discourse was conceptualized before and after the coining of *rhētorikē*. My argument is that the coining of *rhētorikē* was a watershed event in the history of conceptualized Rhetoric in ancient Greece. Specifically, prior to the coining of *rhētorikē*, the verbal arts were understood as less differentiated and more holistic in scope than they were in the fourth century; the teaching and training associated with *logos* do not draw a sharp line between the goals of seeking success and seeking truth as is the case once Rhetoric and Philosophy were defined as distinct disciplines.

The Importance of Naming the Discipline of Rhetoric

The phrase "discipline of Rhetoric" is usefully ambiguous. As Foucault has suggested, the word *discipline* suggests a sense of control, as in the disciplining of a child, as well as a sense of productive rigor, as in the discipline of an athlete or musician. According to Foucault, discipline in practice is "aimed at knowing, mastering, and using. Discipline organizes an analytical space" (1979, 143). Similarly, in scholastic settings, disciplines are recognizable "spheres of relevance" that suppress some ideas to focus efforts on specific problems (Willard 1989, 209–13). Accordingly, the word *discipline* in this book refers to the suppression of Rhetoric vis-à-vis Philosophy, as well as to the productive power that emerged when Rhetoric found its own intellectual space.

As the following discussion illustrates, many contemporary theorists share the belief that naming phenomena alters perceptions of and behavior toward that-which-has-been-named. I contend that this belief is just as relevant to the naming of disciplines as to other social realities. Specifically, the case for the importance of the coining of *rhētorikē* as a disciplinary term can be made on rhetorical, psycholinguistic, and ideological grounds.

The rhetorical case begins with Kenneth Burke's notion of *entitlement* (1966, 359–79). Language sums up situations and makes sense of human experience; language entitles reality: "the mere act of naming an object or situation decrees that it is to be singled out as such-and-such rather than as something-other" (Burke 1973, 4). The creation of a new word provides a somewhat new way of summing up or entitling a portion of human experience. One rhetorical effect of entitling a new "thing" is that it creates the impression that the "thing" has been "out there" all along, waiting to be discovered and described. Nouns, in particular, suggest things-that-already-exist: "And that no doubt accounts for the feeling that when one is using nouns, one is manipulating the symbols of a self-subsistent reality" (Weaver [1953] 1985, 128). Part of the rhetorical power of Plato's *Gorgias,* therefore, is that it persuades the reader that the objective referent of *rhētorikē* has been around for some time. The original appearance of the noun *rhētorikē,* in effect, created the perceived correspondence between word and thing, thereby presenting them both as already given and in place. A similar linguistic process is reported by Bruno Latour and Steve Woolgar in their study of the social construction of scientific facts:

> From their initial inception members of the laboratory [The Salk Institute] are unable to determine whether statements are true or false, objective or subjective, highly likely or quite probable. . . . Once the statement begins to stabilize, however, an important change takes place. *The statement becomes a split entity.* On the one hand, it is a set of words which represents a statement about an object. On the other hand, it corresponds to an object-in-itself which takes on a life of its own. . . . Before long, more and more reality is attributed to the object and less and less to the statement about the object. Consequently, *an inversion takes place;* the object becomes the reason why the statement was formulated in the first place. (1986, 176–77)

Nouns give one the impression of something stable, even permanent and immutable, or at least beyond the immediate limits of subjectivity (Perelman and Olbrechts-Tyteca 1969, 182, 294). Accordingly, Plato's *Gorgias* could be read (as it has been by many) as espousing timeless truths about the nature of Rhetoric.

From a psychological perspective, we know that language affects human perception and cognition. All meaningful human experience is formed experience, organized through a continual process of abstracting, bordering, and categorizing (see Gregg 1984, 25–51). Differences in the way a language encodes a domain of experience influences how individuals conceive of reality in that domain.

Ferdinand de Saussure's theory of meaning clarifies the psycholinguistic importance of the coining of *rhētorikē* (see de Saussure 1973; Culler 1977). According to de Saussure, language is a system of signs. A given sign is made up of a signifier (such as a word) and a signified (concept). Signs possess meaning in a given linguistic community not so much from objective referents as from their relationship to other signs within a language-system (*la langue*).

The introduction of a new signifier, such as *rhētorikē,* simultaneously introduces a new signified and thus expands the spectrum of conceptual possibilities for a given linguistic community. Viewing the process in reverse, *sans* signifier, there is no corresponding signified readily available in the language-system. As demonstrated above, the signs used (signifier + signified) concerning discourse in the fifth and fourth centuries were qualitatively different.[9] Prior to the coining of a term for a distinct art of discourse such as *rhētorikē,* the subject or discipline of Rhetoric was without form or "meaning." The point here is linguistic, not ontological: without the appropriate category of *rhētorikē,* the conceptual space for theorizing was limited to the "predisciplinary" vocabulary.

The categorizing function of language can be a form of symbolic inducement; different terminologies prompt us to perceive the world in different ways (Gregg 1984, 50–51). The creation of a category of human activity known as Rhetoric greatly facilitated the process of theorizing about Rhetoric. The position advanced here does not entail the position, usually attributed to Benjamin Lee Whorf, that language predetermines thought and that meaning is confined to language (Whorf 1956; cf. Gregg 1984, 85–91).[10] *Rhētēr,* or speaker, can be dated at least back to the *Iliad,* where Phoenix reminds Achilles that he has taught him "to be a teller of tales and a doer of deeds" (*Iliad* 9.443).[11] *Rhētōr* is found as a semi-technical term in fifth-century texts. One can, then, think of the concept "the art of the *rhētōr*" and express such a notion in Greek without the word *rhētorikē.* Nonetheless, an examination of selected predisciplinary passages discussed throughout this book demonstrates that the concept of a distinct Art of Rhetoric as detailed by Plato and Aristotle was neither clear nor stable prior to their writings (see also Cole 1991a).

Although one can, in theory, imagine or describe a discipline or subject of Rhetoric without the word *rhētorikē,* naming has the effect in practice of stabilizing the meaning of that portion of human experience being named. Richard Gregg calls this process *linguistic fixing:* "Language helps fix or stabilize tendencies and processes already present in thought and experience" (1984, 87). In fact, empirical evidence supports the relationship between the

9. If the reader prefers Peircean semiotics, the same logic would apply: Regardless of the ontological status of the *object* Rhetoric, the *signs* (Representamens) the Greeks used were qualitatively different in the fifth and fourth centuries, so the *interpretants* the Greeks understood were also qualitatively different. See Justus Buchler (1955, 98–119).

10. For the argument that Whorf's view of language was not deterministic, see Luch and Wertsch (1987, 67–86); Stam (1980, 239–62).

11. μύθων τε ῥητῆρ' ἔμεναι πρηκτῆρά τε ἔργων.

specificity of a given vocabulary and the degree of analytical sophistication and conceptual retrievability.[12] A relationship exists between vocabulary and understanding: the more complex the vocabulary, the more sophisticated the observed learning.[13] Most recent studies tend to presume a relationship between categorical representation in thought and the availability of names for categories (see, e.g., Harnad 1987, 535–65). Though cognitivists sometimes stress the autonomy of language and thought, most acknowledge that there are learning contexts where a change in the lexicon corresponds to a change in "underlying conceptual structure" (Keil 1989, 148). Nouns, in particular, "introduce and arrange new people or objects in the discourse" (Corrigan 1989, 8). Accordingly, one would anticipate that the naming of a distinct art of discourse with a term such as *rhētorikē* would facilitate theory and analysis of that subject.[14]

The name of a discipline also has important ideological implications. The coining of *rhētorikē* enabled Rhetoric to become what Foucault calls an "object of discourse" (1972, 40–49). The objectification of Rhetoric, in turn, facilitated Rhetoric's becoming a vehicle of power and knowledge (Foucault 1980, 92–133). Naming, however, is never neutral. If Plato was the first person to popularize the word *rhētorikē,* he probably did so to depict the teachings of his rival Isocrates (Schiappa 1990a).[15] Isocrates himself portrayed his teachings as philosophy (*philosophia*), a training for the mind as physical training is for the body. Because philosophy teaches all forms of *logos,* according to Isocrates, it makes students stronger in their thinking (*Antidosis* 181–85).[16] The new word *rhētorikē* was a useful label for Plato to use to stress the political aspects of Isocrates' training while diminishing the intellectual con-

12. For a summary of this research, see Rosch (1988, 373–92). For specific studies see Roger W. Brown and E. H. Lenneberg (1954, 452–62); Roger W. Brown (1956, 247–310).

13. See the discussion of *encoding specificity* in Smith et al. (1987, 228–29). Cf. the evidence of a relationship implied between vocabulary and learning in Chiesi et al. (1979, 257–73).

14. It is no accident that the Romans' first use of a word for Rhetoric occurred at about the same time Roman oratory began to flourish and began to be studied. See Kennedy (1972a, 3–7). Cf. the accounts of varying levels of conceptual sophistication regarding oratory in Bloch (1975).

15. As R. L. Howland (1937, 151–59) noted, "The attack on rhetoric [in the *Gorgias*] is intended to refer to Isocrates as the most influential contemporary teacher of it." See also Charlton (1985, 59).

16. For the Greek text see Mathieu and Brémond (1929, 3:103–81). For an English translation see Norlin (1929, vol. 2).

tent. Names imply orientations: *Rhētorikē* as literally the art or skill of the *rhētōr* privileges the ambition of political success, while *philosophia* as the love of wisdom privileges fidelity to the truth. From the beginning, Rhetoric was defined at cross-purposes with the emerging rival discipline of Philosophy.

Once named, intellectual practices can become what we can loosely call a discipline, and a common set of issues can be identified as its focus. At the same time, further categorization and specialization occur. Steven Mailloux describes such a phenomenon as the "institutional need for increasing differentiation and specialization" (1989, 26–27). Foucault refers to disciplines or institutions of knowledge as developing "authorities of delimitation" that, in effect, define the scope of permissible objects and objectives (1972, 41–42). Accordingly, in works such as Plato's *Gorgias, Phaedrus,* and Aristotle's *Rhetoric,* the scope and function of the discipline of Rhetoric are of central concern. Such works provide what Foucault calls "grids of specification": systems according to which the objects and objectives of a discipline are "divided, contrasted, related, regrouped, classified" (1972, 41–42). As a discipline matures, parameters exclude some concerns to focus efforts on others. Disciplinary vocabularies create terministic screens that select and direct attention in certain directions and deflect it from others (Burke 1966, 44–62).

I do not mean to imply here a narrow sense of causality. I do not want to imply that once someone coined the word *rhētorikē* there followed a puff of smoke and a discipline came into being. What I do contend is that the creation of a specific vocabulary to describe the workings of language is a constitutive part of the disciplining of *logos* (cf. Charlton 1985). As our thinking about a given subject becomes more sophisticated, our language evolves. What may begin with general terms becomes increasingly elaborated; what begins with vague metaphors becomes specific and concrete. As André Lardinois notes, the archaic poets refer to proverbial expressions with such overworked general terms as *epos* and *logos,* but during the fifth and fourth centuries, "new terms for proverbial expressions were introduced into the Greek language, including *paroimia, hypothēkē, apophthegma,* and *gnōmē*" (1997, 214). Another obvious example for the discipline of rhetoric is the concept of *style:* what began implicitly with metaphorical descriptions of discourse as "thick" or "thin" became, by Hermogenes' time, a proliferation of types and virtues (O'Sullivan 1992; Wooten 1987).

Ideologically speaking, the irony of Plato's rhetorical maneuvering should be apparent. Plato seems to have coined — or at least borrowed and defined — the new word *rhētorikē* as part of an effort to limit the scope and popularity of Sophistic teaching, particularly that of his rival Isocrates. However, the term quickly became useful as a means of organizing thought and effort around a specific set of problems—those of being a persuasive *rhētōr*. Plato may have helped to empower a discipline that his philosophical outlook found repugnant.

Toward a Revised History of Early Greek Rhetorical Theory

The relatively late appearance of the term *rhētorikē* and the differences between conceptualizations of discourse in key texts of the fifth and fourth centuries B.C.E. warrant several conclusions. First, claims that attribute a disciplinary sense of Rhetoric to fifth-century writers and texts need to be carefully reassessed. Though there are relatively few extended texts concerning persuasive discourse and education from the fifth century, those that survive challenge the standard account of early Greek rhetorical theory. I do not mean to imply that all previous claims about rhetoric in the fifth century are wrong; clearly oratory (or traditional rhetoric) flourished just as "philosophy" and the fine arts did. And, to be sure, one can construct what I would describe as implicit or "undeclared" theories of persuasion and discourse in texts as old as Homer and Hesiod (Kirby 1992; Karp, 1977; Enos 1993).

However, what Kennedy calls "conceptualized" Rhetoric (1980, 8) or "metarhetoric" (1994, 3) was clearly in a predisciplinary stage of development until the early fourth century B.C.E. Claims that project a fourth-century sense of the subject of Rhetoric back into the fifth century require emendation—especially those that imply a sharp difference in Sophistic teaching between "rhetorical" (success-seeking) motives and "philosophical" (truth-seeking) motives. A statement by Carl Joachim Classen provides an example: "The linguistic studies of the Sophists were carried out not for philosophical reasons, not to examine the means by which a statement can be made, but for rhetorical purposes: to persuade people successfully, even at the expense of truth; and it was more or less accidental when some of these investigations produced philosophically important results" (1976, 246–47). A similar sentiment is expressed by Martin Ostwald, who claims that "philosophical" matters entered the teaching of Sophists only "incidentally" (1986, 242–44). The evidence discussed in this book points to a need to modify such claims.

The Sophists' teachings surely belong to the history of the development of rhetorical theory and practice. But their precise place in that history is more complex than most treatments suggest; their contribution is better described as predisciplinary rather than as a consciously held theory or definition of Rhetoric (see Poulakos 1983c, 35–48, 1995; Schiappa 1990b, 192–217).

The process of revising the history of early Greek rhetorical theory will render certain long-standing traditions problematic, including such "givens" as the Corax and Tisias myth and the differences among "technical," "Sophistic," and "philosophical" approaches to rhetoric. If the Greek word for rhetoric emerged later than we usually think, and texts concerning discourse and education are nontrivially different before and after the term's introduction, then how should we revise the standard account of rhetoric's beginning?

3

"Technical Rhetoric" Reconsidered

This chapter develops two main arguments. The first is that there are methodological reasons for reconsidering the standard account of the beginnings of Greek rhetorical theory. The second is that there are textual or "substantive" reasons for questioning the standard account of the "invention" of rhetoric by Corax and Tisias. Specifically, Kennedy's division of Greek rhetorical theory into "technical," "Sophistic," and "philosophical" schools is argued to be an inappropriate and misleading schematization — at least with respect to Greece in the fifth century B.C.E.

Methodological Reasons for Renewed Study

Robert J. Connors's provocative claim that "any scholar who professes to understand classical rhetoric must come to terms with [Eric] Havelock's ideas" (1988, 381) is based on the belief that Havelock's orality-literacy thesis calls for a dramatic paradigm shift in how ancient Greek texts are interpreted. Prior to about 750 B.C.E., reading and writing were largely unknown to most Greeks. Cultural knowledge and tradition were passed on orally. Language in such a culture must meet the needs of memory, since it is only through repetition and memorization that one generation can pass on to the next what has been learned. The vocabulary of a purely oral culture is, as a result, relatively limited compared to literate cultures. Additionally, the needs of memory affect syntax and composition such that verse, song, and story are the best vehicles to "store" the records of a non-book-oriented culture: "Epical verse was the primary mechanism that a sophisticated, preliterate society utilized to preserve and transmit such verbal information as it required for the humanly necessary processes of 'enculturation' or paideia" (Robb 1994, 252).

Havelock's thesis suggests that expression and thought differ significantly from an oral culture to a literate one: "in general the means of communication tends to condition the content of what is communicated" (1982, 2).[1] With widespread literacy in Greece came greater freedom to think "analytically" because formal expression did not have to be crafted with memory as a primary constraint. As Walter J. Ong points out, "once a formulary expression has crystallized, it had best be kept intact. Without a writing system, breaking up thought — that is, analysis — is a high-risk procedure" (1982, 39). Writing facilitates the cognitive ability to objectify people, objects, and events in a way that divorces them from a human action context. For example, the preliterate Greeks thought of "justice" not as an abstract principle but as a concrete practice involving specific experiences: acting unjustly, receiving justice, etc. (Havelock 1982). By the time Plato wrote his dialogues, "philosophers" had advanced the Greek conceptual vocabulary and syntax sufficiently that inquiry could focus, discretely, on "the knower" and "the known" (Havelock 1963). Once "justice" becomes an object of analysis, questions involving intellectual practices such as *defining* ("What is Justice?") are encouraged (see Ong 1982, 53–57).

Havelock's orality-literacy thesis is important for the study of early Greek rhetoric (O'Sullivan 1996; Worthington 1996). For example, certain stylistic changes in the surviving orations of the fifth and fourth centuries are more easily understood if the transition from orality to literacy is kept in mind. Connors' essay "Greek Rhetoric and the Transition from Orality" contends that the highly poetic style of the Older Sophists is a reflection of the influence of orality (1986, 38–65). If the Sophists' discourse seems highly stylized to the modern reader it is because predominantly oral modes of thinking and speaking are foreign to us. Connors concludes that there is a direct correspondence

---

1. Havelock exaggerates the causal powers of literacy, though critics who want to dismiss his thesis altogether are overreacting. Recent work that support Havelock's contention that literacy was much more restricted than is usually thought, and that demonstrate the influence on Greek culture of growing literacy in the fifth and fourth centuries B.C.E. include Cole 1991a; Harris 1989; Robb 1994; Thomas 1989, 1992. I discuss criticisms and attenuations of Havelock's and Ong's treatment of the cognitive effects of literacy in chapter 2 of Schiappa (1991).

between the rise of literacy and the decline of the "grand style" of the Older Sophists. The change in style has less to do with aesthetics than with changing syntax, word meanings, and modes of expression.

In addition to enhancing the study of Greek rhetorical practice, the orality-literacy thesis is also useful to the study of early theorizing. Noting that classicists tend to deny that "theories" or "methods" guide their research, Havelock argues that four unstated assumptions have, in fact, influenced most classical scholarship: "Greek culture from the beginning was built on a habit of literacy; Greek prose discourse was commonly composed and read at least as early as the Archaic age; the Greek language is built up out of a set of interchangeable parts; Greek thought-forms give expression to a common fund of basic values and concepts" (1982, 224). All four assumptions, Havelock claims, either have been successfully refuted or are under serious question. As a result, much of the history of early Greek philosophy must be rewritten. The importance of the four unstated assumptions for the study of early rhetorical theory are noted below. Havelock's point is that the development of philosophical or theoretical thinking is related to the advent of widespread literacy, and that histories of such thinking that do not acknowledge the complex relationship between literacy and philosophical thought may make serious mistakes.

Many comprehensive histories of philosophy, ironically, tend to treat topics unhistorically. Richard Rorty, in an influential article on the historiography of philosophy, has described the genre of works surveying centuries of philosophical thought as "doxography." He complains that such historical accounts treat their topics as "given" or as conceptual constants. Rorty attributes such a tendency to a sort of "natural attitude" on behalf of philosophers toward the objects of their analysis: "the idea [is] that 'philosophy' is the name of a natural kind—the name of a discipline which, in all ages and places, has managed to dig down to the same deep, fundamental, questions" (1984, 63; see also Makin 1988). The typical format of articles in the *Encyclopedia of Philosophy,* for example, is to compare and contrast different philosophers' "approaches," "treatments," or "theories" of "X"—where "X" may be "truth," "ethics," "justice," and so on. Each philosopher is assumed to be addressing the "same" issue and could, in theory, sit down and compare views of "X" with philosophers of other cultures and ages. As Havelock points out, in a critique that parallels Rorty's, such an approach understates important differences between cultures and minimizes or even ignores the role of particular historical contexts. For Havelock, the most significant aspect of the early Greek context is the development of new forms of expression and patterns of reasoning. Anachronistic interjection of a later-developed vocabulary distorts the history of early Greek theorizing by describing it as an activity dealing with problems already "given," rather than as the development of a new language in which such problems slowly come into focus (1983, 57).

Accordingly, historical accounts of early Greek theorizing should include a focus on the evolution of the conceptual vocabulary and syntax, and the related emergence of certain theoretical-philosophical issues. In two provocative studies Havelock has deconstructed the standard accounts of rival presocratic "schools" of philosophical thought (1982, ch.11; 1983). By carefully examining the fragments representing the authentic *ipsissima verba* of the so-called presocratic philosophers, Havelock documents example after example of long-standing misrepresentations. The major source of distortion is the habit of historians and philosophers of taking Aristotle's and Theophrastus' accounts of their predecessors as historically reliable. Once compared to the *ipsissima verba*, the evidence is clear that later doctrines have consistently been read back into earlier thinkers' statements. Certain so-called presocratic schools of thought "dissolve" under careful scrutiny. Havelock concludes that "much of the story of early Greek philosophy so-called is a story not of systems of thought but of a search for a primary language in which any system could be expressed" (1982, 8; see also Havelock 1963, 300–301).

Many previous studies of early Greek rhetorical theory also have operated under assumptions that the orality-literacy thesis call into question. The first two assumptions identified by Havelock—that literacy and prose-writing were common throughout Greek culture—underlie many claims about the written *technai* of the fifth century B.C.E. The second two assumptions—concerning the constancy of Greek word-meanings and thought-patterns—have led to innumerable accounts of Greek history that treat Rhetoric as a relatively unproblematic "given." As noted previously, Kennedy's most influential account of Greek rhetorical theory identified three traditions: technical, Sophistic, and philosophical. These three "views of rhetoric" are "continuing strands" in the long tradition of rhetoric that stretches "throughout the history of western Europe" (1980, 16). Kennedy's treatment of rhetorical theory sometimes parallels the "multiple views of X" approach to the doxography of philosophy mentioned earlier. Though much of Kennedy's work is historical and particularistic, if applied too strictly his tripartite schematization is unhistorical and, in fact, leads to a distorted picture of what transpired in fifth- and fourth-century Greece. It is my contention that rhetorical theory emerged and evolved during the fifth and fourth centuries in a manner somewhat different than is traditionally understood.

A fact undercutting any non-evolutionary approach to early Greek rhetorical theory is that the term *rhētorikē* was not coined until the early fourth century B.C.E. In fact, there were no Greek words or expressions specifically connoting a disciplinary sense of "rhetoric" or "art of rhetoric" until the fourth century B.C.E. The Greek words used during the fifth century by the Older Sophists to describe speech were *logos* and *legein*. The meanings associated with *logos* and *legein* are such that one cannot argue they mean the same thing as was later conveyed by "rhetoric." Accordingly, any thorough historical account of the early development of what is now called rhetorical theory must address the fact that there was a progression from *logos* to *rhētorikē* that took place over a period exceeding a century. Kuhn suggests that intellectual discoveries typically have three stages: a "prehistory" during which the perception of anomaly grows, a period which Kuhn calls the "proper internal history" of the discovery, and a post-history of assimilation and normalization of the discovery (1977, 165–77).

With respect to the "discovery" of Rhetoric as a conceptualized art, I believe that there are three topics worthy of study by the historian of early Greek rhetorical theory. In the fifth century B.C.E. *logos* was the key conceptual term of the Older Sophists. Representative texts of this period include the fragments and surviving speeches of the Older Sophists and the book now called *Dissoi Logoi* or *Dialexeis*. By the first half of the fourth century *logos* had been replaced by *logōn technē*, which was sometimes described by Plato as *rhētorikē*. Isocrates' works (which never use the word *rhētorikē*), Plato's dialogues, and the so-called *Rhetoric to Alexander* (which never uses the word *rhētorikē*) best exemplify this transitional stage of theorizing. By the late fourth century B.C.E. the split between rhetoric and philosophy was more or less successfully reified both conceptually and terminologically in the works of Aristotle and his students.

Each of these periods deserves study in its own right. It is my position that considerable previous scholarship has misunderstood or misrepresented fifth-century thinking by using the later-developed word *rhētorikē* to interpret the texts and fragments of and about the period. Once the methodological necessity of reassessing the standard account of fifth-century Greek rhetorical theory is acknowledged, solid textual or substantive grounds for reconstructing the account become apparent, as the following sections of this chapter illustrate.

Kennedy's "Technical Rhetoric" Revisited

The story that credits Corax and Tisias with the invention of Rhetoric is widely accepted by historians of early rhetoric. Why should it be doubted? To begin with, whatever Corax and Tisias may have taught was not under the rubric of *rhētorikē*. Most accounts agree on an early fifth-century date for

Corax's teaching, around 466–67 B.C.E.[2] Yet the earliest recorded use of the word *rhētōr* is in a decree dated sometime during 446/5–442/1, and the earliest surviving use of the word *rhētorikē* is from Plato's *Gorgias*, dated around 385 B.C.E.[3] If Corax or Tisias had used the word *rhētorikē* as early as 467, surely it would have surfaced again prior to the fourth century B.C.E.

If Corax and Tisias did not literally "invent" *rhētorikē*, per se, then what *was* the nature of their theoretical innovation? Unfortunately, a survey of the available ancient evidence demonstrates that most accounts are notoriously derivative.

The earliest extant reference to Corax or Tisias is in Plato's *Phaedrus*, published sometime around 365 — roughly a century after their "invention." The first reference in the text appears in a section in which Socrates is summarizing the contributions of books on rhetoric: "shall we leave Gorgias and Tisias undisturbed, who saw that probabilities (*ta eikota*) are more to be esteemed than truths, who make small things seem great and great things small by the power of their words, and new things old and old things the reverse, and who invented conciseness of speech and measureless length on all subjects?" (*Phaedrus* 267a).[4] As history the foregoing passage is highly suspect, having little in common with the authenticated teachings of Gorgias and attributing far more to Tisias than is plausible (de Vries 1969, 222–23). The only reference to a doctrine of Tisias that is repeated by any other source is that of "probabilities," which is treated in more depth a little later in the same dialogue. Socrates says that Tisias considers probability (*to eikos*) to mean "that which most people believe" (273b). Tisias' "clever discovery of [this] technique" (273b) is said to lead to the position that what is more believable is more valued by rhetors than what is true — a position Plato critiques at length.

Does the concept of "probabilities" represent an authentic contribution to rhetorical theory by Corax or Tisias? Despite relatively recent arguments in support of the standard account of Corax and Tisias on the subject of probability (Goebel 1989), I believe that it is difficult to consider Plato's testimony in the *Phaedrus* as firm evidence. Plato makes no mention of Corax at all, and soon after his mention of Tisias' "discovery" he hints that "Tisias" may be a pseudonym: "a wonderfully hidden art it seems to be which Tisias has brought

2. See Verrall (1880, 197–210), Smith (1921, 15), Jebb ([1893] 1962, 1: cxxi).

3. See Wilcox (1942, 127), von Gaertringen (1924, 45, line 21), Tod (1985, 88–90).

4. Translations from Plato's *Phaedrus* are the author's adaptations of Fowler (1914) and Hackforth in Hamilton and Cairns (1961). Translations of Isocrates' texts are based on Norlin (1928–29) and Van Hook (1945).

to light, or some other, whoever he may be and whatever country he is proud to call his own" (273c). Pseudo-Tisias' "discovery" is described as part of a *logōn technē* (266d) — an expression found in the fourth century B.C.E. but not in the fifth. The passage (267a) that first mentions Tisias appears to be a direct reference to *Isocrates*' claim that speech can "represent the great as lowly or invest the little with grandeur, to recount the things of old in a new manner or set forth events of recent date in an old fashion" (*Panegyricus* 8). Could the object of Plato's attack on appeals to probability have been Isocrates' teachings? Probably so, since in the *Helen* in the midst of an attack on rival "useless" philosophers — including, it is now generally agreed, Plato — Isocrates makes the explicit claim that "likely conjecture [*epieikōs doxazein*] about useful things is far preferable to exact knowledge [*epistasthai*] of the useless" (5). This and other passages give us reason to believe that the targets of Plato's arguments against *to eikos* are Isocrates and other fourth-century rivals, not long-dead teachers (see Burger 1980; Howland 1937; Nails 1995, 215; Robb 1994, 160; Robin 1985, clxxiii). Plato's attack on the position that "what is more believable is more valuable to rhetors than what is true" need not have been against any particular "doctrine" or "theory." The attack simply represented another level of criticism Plato had for any philosophy that sacrificed "truth" for expediency. No doubt, to Plato, Isocrates' own words convicted him of promoting what was "likely" to the crowd over "truth": "it is evident that those who desire to command the attention of their hearers must abstain from admonition and advice and must say the kinds of things which they see are most pleasing to the crowd" (*To Nicocles* 49).

The somewhat specialized sense of "argument from probability" described by Plato is different than the sense of *eikos* found in fifth-century sources. In Herodotus, Thucydides, Aeschylus, and Sophocles, for example, *eikos* means "likely," "fitting," "meet," "right," or "reasonable" (Liddell and Scott 1940, s.v. *eikos*, 484–85). Even in the fourth-century text on rhetoric by Anaximenes, the sense of *eikos* is simply "that which seems (right)" (Goebel 1989, 45). The technical conceptualization of the term, signaled by the neuter singular paired with the definite article (*to eikos*), cannot be found prior to Plato's writings.[5] Even in Antiphon's *Tetralogies,* where arguments over what is likely or probable play a central role, one does not find *to eikos* used in the way attributed to Corax or Tisias by Plato (Gagarin 1994). Furthermore, the notion that Tisias favored probability *over* "the facts" is obviously a Platonic invention, since prior to Plato's dialogues there is no evidence of this particular epistemological

5. On the conceptual significance of the definite article plus neuter singular construction see Havelock (1983, 55); and Snell (1953, chap. 10).

or logical dichotomy. As Michael Gagarin notes, "there is no evidence to support Plato's claim, echoed nearly unanimously by modern scholars, that Greek orators and rhetoricians valued probability more highly than truth" (1994, 56). The earliest clear use of the concept of "argument from probability" outside of Plato and Aristotle postdates the Older Sophists' writings.[6]

The final reason to doubt the reliability of Plato's account is his implicit claim that Tisias' discovery is found in a book (*Phaedrus* 266d). Yet the earliest surviving prose text is that of Herodotus, who wrote in the last third of the fifth century (Waters 1985).[7] The earliest prose texts remain closely wedded to oral patterns of composition by relying on narrative and often employing mythical themes. Gorgias' *Helen* and Prodicus' *Choice of Heracles* are innovative prose texts for their time (the late fifth century), but are nothing like the sort of dry academic prose one finds nearly a century later in Aristotle. Plato's description seems to fit fourth-century writings such as the *Rhetoric to Alexander* better than anything known from the fifth century. Kevin Robb contends that by the early fourth century, "no logical treatises or exercise manuals as yet existed for use" (1994, 235). The so-called *technai* often attributed to fifth-century Sophists, as Thomas Cole notes (1991a, 71–112), were probably simply collections of speeches. The idea that Corax or Tisias wrote what later authors would call a "handbook" for teaching Rhetoric along the lines of a *Rhetoric to Alexander* is far-fetched, to say the least. In sum, nothing found in Plato can be used as a reliable indication of the contributions of Tisias, and Plato says nothing of Corax.

If Plato's testimony concerning Tisias is dubious, the situation becomes worse in the case of Corax. Noting that "Corax" is Greek for "crow," Cole argues that the name must have been a pejorative nickname: "Greek parents were not in the habit of calling their children crows" (1991b, 81). Observing that it would have been rather ill advised to try "to make a living by teaching the art of public speaking" if one is named Crow, Cole suggests that "Corax" is merely a nickname probably bestowed on Tisias after he began to teach people how to speak (1991b, 81; cf. Kennedy 1994, 34). Despite the durability of the Corax and Tisias origin myth, the earliest evidence for such a narrative virtually disappears into thin air: "Corax" vanishes into pseudonymity, and the earliest mention of "Tisias," already a century after the fact, cannot withstand scrutiny. While numerous versions of the story survive through history (see Cole 1991b), they are inconsistent, often incompatible, and dependent on a story with uncertain parentage.

6. See Anaximenes, *Rhetoric to Alexander* 1433b33–37; 1445a37–38.
7. On the rarity of books in the late fifth century see Turner (1977) and Thomas (1989).

The most commonly cited authority for the story that Corax and Tisias invented rhetoric as an art is Aristotle's *Synagōgē*, referred to by Cicero and Quintilian. Before we examine the testimony of Cicero and Quintilian, Aristotle's surviving references to the Corax and Tisias story must be considered.

There are two extant references by Aristotle to Corax and Tisias. The first is in the *Rhetoric* in a section describing the fallacious use of argument from probability:

> The *Art* of Corax is made up of this topic; for example, if a weak man were charged with assault, he should be acquitted as not being a likely suspect for the charge; for it is not probable [that a weak man would attack another]. And if he is a likely suspect, for example, if he is strong, [he should also be acquitted]; for it is not likely [that he would start the fight] for the very reason that it was going to seem probable. And similarly in other cases; for necessarily, a person is either a likely suspect or not a likely suspect for a charge. Both alternatives seem probable, but one really is probable, the other so not generally, only in the circumstances mentioned. And this is "to make the weaker seem the better cause." Thus, people were rightly angry at the declaration of Protagoras; for it is a lie and not true but a fallacious probability and a part of no art except rhetoric and eristic. (1402a17–28, trans. Kennedy 1991, 210)

It is difficult to ascertain how much "history" can be reliably taken from this passage. As mentioned previously, the odds of "Corax" having published a book constituting a *technē* are slim. Unlike Plato, Aristotle does not attribute a book to "Corax," only a *technē*. It is possible that what is referred to here is not a book, but a set of precepts or examples passed down orally (Lentz 1989, ch. 6). The possibility is heightened by the fact that the strong man versus weak man example is somewhat of a commonplace during the fourth century B.C.E. and is the sort of easily remembered lesson an oral tradition of teaching would produce. There are peculiarities in the attribution, however, that require consideration.

To begin with, it is strange that Corax — whether that be his real name or a nickname — is never mentioned by Plato, nor by any other fifth- or fourth-century writers. In an insightful treatment of Aristotle's and his student Theophrastus' historical summaries of presocratic philosophers, Havelock has noted that figures we now take for granted, such as Anaximander and Anaximenes, had never been mentioned previous to Aristotle (1983, 69–70). Havelock's point is not that such people did not exist, but that Aristotle and Theophrastus demonstrate a penchant for re-writing history, a criticism already thoroughly documented by Harold Cherniss (1935).[8] Aristotle consistently

---

8. See also McDiarmid (1953). For a defense of Aristotle see Guthrie (1957).

sought to identify his predecessors on each subject he wrote about, and to contrast his philosophical system as superior or at least more complete. Havelock suggests that Aristotle sometimes invented anticipations of his own philosophy by stretching what was known about his predecessors.

Is it possible that the attribution of a theory of *to eikos* to "Corax" is an instance of such "stretching"? There are two reasons for suggesting that it might. First, "Corax" is linked to Tisias in a lost writing of Aristotle mentioned by Cicero (*Brutus* 46). It is likely that the reference to Tisias is taken from Aristotle's teacher, Plato. Unfortunately, as explained above, Plato's historical picture of Tisias is probably apocryphal. If Aristotle's description of "Corax" is based on the presumed commonality of doctrine between Corax and Tisias, and if there is reason to doubt the ascription of a theoretical doctrine of *to eikos* to Tisias, then there is cause to suspect that Aristotle's use of "Corax" parallels his unhistorical treatment of other presocratics. The second reason to harbor such a suspicion is the same passage's treatment of Protagoras. After describing the spurious appeal to probability Aristotle claims it is what Protagoras meant by making the weaker *logos* the stronger. However, such a rendering is a distortion. Protagoras' "weaker/stronger" statement is best understood as companion to his "two-*logoi*" thesis. Influenced by Heraclitus' "unity of opposites" thesis, Protagoras claimed that concerning every "thing" (*pragma*) there are two *logoi* in opposition. The same "thing" could be experienced in "opposite" ways: the same food can taste sweet to one person and sour to another, the same wind can feel cool to one person and not cool to another, and the same law can appear just to one person and unjust to another. What Protagoras meant by making one *logos* stronger than its opposite was the substitution of a preferred (but weaker) *logos* for a less preferable (but temporarily dominant) *logos* of the same "experience" (Schiappa 1991, 103–16). As noted by Classen, Aristotle's descriptions of Sophistic doctrines were always in contrast with his own system as superior (in modern terms) epistemologically, ontologically, and ethically (1981, 7–24). Aristotle's treatment of Protagoras in the present case typifies the kind of distortion cited by Cherniss and Havelock.

The careful development of logical theory, including the categorization (based on epistemological criteria) of genuine and spurious arguments from probability, originated no sooner than Aristotle. It is highly probable, therefore, that Aristotle's description of Corax's *technē* is at least anachronistic. It is plausible that the reference to a theory of *to eikos* is based on no more than an orally transmitted anecdote concerning the strong- and weak-man defense. It is even possible, as is suggested below, that the entire Corax and Tisias story is a convenient myth.

The other extant reference to Corax or Tisias by Aristotle is found in a famous passage concluding *Sophistical Refutations*. Noting that his current study might be seen as less than adequate, Aristotle points out that some discoveries are older than others, so it is natural that some arts are more developed than others:

> This is in fact what has happened in regard to rhetorical speeches (*rhētorikous logous*) and to practically all the other arts; for those who discovered the beginnings of them advanced them in all only a little way, whereas the celebrities of today are the heirs (so to speak) of a long succession of men who have advanced them bit by bit, and so have developed them to their present form; *Tisias after the first* [contributors] (*Teisias men meta tous prōtous*), Thrasymachus after Tisias, Theodorus then after them, while several people have made their several contributions to it. Therefore it is not to be wondered at that the art has attained considerable dimensions. (183b25–34)[9]

The passage demonstrates Aristotle's interest in creating a lineage for contemporary rhetorical teaching. His effort here again parallels his efforts in physics and metaphysics to establish a direct line of successors that begins with "first philosophers" and ends with Aristotle's grand synthesis. An additional motivation for this particular bit of history is admitted by Aristotle: he has had less time to develop the particular art he is writing about than those who currently teach Rhetoric. In fact, the passage continues by attacking the recitation methods of current teachers of "contentious arguments." Accordingly, once again it is likely that Aristotle is writing less with the value commitments of an historian than as an advocate for a current school of thought. The people Aristotle mentions may have made contributions to what would later be called the Art of Rhetoric. The evidence concerning Thrasymachus and Theodorus is scanty, but suggestive.[10] What the contributions of Tisias and the first contributors may have been, unfortunately, remains an open question.

Cicero makes mention of the invention of rhetoric by Sicilians twice. The first is in *On Invention* in which he states that "Aristotle collected the early books on rhetoric, even going back as far as Tisias, well known as the originator and inventor of the art" (2.2.6). *On Invention* was written in Cicero's youth and may consist primarily of notes from lectures Cicero attended (Hubbell 1949, 2: vii; Kennedy 1972a, 103–10). Accordingly, it is difficult to know if Cicero had read the *Synagōgē* himself at this point or if the information was derived from a teacher's reading of Plato's *Phaedrus*. The reference in *On*

---

9. Translation adapted from that by Pickard-Cambridge in Barnes (1984).

10. For Thrasymachus see the fragments collected and translated in Sprague (1972). For Theodorus see Kennedy (1963).

Invention does not provide the information necessary to make an assessment of the historical Tisias' contribution to rhetorical theory.

Cicero's other mention of the invention of rhetoric is in the *Brutus:* "Thus Aristotle says that in Sicily, after the expulsion of tyrants, when after a long interval restitution of private property was sought by legal means, Corax and Tisias the Sicilians, with the acuteness and controversial habit of their people, first put together some theoretical precepts; that before them, while many had taken pains to speak with care and with orderly arrangement, no one had followed a definite method or art" (46).

The story provides more detail than other references in Cicero and Quintilian and appears to be a more credible account. Unfortunately, the story may be an imaginative fiction by either Aristotle or Cicero. Commenting on Cicero's *Brutus* 46–48, A. E. Douglas suggersts that, based on what we know of it, Aristotle's *Synagōgē* was "on the historical side highly tendentious" (1955, 536–39). Hypothesizing that the *Synagōgē* may have been written by one of Aristotle's students, Douglas suggests that it may reflect more concern for fourth-century controversies than with portraying the early history of rhetoric reliably (1955, 536–39). Of course, even if Cicero is representing Aristotle faithfully, Aristotle's account has been shown to be in doubt.

Moreover, there is no guarantee that Cicero is representing Aristotle faithfully. As Kennedy notes, Cicero may have had a political agenda in mind in writing the *Brutus*. Cicero despairs of the current political situation, and "it has even been plausibly suggested that one of Cicero's objectives was to incite Brutus to rid Rome of Caesar" (Kennedy 1972a, 247). Cicero cites Aristotle's account in order to provide evidence for the claim found immediately before the Corax and Tisias story: "For the ambition to speak well does not arise when men are engaged in establishing government, nor occupied with the conduct of war, nor shackled and chained by the authority of kings" (45). Cicero's alterations of Aristotle's story, however, are probably minor. The most significant change may have been the substitution of a *forensic* setting for the birth of rhetoric rather than a *deliberate* setting (as found in other versions), as in Cicero's time the courts "were the arena for the structure and maintenance of Roman values" and hence they "served as a forum for public articulation of political positions" (Enos 1988, 20).[11]

Even if Cicero did not alter Aristotle's story in order to provide an analogy to his own political-rhetorical scene, it is entirely possible that Aristotle's version of events was motivated by the desire to make the same point that

11. See also Wood (1988, 53). Wood makes it clear that Cicero was not a democratic reformer, however.

Cicero wanted to make: "Upon peace and tranquility eloquence attends as their ally, it is, one may say, the offspring of well-established civic order" (*Brutus* 45).

Quintilian's claim that Corax and Tisias were "the earliest writers of text-books" (*Institutio Oratoria* 3.1.8; cf. 2.17.7) on rhetoric is apparently derived from Cicero, so it does not offer independent corroboration of the Corax and Tisias story. Furthermore, the claim that Corax or Tisias wrote a textbook is highly dubious, for reasons cited above.

The remaining ancient authorities who refer to Corax and Tisias have been preserved in the introductions to rhetoric and the prefaces to commentaries on Hermogenes, which were written after the third century CE (Wilcox 1943a, 1–23; see also Cole 1991b). These are referred to as the *Prolegomena* and were collected in the 1830s in Christianus Walz's *Rhetores Graeci* (1832–36) and reedited by Hugo Rabe a century later (1931). A representative passage, quoted below, narrates three origins of the art of rhetoric — one among the gods, one among heroes, and a third among mortals:

> We must look into the following matters with regard to the third major point which needs investigating: how rhetoric came to men. After the already mentioned divine heroes, we are justified in demonstrating its in-born rational nature. The Syracusans were accordingly the first men to display it. Sicily . . . was ruled as a tyranny by Gelon and Hieron, very savage tyrants, who strengthened the force of their tyranny against the Syracusans to the point where the Syracusans rejected them and escaped from this cruel slavery. It is said that the tyrants indulged their savagery to the extent of forbidding the Syracusans to utter any sound at all, but to signify what was appropriate by means of their feet, hands, and eyes whenever one of them was in need. It was in this way, they say, that dance-pantomime had its beginnings. Because the Syracusans had been cut off from speech (*logos*), they contrived to explain their business with gestures. Because, then the Syracusans were ruled so harshly and savagely and because they prayed to Zeus the deliverer to free them from this cruel slavery, Zeus, acting as both savior and deliverer, liberated the Syracusans from tyranny by destroying the tyrants. Then, since the citizenry (*dēmos*) among the Syracusans feared that they might in some way fall upon a similar tyrant, they no longer entrusted their government to a tyrant. The people (*dēmos*) themselves wanted to have absolute control over all things. (Rabe 1931, 245, no. 4 trans. Farenga 1979, 1035)

The preceding passage is from what is generally regarded as the oldest and "purest" account of the Corax and Tisias legend (Wilcox 1943, 19). It has been conjectured that the passage was originally derived from the writings of the fourth-century (B.C.E.) historian Timaeus, but the attribution is both unlikely and uninformative (Wilcox 1943, 20–23).[12] It is uninformative because the highly mythologized retelling of the fall of the Syracusan tyrants suggests that any subsequent claims about a Syracusan invention of rhetoric must be considered as similar historical legend-building. It is unlikely because the extant text is filled with historically impossible claims such as that Corax defined rhetoric as *peithous demiourgos* — the producer of belief. The practice of definition originates with Socrates and cannot be documented in the first half of the fifth century B.C.E. Furthermore, as Hermann Mutschmann argued decades ago, the definition of rhetoric as *peithous demiourgos* first appeared in Plato's *Gorgias* (453a) and has nothing to do with Corax and Tisias (1918, 443; see also Dodds 1959, 203).

An additional passage from the *Prolegomena* preserves the legend that rhetoric originates from the disputes after the fall of the Syracusan tyranny:

> And thereupon, democracy came once again to the Syracusans. And this man Korax came to persuade the crowd and to be heard . . . He observed how the people had produced an unsteady and disorderly state of affairs, and he thought that it was speech by which the course of human events was brought to order. He then contemplated turning the people toward and away from the proper course of action through speech. Coming into the assembly, where all the people had gathered together, he began first to appease the troublesome and turbulent element among them with obsequious and flattering words, and he called such things "introductions." After this, he began to soothe and silence the people and to speak as though telling a story, and after these things to summarize and call to mind concisely what had gone before and to bring before their eyes at a glance what had previously been said. (Rabe 1931, 270, no. 17 trans. Farenga 1979, 1035–36)

The unreliability of the story is underscored by the fact that two traditions exist about the nature of Corax's "teaching": one, represented by the above passage, that suggests his teaching was geared for the assembly, and another that suggests it was used only in the law-courts.[13] Interestingly, Corax is not

---

12. Wilcox's logic is as follows: (1) Dionysius of Halicarnassus and Diodorus Siculus both relate the story of Gorgias' first visit to Athens. (2) Since Dionysius says that his source is Timaeus, Timaeus must also be Diodorus' source. (3) Since Timaeus the Sicilian glorified his homeland by recording and embellishing the Gorgias story, it is likely he would have recorded the story of Corax and Tisias. (4) Since Diodorus' account of Sicilian history is similar to Rabe #4, Timaeus must be the source for both. Steps 2 and 3 are obviously *non sequitur* arguments. Step 4 would tend to *disprove* the assertion Timaeus was the basis of Rabe #4 since Diodorus does *not* mention Corax *or* the invention of rhetoric — a remarkable omission by a fellow proud Sicilian historian.

13. See Wilcox (1942, 1943a), Hinks (1936, 170–76), Kennedy (1959, 169–78).

described as teaching rhetoric or even *logos* (the word translated as "speech" above). His primary contribution is the introduction of names for parts of a speech, a contribution credited also to Theodorus and Protagoras.[14] Furthermore, the Sophist Antiphon is said by Hermogenes to be "the absolute inventor and originator of the political genre" (DK 87A2).

While it is impossible to ascertain who first codified the traditional terminology for the parts of a classical oration, it is unlikely that it was Corax or Tisias (cf. Cole 1991b). The evidence concerning Corax and Tisias is notoriously inconsistent, describing as few as three and as many as seven parts of speech. While most preplatonic Greek speeches can be said to have a three-part organization of introduction, argument, and conclusion, such a pattern is most likely the result of performing "ring composition" rather than a particular theory of prose arrangement (Major and Schiappa, 1997). The pattern of beginning and ending with the same idea is common in archaic Greek composition, already found in full flower in Homeric epic. Under the rubric of "ring composition" scholars have documented its prevalence in ancient poetry from epics and hymns of the eighth century B.C.E. to the choral odes of the fifth (Edwards, 1991, 44–48; Otterlo, 1944; Reid 1997, 72–80). The innovation of the canonical quadripartite division of speeches cannot be dated with confidence before the fourth century B.C.E. (Major 1996).

Furthermore, it is possible that the whole legend is ideologically inspired and that Tisias (a.k.a. "Corax") did no more or less than become a successful *rhētōr* (politician and speaker) after the fall of the tyranny. An alternative hypothesis concerning the different parts of speech would preserve the originality of Tisias' contribution without making obviously anachronistic assumptions about the invention of rhetoric. It is possible that what is commonly referred to as the early Sophistic "rules" for speaking before the law-courts and the assembly were just that-regulations governing speaking procedure on par with the water-clocks of the time. Such a possibility has been anticipated by Havelock, who has suggested that Plato's *Protagoras* and other fifth-century writings imply that the Sophists first promulgated norms for the conduct of political discourse (1957, ch. 8). Given that Protagoras was selected by Pericles to write the laws of the new colony of Thurii in 444 B.C.E., it is possible that the early *technai* ascribed to Corax and Tisias was simply a description of the procedure of the courts and the assembly. The basic structuring of the parts of speech attributed to Corax and Tisias would have been as useful for the audience as for the speaker as analytical and organizational guides. Such a possibility gains further credence when it is recalled that the

14. For Theodorus see Plato, *Phaedrus* 266d7–e6. For Protagoras see DK 80A 1.

court system in Greece evolved during roughly the same time as the Older Sophists. Homicide courts may have an older history, but the popular law-courts in which so many fortunes were won or lost flourished in the fifth century B.C.E. along with the Older Sophists (Garner 1987; Ostwald 1986). This hypothesis is highly speculative and is likely to remain so, but for me the alternative is to abandon Corax and Tisias altogether.

What is left of the tradition of "technical rhetoric"? Unfortunately, very little. The various rhetorical *technai* attributed to fifth-century Sophists are without authority. As Cole argues (1991a, 71–112), there may have been collections of speeches dubbed "manuals" of rhetoric in the fourth century B.C.E., but no fifth-century Sophist wrote a treatise on *rhētorikē,* per se. His-torically, no "Art of Rhetoric" is attributed to Protagoras, Hippias, Prodicus, or Critias. The "Arts" attributed to Gorgias, Thrasymachus, and Antiphon are probably the result of the publication of exemplary speeches. Kennedy asserts that "the existence of Aristotle's summary [the *Synagōgē Technōn*] seems to have rendered the survival of the original handbooks superfluous" (1980, 19). A more likely explanation is that there were no theoretical "Arts of Rhetoric" written in the fifth century B.C.E..

What Do We Know of "Technical Rhetoric" in the Fifth Century B.C.E.?

This chapter has offered a case for the renewed historical study of the beginnings of Greek rhetorical theory. Paralleling Havelock's reexamination of the standard account of early Greek philosophy, this chapter suggests that a careful reading of important fifth- and fourth-century texts calls into question much of the standard account of early Greek rhetorical theorizing. What, then, can reasonably be taken from the various accounts of Corax and Tisias and the tradition of fifth-century "technical rhetoric"? Let us return to the claims delineated in this book's first chapter:

1. The Art of Rhetoric originates with Corax of Sicily around 467 B.C.E.

2. Corax was probably the teacher of Tisias, a fellow Sicilian.

3. Corax and/or Tisias authored the first technē, or book designated as an Art of Rhetoric.

These three claims are doubtful because "Corax" is probably a fictitious name, Tisias' role cannot be independently corroborated apart from a suspect account by Plato, no record of a "book" can be dated to this period, and whatever "they" did was not under the rubric *rhētorikē.*

4. Corax/Tisias may have been the first to define rhetoric, specifically as "the artificer of persuasion." This claim is highly unlikely because the practice of

definition cannot be dated confidently prior to Socrates and Plato, and the specific definition is almost certainly Plato's innovation in his *Gorgias* (453a).

5. An important contribution of Corax's and/or Tisias' handbook was the identification of the parts of forensic speeches. Though the specific number of parts differs from account to account (3, 4, 5, or 7), few scholars doubt that some practical system of division was introduced by Corax, Tisias, or both. There is insufficient evidence to support the notion that "handbooks" other than collections of speeches were published in the fifth century. The extant texts suggest that nothing more sophisticated than ring composition was taught prior to the fourth century B.C.E.

6. The primary theoretical contribution was their identification of the "argument from probability." While it is possible that the "weaker and stronger man" anecdote is a fifth-century oral lesson, the technical conceptualization of "the probable," signaled by the neuter singular construction (*to eikos*), cannot be found prior to Plato's writings; it is particularly anachronistic to attribute to fifth-century figures the notion that "the probable" is preferable in argument to "the truth."

7. By the end of the fifth century B.C.E., written technical handbooks (*technai*) were commonly available to which people could turn to learn Rhetoric. As Cole argues (1991a), if such *technai* existed at all, they were simply collections of speeches. As I have argued previously, if such texts existed, they were not called arts of *rhētorikē*. To the extent that the assumed existence of such handbooks depends on the legacy of the Corax and Tisias myth, it is difficult to make anything more than highly speculative attributions about them (cf. Kroll 1940, 1046).

8. Most early teaching of the Art of Rhetoric, including that of Corax/Tisias, concentrated on forensic rhetoric; that is, the successful pleading of one's case in a law-court. Since the Greek judicial system required individuals to defend themselves, Rhetoric quickly became an attractive subject of study. Two immediate problems with this claim are its assumption of the veracity of the Corax and Tisias myth and its use of the rubric "Rhetoric." I argue in the next two chapters, additionally, that the teaching of certain fifth-century figures, such as the Sophists, is misleadingly "reduced" by such an account.

9. At least some of the handbooks included discussions of style, specifically of the various kinds of diction and forms of linguistic ornamentation available to the orator. The problematic status of the "handbook" tradition should be sufficient to cast some doubt on this claim. While O'Sullivan (1992) is surely correct to draw our attention to a nascent fifth-century awareness of "thick" versus "thin" discursive styles, I argue at several points later that "style" is not

explicitly theorized or "disciplinized" by rhetorical theorists until well into the fourth century B.C.E.

10. No fifth-century rhetorical handbooks exist because Aristotle's *Collection of the Arts* made them obsolete. This claim is impossible to disprove. Given the preceding analysis, however, a more plausible explanation is that no such handbook survives because there were no such handbooks — as they traditionally have been described.

While I do not expect that I have delivered a death blow to the Corax and Tisias myth, it is my hope that this chapter has created enough doubt about key aspects of the narrative to open a space from which to reconsider the origins of Greek rhetorical theory.

4

4

"Sophistic Rhetoric" Reconsidered

The notion of a distinctive "Sophistic Rhetoric" is popular with both friends and foes of the fifth-century figures often referred to as the Older Sophists. Edward M. Cope's account of "Sophistical Rhetoric," now over a century old, was written in response to George Grote's efforts (1851) to restore the damaged reputation of the Sophists. His assessment is fairly typical of critics of the Sophists: "I think that I shall be able to show that this rhetoric [Sophistical Rhetoric], the principal instrument of instruction employed by most of the Sophists, and the principal means by which they acquired their great fame and influence, was as unscientific and unprincipled as the rest of the arts and philosophy they taught; and that all the hard words which Plato and Aristotle applied to it were fully warranted by the character of the things which they described: that the style which the Sophists cultivated was often vicious, the treatises they wrote mostly frivolous, and the practice they encouraged and the notions they instilled demoralizing" (1855, 147). As there are already several competent accounts of the opprobrious histories of the Sophists and Sophistic Rhetoric, there is no need to repeat an account here.[1] It is sufficient to note that most negative descriptions share the following two

1. See Classen (1976, 1–18), Kerferd (1981a, 1–6; 1981b, 4–14), Guthrie (1971, 3–13), Mailloux (1995, 1–31), Schiappa (1991, 3–12).

48

claims, previously identified as part of the standard account of the beginnings of Greek rhetorical theory as described in chapter 1:

11. Though specific doctrines may have varied, there was a commonly identified group of individuals in the fifth century known as Sophists. The group included Protagoras, Gorgias, Hippias, Prodicus, Thrasymachus, Critias, and Antiphon.

12. The most important shared characteristic of the Sophists was that they all taught the Art of Rhetoric.

Equally important, in recent years there has been a distinct turn toward a more positive assessment of Sophistic Rhetoric. For a variety of writers, Sophistic Rhetoric represents a veritable oasis of ideas for contemporary theories of discourse, composition, and argumentation. Consider a few manifestations of a Sophistic turn: John Poulakos has developed a "Sophistic definition of rhetoric" that he believes provides an important contribution to a contemporary understanding of discourse (1983), and that he offers as a model of liberating rhetoric (1987, 1995). Declaring himself a Sophist, Jasper Neel advocates "Sophistical rhetoric" as "a study of how to make choices and a study of how choices form character and make good citizens" (1988, 211). Roger Moss has made a "Case for Sophistry" (1982) as an antidote to the paralyzing influence of realism, and Sharon Crowley has made "A Plea for the Revival of Sophistry" (1989) to encourage a more sociopolitically engaged model of pedagogy. These examples can be multiplied, but I think they suffice to show that the concept of Sophistic Rhetoric has grown in popularity in a variety of ways.[2]

The turn to Sophistic Rhetoric is, in many ways, attractive and productive. To those who see our understanding of the workings of discourse theory as inescapably rooted in ancient Greece, the turn to Sophistry provides a valuable alternative to Platonic and Aristotelian pedagogical traditions. The contemporary appropriation of specific fifth-century texts, ideas, or practices has proven its usefulness.[3] Nevertheless, my admittedly narrow interest in this chapter is

2. See also Jarratt (1991), Mailloux (1995), McComiskey (1993, 1994), Poulakos (1984), and Vitanza (1997).

3. In earlier work I argue that there is a difference between scholarship that makes claims about how the discourse communities of fifth- and fourth-century B.C.E. Greece interpreted and understood the texts of the Sophists (*historical reconstruction*), and scholarship that seeks to draw upon Sophists' texts in order to inform contemporary theoretical or pedagogical interests (*contemporary appropriation*) (1990b, 1990c). To be sure, such activities overlap considerably. But our ability to identify clear exemplars of each persuades me that the distinction is still useful (Schiappa 1991, 66–67). In a nutshell, the charge of anachronism bothers the historian, while it is irrelevant to those

historical. I want to challenge the notion that there was a monolithic or unified Sophistic Rhetoric that was taught by the fifth-century group of seven individuals known as the Older Sophists. My position is that we are unlikely to come up with a historically defensible definition of Sophistic Rhetoric that is nontrivial and uniquely valuable, and that several alternatives should be considered. I believe that we should realize the difficulty of identifying a specific and distinct group known as "Sophists"; understand that what the Sophists taught was broader than what is typically understood as Rhetoric; resist reducing the variety of theories, practices, and ideologies of the Older Sophists into *one* Sophistic Rhetoric and instead recognize their diversity; and recognize contemporary appropriations of specific Sophists' doctrines or practices as contributions to "Neosophistic" rhetorical theory and practice. Such steps allow us as scholars and teachers to retain the most useful contributions of such fifth-century thinkers without engaging in anachronism.

Who Were the Sophists?

The first problem with the notion of Sophistic Rhetoric is identifying what is meant by "Sophistic." Most scholars take the word as meaning literally belonging to the Sophists, and refer to the group of individuals of the fifth century B.C.E. that Plato denotes as such.[4] The standard list, canonized by Diels and Kranz (1951–52) and adopted by scholars such as Poulakos (1983), includes Protagoras, Gorgias, Hippias, Prodicus, Thrasymachus, Critias, and Antiphon. Unfortunately, canonized or not, the list is somewhat arbitrary and cannot be squared with the available ancient testimony.

The word "Sophist" is in Greek *sophistēs,* meaning a person of wisdom (*sophia*). The term first appears in Pindar in the early fifth century and predates the appearance of the group of so-called Older Sophists identified as such by Hermann Diels and Walther Kranz. The notion that there was a distinctive Sophistic Rhetoric seems to have originated in the writings of Plato, and it has been reified through a series of accounts that (mistakenly) take Plato

---

whose primary purpose is to inform contemporary theory, practice, or pedagogy. This is why I am skeptical of the rubric Sophistic Rhetoric while I encourage the title Neosophistic. Historical reconstruction and contemporary appropriation are *both* important activities, and fifth-century texts are rich enough to supply ample work for all concerned.

4. As the texts of writers such as Diogenes Laertius (C.E. third century), and Philostratus (C.E. second or third century) demonstrate, later antiquity clearly recognized a specific profession of "Sophist." What is at issue in this chapter is the usefulness of such a label for describing a consistent position toward Rhetoric in the fifth and early fourth centuries B.C.E.

seriously as a historian of fifth-century thought (see, e.g., Cope 1855, 1856; Guthrie 1971). But Plato's references to "Sophists" include people normally not included in the standard list (Miccus, Proteus), and though he refers to four of the standard list as "Sophists" (Protagoras, Gorgias, Prodicus, Hippias) he does not do so with the other three (Thrasymachus, Critias, Antiphon). When he uses the term generically, such as in his *Sophist,* it appears that he is often referring to fourth-century rivals rather than fifth-century Sophists. It is noteworthy that Plato's *Sophist,* dedicated to defining what it means to be a Sophist, never once uses the word *rhētorikē* to describe their teachings or doctrines (in contrast to his *Gorgias*). In both Plato's and Aristotle's writings there is evidence of different kinds of "Sophists" that they sometimes take pains to distinguish and sometimes lump together (Classen 1981). In other words, even in the corpus of texts that has most influenced our conception of Sophistic Rhetoric, there is sufficient equivocation to warrant another look at the evidence.

Aristophanes' comedy *Clouds* is the only surviving preplatonic text that discusses Sophists at length, and it provides a perspective quite different than that found in Plato. The main Sophist lampooned is Socrates, and decades later the label "Sophist" was still commonly applied to him despite Plato's protests (Nehamas 1990). Most of the play's action takes place at the "Thinkery" (*phrontistērion*), and the object of Sophistic training is portrayed as to produce a "person of wisdom" (*sophistēs*) or "thinker" (*phrontistēs*). When Strepsiades comes to the Thinkery to learn how to avoid paying his debts, Socrates requires him to learn to reason analytically. Socrates' lesson concerning how to win a lawsuit is an exercise in the invention of creative arguments that has little in common with the discussions of forensic rhetoric found in the fourth century. The play never once mentions "Rhetoric" (*rhētorikē*) or "Oratory" (*rhētoreia*), yet there is a surprising variety of subjects explored at the Thinkery. The subjects include what are now called astronomy, surveying, geometry, and meteorology; all are treated as serious interests of the Thinkery's inhabitants. Throughout the play, Aristophanes portrays the process of learning to speak (*legein*) as a natural consequence of learning to engage in "sophisticated" reasoning.

As documented in detail by Kerferd (1950) and G. E. R. Lloyd (1987, 83–98), a wide variety of people occupying an assortment of professions were called Sophists in ancient Greece, including poets (such as Homer and Hesiod), musicians and rhapsodes, diviners and seers, and an assortment of "wise men" we now would categorize as presocratic philosophers, mathematicians, and politicians. According to Kerferd, "the term *sophistēs* is confined to those who in one way or another function as the Sages, the exponents of knowledge in early communities" (1950, 8). In fact, the term "Philosopher" was not used to demarcate a specific group of thinkers until well into the fourth century B.C.E. (Charlton 1985; Havelock 1983; Striker 1996, 5). As Ostwald notes, "the Athenian public made no attempt to differentiate sophists from philosophers" (1986, 259). We are reading history backward when we call presocratics such as Thales and Pythagoras "Philosophers" because prior to Aristotle they would have been described as "Sophists." Even in the fourth century, Isocrates and Plato called each other "Sophists" and themselves "Philosophers," making it purely a modern bias to label either definitively (cf. Quandahl 1989; Striker 1996).

Despite the ancient evidence suggesting that "Sophist" was a label used to describe a variety of people, a common means of identifying a specific group of fifth-century Sophists is by reference to their professionalism; that is, some distinguish Sophists from non-Sophists by whether or not they charged fees for their teaching (Kerferd 1981b, 25). Such a strategy would delineate a specific group of "professional" fifth-century teachers, and there are sound reasons to use such a criterion for defining and studying the cultural place of professional educators in the fifth century (O'Sullivan 1996). The purpose here, however, is more narrow. The question becomes: Why is this a useful litmus test for defining Sophistic *Rhetoric* for the purposes of the history of rhetorical theory? If some substantive differences can be identified between the teachings of those who charged for their services and those who did not, then would not those doctrinal differences be more appropriate defining variables? One attraction of the "Sophistic movement" that is often claimed is that it helped provide an education useful for a democracy. Accordingly, defining "Sophist" as a "professional educator" has a certain egalitarian appeal. The evidentiary merits of such a view are dubious, however (see below), and even if true it would follow that those who taught for free would be even more useful for the democratic masses. In short, there seems to be no good reason why the charging of fees ought to be considered a necessary condition for defining a Sophistic Rhetoric.

In ancient as well as modern times the label "Sophist" is assigned rather inconsistently according to the biases of the writer. In ancient times, persons as diverse as Prometheus, Homer, Hesiod, Damon, Solon, Thales, Pythagoras, Anaxagoras, Empedocles, Zeno, Plato, Socrates, and Isocrates were called "Sophists" (Blank 1985; Kerferd 1981b). Aeschines, Eudoxus, and Protagoras are included in Philostratus' *Lives of the Sophists*, as well as in Diogenes Laertius' *Lives of Eminent Philosophers*. In modern times, even the seven Sophists listed by Diels and Kranz is far from universal. Grote omits Critias and adds Polus, Euthydemus, and Dionysodorus (1851, 486); Kerferd adds

Callicles and Socrates, as well as the authors of the *Dissoi Logoi* or *Dialexeis,* the *Anonymus Iamblichi,* and the *Hippocratic Corpus* (1981b); and Guthrie adds Antisthenes, Alcidamas, and Lycophron (1971).

Whom we choose to call a "Sophist" necessarily affects how we describe Sophistic Rhetoric. As Kerferd points out, the process of designating certain individuals as "Sophists" necessarily influences what "Sophistic" doctrine or curricula turn out to be (1981b, 35). If "Sophist" includes the presocratic philosophers, Socrates, Plato, and Isocrates, then the resulting picture of Sophistic Rhetoric is considerably different than if a smaller group of people is so designated.

To summarize the argument thus far, it is difficult to identify a defining characteristic of "the Sophists" that allows us to narrow the group to a degree sufficient to adduce a common perspective or set of practices. Either we treat the term as broadly as did the ancient Greeks, in which case almost every serious thinker must be included, or we are forced to pick a trait that serves no useful function other than to confirm some preconceived preference. Any account of Sophistic Rhetoric will tend to beg the question because it will presuppose who should be called a "Sophist" — a determination that must be made on doctrinal grounds. The circularity of the reasoning seems to be unavoidable, and is part of the reason Sophistic Rhetoric should be considered a problematic historical construct.

What Counts as Sophistic "Rhetoric"?

Even if we were able to agree on who to call Sophists, a clear notion of Sophistic "Rhetoric" would not necessarily result. There are three senses of "rhetoric" that need to be distinguished at this point — rhetorical theory, practice, and ideology. Rhetorical theory is what Kennedy (1980) refers to as "conceptual" or "meta" rhetoric, and is what scholars generally mean when they say that the Sophists "taught rhetoric." Some (but not all) writers advocating Sophistic Rhetoric imply that there was a distinctly "Sophistic" definition or theory of rhetoric attributable to the Sophists. Unfortunately, there are good reasons for challenging any claim that such a thing as a distinct and explicit Sophistic theory or definition of rhetoric ever existed. A host of philological sources claim that the Greek word for rhetoric (*rhētorikē*) originates no earlier than Plato's writings, and it is possible that Plato himself coined the word (see chapter 2). *Rhētorikē* appears nowhere in any document or fragment attributable to a fifth-century source, nor does it appear in the writings of Isocrates — the most famous teacher of oratory in the fourth century B.C.E.

If one cannot identify an explicit Sophistic theory of rhetoric, one is left with ferreting out an implicit theory. But this task is also difficult — even if one treats the Diels and Kranz list of Sophists as definitive. The pivotal theoretical term or keyword found in the few surviving doctrinal fragments of the Sophists is *logos* — one of the most equivocal terms in the Greek language. The implicit theory of language one finds in Protagoras and Gorgias (the two Sophists we know the most about) have little in common: Gorgias treats persuasion as a matter of deception and questions the possibility of communication altogether, while Protagoras' fragments suggest that he viewed "making the weaker account the stronger" as a matter of improving a person's (or city's) objective condition.[5] In a critique of Poulakos' "Sophistic definition of rhetoric," I argue that while it might be possible to identify the incipient rhetorical theory of individual fifth-century figures, the available ancient evidence renders suspect any generalization about a common "Sophistic" theory of rhetoric (Schiappa 1991, 64–81; cf. Cole 1991a).

It is equally difficult to identify anything like a common set of Sophistic rhetorical practices (Cole 1991a, 71–112). Some portrayals of Sophistic Rhetoric suggest that the speeches of the Sophists shared certain stylistic characteristics. Moss's "case for Sophistry," for example, notes the "highly-wrought use of alliteration, assonance, rhyme and other parisonic devices, parallelisms of all kinds" that "define Sophistry" (1982, 213). There are two problems with such portrayals. First, even working with the "standard" list of seven Sophists, one finds little evidence of stylistic commonality. Among the standard list one finds both the "thick" style of Gorgias and the "thin" style of Prodicus that represent the range of prose style noted in the fifth century (O'Sullivan 1992). Most writers who take a "tropical" approach to Sophistic Rhetoric rely extensively on the example of Gorgias' highly poetic style.[6] But Gorgias was virtually unique among the public speakers of his time, a fact that undercuts any effort to equate his style with that of a general Sophistic style. Accordingly, it would be more appropriate to espouse a Gorgianic rhetoric than a Sophistic rhetoric. Second, stylistic accounts of Sophistic Rhetoric confuse cause and effect. As argued by Thomas Cole (1991a) and Robert Connors (1986), the stylistic innovations found in surviving "Sophistic" treatises are a manifestation of the widespread changes associated with the shift from oral to "literate"

5. Crowley's "Plea for Sophistry" cites only Protagoras and Gorgias as examples of Sophists, and her analysis acknowledges that the two perspectives conflict (1989, 327). Similarly, Renato Barilli's (1989) treatment of "the Sophists" includes only Protagoras, Gorgias, and Isocrates. For Gorgias see Verdenius (1981) and Segal (1962); for Protagoras see Cole (1972) and Schiappa (1991). For a comparison of their perspectives on language see Kerferd (1981b, 68–82).

6. See, for example, Moss (1982, 213–17) and Kennedy (1980, 29–31).

modes of composition. Paradox, allusion, antithesis, and the like can be found in a wide variety of fifth-century texts by Sophists and non-Sophists alike (Solmsen 1975, 83–125; see also Quandahl 1989), as can the the earliest examples of plain versus grand prose styles (O'Sullivan 1992). Hence the appearance of these devices or styles is not a sufficient criterion by which to differentiate between Sophistic and non-Sophistic discourse.

The third sense of rhetoric that one finds linked to the Sophists is best described as an ideology. Describing "Sophistical rhetoric" as "emancipatory," John Poulakos suggests that "the Sophists' rhetorical lessons were subversive in that they aimed to disempower the powerful and empower the powerless," and that "Sophistical rhetoric flourished as a radical critique of the Hellenic culture in the fifth century B.C." (1987, 99). Subsequently Poulakos claims that "the sophists' motto was not survival of the fittest but fitting as many as possible for survival" (1995, 14). The Sophistical promise to turn "the weaker argument into a stronger one" must have "inspired some hope among the 'lesser,' that is, the poor, the common, and the marginalized" (1995, 29). Similarly, Harold Barrett (1987) and others (Kennedy 1980, 18–19; Müller 1986) contend that the most useful aspect of Sophistic teaching was that it aided participation in the democracy. Unfortunately, such idealistic accounts of the Sophists cannot be squared with the historical evidence.

It is simply wishful thinking to describe the Sophists collectively as populist-minded teachers wishing to aid the "hitherto voiceless and marginalized" (Poulakos 1987, 101). Whoever the Sophists were, the ancient authorities are virtually unanimous in their assessment that the fees the Sophists charged were very high (Blank 1985). Ostwald contends that "only the wealthy" could afford to hire a Sophist, and that their followers "consisted largely of ambitious young men of the upper classes" (1986, 237, 242). Kerferd concludes that "what the Sophists were able to offer was in no sense a contribution to the education of the masses" (1981b, 17). The verdict, in ancient times as well as the present, is that the most appreciative audience was an aristocratic one and, indeed, most of the political leaders who managed to overcome a nonaristocratic birth were rather suspicious of the Sophists (Blank 1985, 14–15).

We would do well not to over-romanticize the relationship between "the Sophists" and Athenian democracy. Every age evaluates Athenian democracy by its own ideological lights (Roberts 1994), and by contemporary standards it is unlikely that we will want to imitate what we find. True, Protagoras is credited with providing the first theoretical defense of democracy (Menzel 1910), but even the most advanced stage of Athenian democracy still limited citizenship to a minority of the adult male population, retained the institution of slavery, and was thoroughly misogynist (Cantarella 1987; Keuls 1985). Furthermore, there was by no means a consensus among "Sophists" about the value of democracy (cf. Dupréel 1948; Guthrie 1971; Ostwald 1986, 229–50). Antiphon, Critias, and Socrates were all "Sophists" who eventually were put to death for their *anti*-democratic teachings or activities.[7] In addition, some Sophists explicitly championed the doctrine of *physis,* or "nature," over *nomos,* democratically derived custom-law: "For a price only the well-to-do could afford, Sophists promised to provide the disenchanted younger generation with rhetorical and other training. . . . By and large, *nomos* identifies the conventions, traditions, and values of the democratic establishment, which the older generation tended to regard itself as guarding; arguments from *physis* were marshaled by an intelligentsia that took shape in the Periclean age and from the 430s attracted the allegiance of young aristocrats" (Ostwald 1986, 273). In short, even if we stipulate the traditional list of Sophists as definitive, there is no consistent ideology that could be called a distinct Sophistic Rhetoric.

As there is no unifying essence of the term "Sophistic," then one needs to stipulate a particular group of individuals dubbed "Sophists" for a particular purpose; otherwise, the variety of theories, practices, and ideologies among fifth-century intellectuals makes the label "Sophistic" more misleading than useful in terms of describing a unitary view of discourse, persuasion, or education. The attributes one finds on all or most of the standard lists of Sophists are also common to many other thinkers of the fifth century; such as their questioning of the dominant religious dogmas, their innovation in compositional style, and their roles as teachers. When one finds an authentically unique contribution, such as Gorgias' account of the power of *logos,* the very uniqueness that makes the contribution noteworthy makes the label "Sophistic" an overgeneralization.

The Uses and Limits of Interpretation

Despite charges to the contrary, my objective is not to "kill off" those figures commonly referred to as the Sophists, but to reanimate them in their rich respective particularity and to understand the contributions they made to their own time.[8] There are many aspects of specific Sophists' writings that can and should be recovered and appreciated for their contributions to the de-

7. For Socrates see Stone (1988); for Critias see Sprague (1972, 241–49); for Antiphon see Sprague (1972, 108–11, 127–28).

8. That is, after all, why I have devoted a book to Protagoras and a substantial part of this book to Gorgias. For the charge that I want to kill off the Sophists, see Vitanza (1997, 11, 27–55). For the charge that I want to turn them into Philosophers, see Consigny (1996) and my response (Schiappa 1996).

velopment of what later became recognized as rhetorical theory. It is my belief that such contributions will be understood better absent the imposition of later-developed terminology, including the potentially reductionist label Sophistic Rhetoric (usually contrasted to a Platonic/Aristotelian "Philosophical Rhetoric").

While in chapter 2 of this book I needed to respond to certain objections of colleagues in classics, in the remainder of this chapter I want to engage the concerns of interlocutors from English and communication studies. One defense of the notion of Sophistic Rhetoric is to admit that it may be, in some sense, a mirage, but to insist that it can be retained as a useful fiction. After all, history is a form of storytelling that is interpretive and rhetorical through and through; the myth of a single, authoritative "objective" historical account has been exploded. Furthermore, Sophistic Rhetoric forms part of a useful narrative with which to explore certain recurring issues in the history of ideas. As Poulakos puts it, "because cultural conflicts and contradictions are still with us, because no utopia has yet been devised, and because rhetoric pervades so many human practices, the story of the Sophists is still relevant" (1987, 100). Specifically, as Jarratt has argued (1991), Sophistic Rhetoric provides a point of departure from "classical philosophy" that allows us to identify and deconstruct certain persistent "binary structures" (such as rhetoric/philosophy) that are prototypical of hierarchical strategies used to displace and marginalize people and ideas.

I am sympathetic toward such an argument. In fact, the sort of narrative that pits the provocative "revolutionary" Sophists against the "establishment" figures of Plato and Aristotle is exactly what attracted me to study the Sophists in the first place (see Pirsig 1974). And clearly any theory of History that asserts that a single objective true account of an era or event is possible is no longer tenable (Novick 1988). Are there any good reasons, therefore, to resist the turn to a monolithic Sophistic Rhetoric, even if such a notion is granted to be a fiction? I believe that there are, and consequently will proceed to defend three propositions: first, that there are important socially constructed limits to interpretive variability; second, that there are more useful constructs to study for political and social critique than Sophistic Rhetoric; and third, that Sophistic Rhetoric fails to overcome the binary oppositional structures it is credited with challenging.

One reaction to my previously published claim that the historical construct Sophistic Rhetoric is problematic has been to suggest that I fail to acknowledge that the "past-as-it-was is irretrievable," because "any statement we make about the past is anchored in the present" (Poulakos 1990, 221; cf. Consigny 1996). That is, all historical writing cannot help but be influenced by the historian's own set of historically conditioned values and beliefs. As I understand the objection, I cannot claim that my historical account is superior because to do would imply I have access to "foundational" and "objective" facts, which any contemporary language theorist will tell you is impossible. Contrasting his reading of Protagoras's fragments to mine, neosophist Scott Consigny suggests that "we can neither 'contradict' nor 'prove' either account by reference to the putative historical 'facts' about Protagoras, simply because there are no such objective and uninterpreted facts to which we can appeal" (1995, 220). Though I respect such critics and have learned from their responses, they underestimate our ability to learn from texts and undervalue the concept of "facts" and the genre of writing known as "history."

Those who defend a radical version of reader-response theory with respect to historical texts find themselves in a dilemma. If, on the one hand, history is merely a matter of personal interpretation, then the question becomes: Why trouble ourselves with the Sophists at all? If we cannot learn something new from the Sophists' texts because all history is merely self-affirmation, then why bother with such texts at all? If all we will ever find in "Sophistic" texts is what our contemporary presuppositions tell us we'll find, then why bother? Why not instead simply formulate those presuppositions into a contemporary, postmodern theory of rhetoric, and wash our hands of dead Greeks altogether? So the first part of the dilemma is that if there is no way to escape the present by engaging ancient texts, then there is no apparent reason for considering "Sophistic" texts.

If, on the other hand, we admit that our interactions with colleagues and ancient texts resist some interpretations more than others, then we are encouraged to accept the idea that interpretations may be evaluated and compared. Consider the case of the writings of Friedrich Nietzsche, the writer most often credited with formulating the position that "there are no facts, only interpretation." Why couldn't I simply declare that my reading of Nietzsche revealed that he was really a Platonist? What is it about his texts or us that resists such a reading? Similarly, what is it about the texts of the fifth century B.C.E. that prevents me from arguing that they articulate a Sophistic calculus or a Presocratic Lutheranism? Nehamas argues that even Nietzsche insists that some interpretations are better than others. The problem with some renditions of Nietzschean perspectivism "is that they have been too quick to equate possible with actual falsehood, interpretation with mere interpretation" (1985, 67). Noting that Nietzsche sought to replace the standard Christian interpretation of morality with his own, Nehamas argues that those who equate interpretation with mere interpretation "presuppose that to consider a view an interpretation is to concede that it is false" (1985, 66).

Even Jacques Derrida, famous for his claims about interpretive variability, notes that while there be no such thing as "the final, correct" pure interpretation, this does not level all interpretations as equal (1988, 144–46): Though even paraphrase is interpretation, he says, there are historically situated dominant "conventions" and "contracts" that inform judgments about better and worse readings. There is a good deal of "stability" (though "such stabilization is relative") about the shared language that "grant a minimum of intelligibility" to our readings of texts (1988, 144). Derrida refers to evidence concerning an author's intentions, what texts might have informed the writing/reading of the text under study, and what a historically situated audience may have gleaned from a particular text. Without such historical information, "one could indeed say just anything at all and I have never accepted saying, or encouraging others to say, just anything at all, nor have I argued for indeterminacy as such" (1988, 144–45).

Indeed, at least one of my critics acknowledges that it is untenable to reason from the premise that all history is interpretive to the conclusion that all interpretations are of equal value: "Neosophists are not 'subjectivists' for whom readings are arbitrary personal fabrications; for neosophists also reject the notion of individualistic 'free readers' who are able to interpret the texts in any way they choose, and still remain members of the interpretive community" (Consigny 1996, 254). Similarly, Steven Mailloux has described a "rhetorical hermeneutics" that rejects foundationalism but leaves room for historically situated argument over competing interpretations: "Putting aside realist and idealist foundationalism . . . does not mean that just anything goes" (1989, 145). Furthermore, Mailloux points out that "referring to textual details during an argument is not the same as trying to construct a general realist theory of reading" (1989, 146). In short, one can make text-based arguments without collapsing into foundationalism as long as one acknowledges one's presuppositions and the historical contingency of any given interpretation.

There are no magic formulas for knowing in advance the difference between good and bad interpretations or a more or less defensible historical account. But some interpretations are more persuasive than others, and hence display a longer shelf life. Some interpretations even become "facts." As long as we treat "facts" as temporarily reified interpretations that are socially constructed and subject to deconstruction, it does no harm to refer to facts, and their use even helps to explain the difference between more or less reliable historical accounts.

An example can illustrate the relationship between the process of reification/deconstruction and the social utility of facts. Consider the statement "John F. Kennedy died in 1963." I think it is fair to call this statement a reliable fact that most, if not all, readers would accept, and that is more persuasive than some alternatives ("JFK died in 1881") or the statement's contrary ("JFK did *not* die in 1963"). Nonetheless, it is possible to imagine that our fact could someday be rejected by the vast majority of people. Aside from the phenomenon of new theories that challenge the statement (such as clear proof of a secret conspiracy), the concepts and presuppositions underlying the statement could be revised. Postmodern challenges to the concept of "self" or "personhood" might render the notion of "John F. Kennedy" problematic; our understanding of *death* might change in such a way as to require revision of the statement; and, alternative calendar systems (or even a rejection of linear time) could make "1963" obsolete. But until we are willing to pay the conceptual cost of rejecting present notions of identity, death, or time, "John F. Kennedy died in 1963" can be regarded as a reliable fact.

Recent philosophers of science talk of facts and observations being "theory-bound." That is, even the simplest measurement or observation in science is made possible only through a host of conceptual commitments (Latour and Woolgar 1979). A scientist rejects a fact only at the cost of giving up the conceptual apparatus producing it, which is why Kuhn (1970) says that scientists abandon one theory only when a suitable alternative is available that also can account for certain facts. It is also the case that new theories sometimes have rendered old facts obsolete. Knowing that scientific facts are socially constructed, historically contingent, and theory-bound does not make them any less useful or reliable — it simply helps us to understand scientific research as a human activity. Similarly, the more general statement that "all facts are interpretations" does not vitiate the utility of facts. It simply helps us to understand the social processes that construct facts, and it points out that there is a conceptual cost to rejecting those that are widely shared and well established.

Accordingly, we can conclude that the interpretive, narrative, and rhetorical aspects of writing history do not require a cessation of efforts to evaluate competing historical accounts. To claim that an account is "not historically defensible" or problematic as a historical construct simply means that I find it difficult or impossible to reconcile that account with interpretations I have been persuaded to count as facts. The claim that the Sophists were all champions of democracy, for example, runs counter to my beliefs about who "counts" as Sophists, what "all" means, and how I understand "democracy." Unless I revise those beliefs, I will reject the statement as false, just I would reject as false the statement "JFK died in 1881." Doing so does not make me a traditionalist, positivist, objectivist, foundationalist who labors under the delusion that I have access to objective and uninterpreted facts. It means that I can acknowledge the contingency, rhetoricity, and constructedness of those claims

I treat as facts yet still believe them to be useful until persuaded to do otherwise. Though historians must concede that any account is potentially subject to later revision, they need not abandon their efforts to produce accounts that make sense of the available socially constructed, historically contingent facts.

The price we pay for giving up facts altogether is that we must give up history as well. Perhaps the most salient difference between the genre of literature called "history" and various sorts of fiction is that the former has something to do with using facts and avoiding anachronism (Schiappa 1995, 1996). In other words, being part of the interpretive community that engages in the language-game known as "writing history" means that one tries to avoid anachronism and factual errors. Note that this is a sociological contention, not one based on metaphysics. As Richard Rorty puts it, "What excites and convinces is a function of the needs and purposes of those who are being excited and convinced" (1992a, 105). The existence of differences between the needs and interests of different interpretive communities is why I have suggested that we, at times, distinguish between scholarly efforts aimed at historical reconstruction and those aimed at contemporary appropriation for use in theory development. Anachronism is a far more significant problem for the former than it is the latter.

If all interpretations were equally useful as history, then Ronald Reagan's history of the Vietnam War would be as reliable as that of Stanley Karnow, and his account of the Iran-Contra affair would be as good as that of Bill Moyers.[9] I hope these examples challenge the often implicit assumption that radically relativizing history is an emancipatory move; "it ain't necessarily so." "Facts" figure crucially in the power/knowledge dynamic problematized by Michel Foucault (1980). If power is all that writes history, then there is no basis for reclaiming marginalized histories, no basis for critiquing establishment narratives, and no basis for curing cultural amnesia about past genocide, misogyny, and racism. In the face of poststructuralist critiques of facts, one historian of rhetoric reports, "I feel almost paralyzed by the impossibility of writing history" (Crowley 1988, 13).[10] Her testimony suggests that — far from emancipation — excessive cynicism toward historical facts can induce intellectual self-imprisonment.

9. For a compelling analysis of Reagan's abuse of "facts," see Mark Green and Gail MacColl (1983).

10. James J. Murphy, describing a set of essays that explore various postmodern critiques of historiography, notes: "The impressive array of 'anxieties,' post-constructionist alarms, and post-Marxist shibboleths gathered here could well paralyze the would-be historian of rhetoric into a permanent state of writer's block" (1997, 267).

Sophistic Rhetoric has been and can be used to critique various sociopolitical arrangements and modernist notions of disciplinarity (Poulakos 1989a). Hence the Sophists' story is sometimes revisited as a useful chapter in the history of ideas. While I am in sympathy with the motivations of such endeavors, I also think it is important to recognize that such a turn can be as misleading as it is useful. From a host of perspectives — political, social, demographic, technological, economic, aesthetic, linguistic, and others — contemporary American life has little in common with ancient Greece. At a superficial level, one can find similarities between contemporary sociopolitical or educational arrangements and virtually any culture. Far more useful "chapters" in intellectual history abound, and most of them offer far more textual and other sorts of data than do the ancient Greeks. We need not turn to Athens to find strategies of oppression and marginalization; we need only look around us. We need not turn to ancient Greece to understand how power/knowledge relationships are manifested through disciplinary arrangements; we need only consider the past two centuries of the relationship between capitalism and higher learning. In short, we do not need the fiction of Sophistic Rhetoric as a way into pressing contemporary issues. In a culture saturated by rhetoric, we need not seek refuge in a romanticized fictionalization of a place long ago and far away.

There is an important sense in which the turn to Sophistic Rhetoric ideologically supports the status quo. By promoting a historical fiction we legitimize political leaders who do the same. By suggesting that there is a sort of transmillennial "essence" of Sophistic Rhetoric, we promote an outdated metaphysics that obfuscates our own contingency in history. Richard Rorty notes that historicist "writers tell us that the question 'What is it to be a human being?' should be replaced by questions like 'What is it to inhabit a rich twentieth-century democratic society?' . . . This historicist turn has helped free us, gradually but steadily, from theology and metaphysics — from the temptation to look for an escape from time and chance" (1989, xiii).

I am not saying that historians should ignore ancient Greece, or the group of individuals known as the Sophists. My point is only that once we grant that Sophistic Rhetoric is a problematic historical construct, we need not use it as a route to studying other topics. Instead, we should skip the detour and move directly to the contemporary sites of social and political struggle. As my late colleague James A. Berlin put it: "Rhetorics interpellate us, hail us, position us, subject us, put us in our places — and not in others. The places, the positions, the subjects, and subjectivities are not eternal and true, are not timeless and trusty. . . . *We need new rhetorics.* . . . We need rhetorics that allow new voices to be heard, new audiences to act, new actions to be taken, new actors for these actions, new ways of figuring the ways language figures us" (1990, 6–10).

Sophistic Rhetoric also has been invoked as a means for transcending certain philosophical dualisms that poststructuralist and postmodernist critiques have called into question. Aside from the obvious reply that these contemporary critiques make such a "Sophistic" turn superfluous, it is arguably the case that the notion of Sophistic Rhetoric reproduces such binary thinking (Schiappa 1996). Even if some scholars have succeeded in reversing the verdict on the case of *Plato v. Sophists,* they have not transcended the dualities implicit in the conflict. The postmodern challenge is not merely to reverse our evaluation of such pairs as rational/emotional, literal/figurative, truth/opinion, *physis/ nomos,* and Philosophy/Sophistry, but to deconstruct and replace the pairs.[11] Hegel portrayed the presocratics as Objectivists (thesis), the Sophists as Subjectivists (antithesis), and Plato/Aristotle as providing the proper synthesis. We do not overcome such binary oppositions by preferring one over the other; we overcome them by moving beyond the Hegelian framework.

The Rhetoric of Definition

A basic assumption of this chapter is that definitions are both normative and important. Most readers will concede the point that there is no correct definition of a word in any absolutist, metaphysical sense. One can either surrender to the conventional definition of a word—the most common or predominant definition—or one can defend an alternative. Accordingly, any discussion of a concept such as Sophistic Rhetoric unavoidably involves what can be called the rhetoric of definition—persuasion about how some facet of our experience ought to be labeled and defined (Schiappa 1993). Scholars defending Sophistic Rhetoric typically must engage in some act of defining what the terms mean to them, or else rely on readers' intuitions as to what the terms denote. Similarly, my efforts in this chapter have been concerned with the meaning(s) of "Sophistic Rhetoric." What is at stake is how we as a group of specialized language-users ought to define and use the phrase Sophistic Rhetoric—or whether it should be used at all. The question is normative because "all those who argue in favor of some definition want it . . . to influence the use which would probably have been made of the concept had they not intervened" (Perelman and Olbrechts-Tyteca 1969, 213).

My argument is that a historically defensible definition of a singular Sophis-

---

11. See, for example, Jarratt's (1991, 31–61) useful reworking of the *mythos/logos* pair into a fifth-century-inspired *mythos-nomos-logos* schema. Even though Jarratt's title refers to "the Sophists," she avoids most of the criticisms launched in this chapter by grounding her claims with specific fifth-century texts (mostly those of Protagoras and Gorgias) and by demonstrating considerable historiographical reflexivity.

tic Rhetoric derived from fifth-century Greece is improbable, and that ahistorical definitions are misleading, unhelpful, or superfluous. The principle of Ockham's Razor suggests that the notion of a monolithic Sophistic Rhetoric is expendable. If we want to empower certain contemporary discourses with identifying labels, then let us use labels that are more straightforward: feminist rhetoric, oppositional discourse, and cultural critique are three examples.

Or, if borrow we must, then let us be explicit about our debts. If we find more inspiration in Isocrates' educational program than in Plato's, then let us invoke Isocrates rather than the label "Sophistic," or at least pluralize our readings to acknowledge a number of Sophistic Rhetorics. Kathleen Welch's book (1990) is a positive model in this regard: she self-reflexively describes her efforts as "appropriations" of classical discourse, and she focuses on the contributions of specific individuals (Gorgias, Isocrates, and Plato) rather than on an artificial grouping. Alternatively, if we need a specific rhetorical antidote to competing appropriations of classical texts, then at least such labels as "Modern Sophistic" or "Neosophistic" acknowledge that it is we who have formulated the rhetoric, and that we are bracketing consideration of what "Sophistic" rhetoric might or might not have been (see, e.g., Haslett 1995; Lindblom 1996; McComiskey 1993, 1994).

Though most of my examples in this chapter have been drawn from recent champions of Sophistic Rhetoric, my argument cuts both ways in the dispute between those who praise or condemn the Sophists. That is, if it is anachronistic to praise fifth-century Sophistic Rhetoric, so too is it fallacious to castigate it (see Kastely 1997). Those who would praise Plato's or Aristotle's treatment of Rhetoric must do so on grounds other than by comparison with a hypothetical Sophistic Rhetoric if they want to avoid the charge of attacking a construct of straw. Anti-platonist historians of rhetoric may want to reconsider their use of Plato's terminology if they want to escape his dichotomous categories. Writers as diverse as Havelock (1963) and Derrida (1981, 106–17) have done much to undercut the Sophist/Philosopher distinction in Plato, and our theorizing of Rhetoric should be too quick to give back to Plato what has taken centuries to undo. There are important ways in which the Sophists' texts defy the labels "philosophy" and "rhetoric," "foundationalist" and "antifoundationalist," and "rationalistic" and "mythic-poetic," and thus give us way out of long-standing binary oppositions.

Approaching the sophists historically means, to me, approaching their texts with sufficient openness that one might learn something new. In chapter 10 I argue that there is a parallel between approaching a historical text and an Other human being. In addition to valuing what we may have in common (that which we see as "sameness") it is ethically imperative that we also seek and value that which we see initially as "strange" and "different." We learn more by trying to inhabit their world than by simply seizing on similarities and ignoring differences. What I find fascinating about the Sophists' texts is that the more I value their differences, the more I learn about how they bridge, transcend, or otherwise avoid certain dualities that have plagued us since Plato.

I believe that Sophistic Rhetoric is a construct that we can do without—a fiction originally invented by Plato for his own ends. We no longer need to maintain the fiction for ours.

5

"Philosophical Rhetoric" Reconsidered

This chapter reconsiders the remaining claims identified as part of the standard account of the beginning of Greek rhetorical theory:

13. The rhetorical teachings of the Sophists were amoral.

14. The Sophists were relativists who eschewed any positive notion of "truth" in favor of subjectivism. This claim is closely related to the next.

15. The Sophists were more concerned with teaching political success than pursuing truth, per se.

16. Plato's philosophical rhetorical theory was formulated primarily in response to fifth-century Sophistic rhetorical theory.

17. Plato's philosophical rhetorical theory can be distinguished from sophistic rhetorical theory by its commitment to truth — even when such a commitment conflicts with successful persuasion.

George A. Kennedy describes the Sophists as "self-appointed professors of how to succeed in the civic life of the Greek states." Though a few of the "leading" Sophists can "rightly be thought of as philosophers," most were "little more than teachers of devices of argument or emphasis" (1980, 25). Kennedy's treatment of the Older Sophists, like many other standard accounts, is based upon the assumption that the teaching of Rhetoric is the most fundamental defining characteristic of being a Sophist: "Sophistry was in large part a product of rhetoric, which was by far the older and in the end the more vital [art]" (1963, 26). All too often, Platonic or other pejorative senses of Rhetoric are assumed, rather than proven, to describe aptly what the Sophists were all about. Once the Sophists are equated with Rhetoric, it is difficult to resist the centuries-old tradition of defining them as distinct from and opposed to Philosophy — as the quotations cited in chapter 1 illustrate. My argument in this chapter is that the absence of a clear concept of *rhētorikē* or even *logōn technē* in the fifth century B.C.E. requires a careful reconsideration of what is asserted in statements defining or describing the Sophists with the term Rhetoric. Such a reconsideration, I believe, will cast doubt on the remaining claims of the standard account cited above.

I begin by contending that theoretical treatises written before and after the appearance of the word *rhētorikē* differ substantially. Since the definitions and systems of classification of Rhetoric and Philosophy in Plato's and Aristotle's work are well known,[1] this section surveys a series of passages from earlier works to provide an illustrative contrast. Explicit and implicit textual evidence supports the claim that teaching discourse was conceptualized in very different ways in the fifth and fourth centuries. Specifically, in the texts of the fifth century one does not find an explicit sense of a delimited art of the *rhētōr* that is restricted to political contexts or that is somehow distinct from the skills involved with being a philosophical thinker. There is no clear evidence of what I have called the disciplinary sense of Rhetoric. Furthermore, no necessary conflict emerges in the most significant texts of the fifth century between the goals of seeking successful persuasion and seeking "the truth." This is important because most scholars share Jacqueline de Romilly's belief that for the Sophists' "rhetorical" education, "success mattered more than the truth" (1992a, 82). After all, "unlike the philosophers, the new teachers were not disinterested theorists in quest of metaphysical truths" (1992a, 33). The basic point I wish to make, both here and in the succeeding chapters, is that the Rhetoric/Philosophy binary is an inappropriate framework within which to make sense of preplatonic texts, and thus the notion that "Philosophical Rhetoric" developed in response to a distinct fifth-century Sophistic Rhetoric is problematic.

A search for key terms provides evidence that no precise equivalent to the fourth-century term *rhētorikē* appears in the vocabulary of fifth-century texts. An intertextual comparison suggests a substantial difference between the explicit predisciplinary terminology of the fifth century and the technical vocabulary that emerged in the fourth. Obviously I cannot discuss every potentially relevant preplatonic text for comments about discourse, art, and persuasion.

1. See, e.g., Hunt (1925, 3–60); Baldwin (1924); Erickson (1974, 1979); and Kennedy (1963, 74–113; 1980, 41–85).

Fortunately, computer searches through the texts of the *Thesaurus Linguae Graecae* include all extant writings from the classical era. Personal inspection of the most relevant texts, complemented by *Thesaurus Linguae Graecae* searches for key terms in all preplatonic texts, allows us to generalize about the status of predisciplinary theory with some confidence.

The two specific concepts that combine to form *rhētorikē* are *technē*, as art or skill, and *rhētōr*. Significantly, one does not find the two terms explicitly linked in fifth-century texts, nor does one find an explicit reference to an art of persuasion.[2] The word *rhētōr* was a legal term denoting a specific class of people: those who often put forward motions in the law-courts and the assembly.[3] *Rhētōr* was not a very old term—the earliest extant use is from 445 B.C.E.; it appears far less in the fifth century than it does in the fourth.[4] Herodotus, for example, never used the word *rhētōr* (Powell 1977), and Thucydides refers to orators (*rhētores*) only three times.[5] And no surviving preplatonic text refers to a Sophist as a *rhētōr*. One cannot, then, explain the absence of *rhētorikē* in the fifth century by claiming that two words were used to delineate what Plato denoted with one word. The available evidence strongly suggests that the explicit notion of a specific art of the *rhētōr* was not yet fixed in Greek consciousness.

That both Plato and Aristotle use the expression *logōn technē* as an equivalent to *rhētorikē* to refer to the "art of speech"[6] has led scholars such as W. K. C. Guthrie to project the same usage back to the fifth century: "The rhetorical art was also known [among the Sophists] as 'the art of the *logoi*'" (1971, 177). However, the expression *logōn technē* appears very rarely in the fifth century, and when it does, it has a broader meaning than Rhetoric.[7] The reconstructed

2. According to a search with *Pandora* 2.1 for techn- near rhē-, and peith- near techn- in all preplatonic texts in *Thesaurus Linguae Graecae* Compact Disc version C. That the phrase πειθοῦς δημιουργός originates with Plato has been established by Hermann Mutschmann (1918, 440–43).

3. See Hansen (1981, 345–70); Ober (1989, 104–27); Sinclair (1988, 136–37). See also Hansen (1983a, 33–55; 1983b, 151–80).

4. See Wilcox (1942, 127); Tod (1985, 88–90); Meiggs and Lewis (1969, 128–33).

5. See 3.40.3, 6.29.3, and 8.1.1 in H. S. Jones and J. E. Powell (1942).

6. See, e.g., Plato, *Phaedrus* 260d4, 261b4–6, 263d5, 266c3, 266d6, 267b4, 267d7–8, 270a7, 271c2, 272b1–4, 273d7, 273e3; Aristotle, *Rhetoric* 1354a12, cf. 1356a11, 1356a17. The standard edition of Plato's *Phaedrus* is Burnet (1959), but cf. the text and commentary by Rowe (1986). For Aristotle's *Rhetoric*, see Kassel (1976) and Kennedy's translation (1991).

7. Investigated with a search using *Pandora* 2.1 for τεχν- proximate to λογ- or λεγ- in all preplatonic texts in *Thesaurus Linguae Graecae* CD-ROM version C.

treatise known as the *Anonymus Iamblichi* makes a passing reference to how quickly one could learn "the *technē* concerning arguments," but the syntax is different from the stock phrase *logōn technē,* perhaps because it was unfamiliar or not yet known.[8] The same is true of Gorgias' reference, in his *Helen,* to a speech "written with skill" (*technēi grapheis*).[9] The sophistic tract *Dissoi Logoi* or *Dialexeis* (hereafter *Dialexeis*) explicitly refers to *logōn technē,* but in that context the skill is described as distinct from the abilities "to plead one's court-cases correctly" and "to make popular speeches."[10] Thomas M. Robinson aptly translates *logōn technē* in this passage as "argument-skills."[11] Accordingly, if *logōn technē* in *Dialexeis* is the art that is the object of Plato's critique, it is clearly much broader than what would later be defined as Rhetoric.

Perhaps the most interesting early instance of *logōn technē* appears in Xenophon's *Memorabilia* from the early fourth century.[12] Xenophon claims that Critias the Tyrant, who bore a grudge against Socrates, issued an edict outlawing the teaching of *logōn technē:* "It was a calculated insult to Socrates, whom Critias saw no means of attacking except by imputing to him the practice constantly attributed to the philosophers" (*Memorabilia* 1.2.31).[13] A few sentences later Xenophon equates *logōn technē* with the Socratic practice of *dialegesthai* — "holding discussion" (*Memorabilia* 1.2.33–34). Regardless of the truth of the story about Critias' edict, clearly the scope of activities denoted by *logōn technē* was, even in the early fourth century, considerably broader than the art of political speechmaking. *Logōn technē* was sufficiently co-extensive with philosophical argumentation and discussion for Xenophon to believe that the phrase could be credibly linked to, and even spoken by, his hero Socrates. The usage of *logōn technē* in *Dialexeis* and by Xenophon both describe an art of discourse that show the early signs of professionalization and disciplinization — insofar as the skills described are specialized and not

---

8. καὶ τέχνην μὲν ἄν τις τὴν κατὰ λόγους πυθόμενος καὶ μαθὼν οὐ χείρων τοῦ διδάσκοντος ἂν γένοιτο ἐν ὀλίγωι χρόνωι (89 §2.7). For the Greek text see section 89 in DK, or Untersteiner (1949). For an English translation see section 89 in Sprague (1972). On the passage in question see also Kerferd (1981b, 126–27).

9. For the Greek text see DK or Untersteiner (fasc. II), sec. 82 B 11.13; for an English translation see the corresponding section in Sprague (1972), or Kennedy's updated translation in Matsen, Rollinson, and Sousa (1990, 34–46).

10. For the Greek text see DK or Untersteiner (fasc. III), sec. 90.8.1; for an English translation see the corresponding section in Sprague (1972), or Robinson (1979).

11. Robinson (1979, 227) correctly suggests that Sprague's translation of *logōn techne* (1972, 291–92) as "art of oratory" is overly restrictive.

12. For the dating of Xenophon's *Memorabilia* see Marchant (1923, xi).

13. Translation adapted from that by Marchant (1923).

accessible to all — yet are not as specifically delimited as the art of Rhetoric would be in the texts of Plato and Aristotle.

Fifth-century language use did not clearly delineate an explicit art of the *rhētōr*. Possibly, of course, such a notion could be pointed to within a given text even without a distinct lexical marker.[14] Implicit, intratextual evidence concerning such a conclusion is largely a matter of interpretation. Nevertheless, if one brackets the fourth-century notion of *rhētorikē* when reading several key fifth-century predisciplinary texts, it is apparent that the art of discourse is conceptualized in terms broader and less differentiated than that found in fourth-century texts. The three texts discussed here are Aristophanes' play *Clouds,* Gorgias' *Helen,* and the sophistic tract *Dialexeis.*

These three texts are arguably the best extant sources for evidence about the language used to describe sophistic teaching in the fifth century. Because the point of Aristophanes' *Clouds* was to parody the Sophists, and because Aristophanes has a documented penchant for borrowing and making fun of new technical jargon (Denniston 1927, 113–21; Chantraine 1956, 98–99; O'Sullivan 1992, 7), *Clouds* is a very valuable source for evidence about sophistic theorizing — as long as it is kept in mind that Aristophanes was writing a comedy, not a history.[15] Gorgias' *Helen* is the most theoretical discussion of persuasive speech found in the fifth century. Kerferd claims that it provides "our best insight" into sophistic rhetorical theory (1981b, 78). And, though it has been largely overlooked by historians of rhetoric, *Dialexeis* is an important sophistic text that includes an enumeration of specific verbal activities and skills. Particularly in light of the fact that all three texts date from very late in the fifth century, they are our most useful guides to the preplatonic, predisciplinary vocabulary concerning discourse.

Aristophanes' Clouds

Three aspects of Aristophanes' *Clouds* are particularly noteworthy. First, as noted in the previous chapter, the play posits a close relationship between thinking and speaking, and between acquiring wisdom and the abil-

14. See, for example, the relatively late (340 B.C.E. at the earliest) treatise known as the *Rhetoric to Alexander* that, while not using the word *rhētorikē,* clearly belongs to the "disciplined" writings of the fourth century rather than the predisciplinary writings of the fifth. For Greek text and an English translation, see Rackham (1937).

15. The best critical edition of the *Clouds* is that by Dover (1968a); see also Reckford (1987, 388–402). The surviving version of *Clouds* has been dated to ca. 418 B.C.E. (see Storey's 1993 reply to Kopff 1990).

ity to persuade. When prompted by Socrates[16] to explain how he will avoid paying his debts by "analyzing correctly" (*orthōs diairōn*), Strepsiades suggests three solutions: hire an enchantress to steal the moon, for without the moon there would be no way to compute monthly payments; use a "burning-glass" to burn up the written summons for his debt from a distance; or, if all else fails, hang himself so that no one can bring suit to collect (*Clouds* 737–84).[17] Pheidippides, Strepsiades' son, shows his ability to win a suit after attending the Thinkery through the use of clever reasoning, not through formal speechmaking. Pheidippides argues that creditors cannot force payment on the traditional collection day, called "Old-and-New Day," since it is as impossible for a day to be both old and new as it is for a woman to be old and young (*Clouds* 1178–1200).[18] Throughout the play, Aristophanes portrays the process of learning to speak (*mathōn legein*) as a natural consequence of learning to engage in "sophisticated" (though sometimes absurd) reasoning.

The second noteworthy aspect of *Clouds* is the surprising variety of subjects explored at the Thinkery. The subjects include what are now called astronomy, surveying, geometry, and meteorology; all are lampooned as serious interests of the Thinkery's inhabitants.[19] Third, there is a noticeable lack of the sort of disciplinary jargon one might expect to be associated with sophistic teaching concerning Rhetoric. Neither *technē* (in the sense of art or skill) nor *rhētōr* are mentioned — even when the Clouds promise Strepsiades that no one will pass more motions in the assembly than he (*Clouds* 431–32).[20] Although in *Clouds* a general art of persuasion is implicit and a specific art of the *rhētōr* is nascent, Aristophanes clearly did not reduce all sophistic teaching to training in public speaking. Furthermore, he portrays sophistic training as involving what we would now call critical reason and a scientific outlook. In many

16. Most commentators agree that Aristophanes used "Socrates" as his central character for dramatic reasons and that his treatment was directed at Sophistic education in general (which, for Aristophanes, included Socrates' pedagogical habits). See Dover (1968, xxxii–lvii); W. J. M. Starkie (1911, xlvi–l); B. B. Rogers (1924, 263–64).

17. See Dover 1968a, 191–96; Starkie 1911, 172–81.

18. See Dover 1968a, 235–37; Starkie 1911, 256–61.

19. For historical evidence supporting the notion that the Sophists investigated a broad variety of subjects, including those we now call scientific, see Kerferd (1981b), and Dupréel (1948).

20. True, *pasēi technēi* appears at 885 and 1323, but as Dover (1968, 208, cf. 249) notes, "this expression does not refer to sophistic technique, but makes an imperative or its equivalent into an urgent plea." The lack of such terminology is particularly noteworthy since "La parodie d'Aristophane définit à merveille le ton des adjectifs nouveaux en *-ikos*" (Chaintraine 1956, 99).

ways, even discounting the playwright's hostility, the thinkers of Aristophanes' Thinkery are difficult to distinguish from those who would soon be called philosophers. This point is not surprising if we recall that the Athenian public — unlike Plato — "made no attempt to differentiate sophists from philosophers" (Ostwald 1986, 259). With hindsight we can interpret specific portions of *Clouds* as an attack on Rhetoric, but a more historical reading suggests that the play was an attack on the newfangled "higher education" in general. Rhetoric — though it would later become a distinct subject — was still a largely undifferentiated part of skill in *logos*.

Gorgias' Helen

Although scholars disagree about the precise purpose of Gorgias' *Helen,* most agree that the speech contains Gorgias' most explicit analysis of *logos.*[21] Gorgias' *logos* should be understood as broad in scope and holistic in function, the result being a relationship between Sophist and *logos* not unlike that found in Aristophanes.[22] To understand the persuasive effects of *logos,* Gorgias outlines what one must study: "[F]irst, the arguments of the astronomers (*tōn meteōrologōn logōn*) who, substituting opinion for opinion (*doxa*), removing one and instilling another, make what is incredible and unclear appear true to the eyes of opinion; second, the forceful contests of argumentation,[23] where one side of the argument, written with skill but not spoken with truth, pleases a large audience and persuades; third, the debates of rival philosophers (*philosophōn logōn hamillas*), in which swiftness of thought is also exhibited, making belief in an opinion easily changed" (*Helen* 13). The breadth of activities associated with persuasion by means of *logos* demonstrates that, for Gorgias, the skills of *logos* were much broader in scope than those of the discipline *rhētorikē* as explicated by Plato and Aristotle.[24] Gorgias' description of *logos* as "a powerful lord" is well known. For Gorgias, *logos* is "an independent external power which forces the hearer to do its will" (Segal 1962, 121).[25] Since his *logos* is a psycho-physical force that acts directly on the

21. Translations of Gorgias' *Helen* are based on Kennedy (1972b; 1991, 284–88). For text see Buchheim (1989) and DK 82 B11.

22. If one finds a "theory of deception" in Gorgias' views on language, it would be the case that *all* discourse is "deceptive." As the *Helen* shows (13), philosophers and rhetoricians are equally close to, or distant from, "the truth" in their efforts to persuade. Cf. Verdenius (1981, 116–28).

23. Cf. Kennedy's alternate translation of τοὺς ἀναγκαίους διὰ λόγων ἀγῶνας as "logically necessary debates" (1972b, 53).

24. On the breadth of the Sophistic senses of *logos* see Kerferd (1981b, 83).

25. See also Mourelatos (1985, 607–38).

psyche, his analogy between the effect of drugs and that of *logos* is literal (Segal 1962, 104–7): "for just as different drugs dispel different secretions from the body, and some bring an end to disease and others to life, so also in the case of *logos* — some bring pain, others pleasure, some bring fear, others instill courage in the hearers, and some drug and bewitch the psyche with a kind of evil persuasion" (*Helen* 14).

In Plato's and Aristotle's writings, the psyche becomes the composite of distinct specialized functions (such as in Plato's myth of the charioteer) wherein *logos* is contrasted to the emotions (Guthrie 1975, 421–25; 1981, 277–327). Gorgias' theory of *logos* culminates, according to Charles P. Segal, as a "full-blown 'scientific' theory in the *Poetics* of Aristotle" (1962, 134). Once contrasted to Plato's and Aristotle's compartmentalization of different verbal arts (poetic, eristic, dialectic, rhetoric, etc.) and their corresponding forms of comprehension, the holistic and largely undifferentiated sense of Gorgias' *logos* becomes apparent:[26] "The consequent division of the psyche, with a hierarchical ranking of its parts, represents in a sense a narrowing in the attitude toward the psyche and a relinquishing of the sense of the organic relationship and balance between rational and emotional capabilities that characterized the fifth century" (Segal 1962, 134). It is appropriate, therefore, to categorize Gorgias' treatment of *logos* as prediscrimary.

Dialexeis

The third fifth-century text examined here is the treatise *Dialexeis,* dated ca. 400 B.C.E.[27] Attempts to identify the author have been inconclusive; one explanation is that the *Dialexeis* is a collection of notes, never intended for publication, gleaned from lectures by one or more Sophists (Robinson 1979, 41–54). Most of the surviving text consists of illustrations of Protagoras' thesis that "About every 'thing' there are two *logoi,* opposed to each other" and a discussion of the semantic implications of the thesis.[28] The remaining chapters drop the two-sided approach and directly address topics of popular interest among intellectuals. Of the nine chapters, three are of special value for the purposes of this chapter. Chapter two is entitled "On Seemly and Shameful." After describing a variety of "things" that are seemly to some but shameful to others, the author interjects the notion of *kairos* — a concept often asso-

26. On Plato's division of verbal arts see Kerferd (1981b); Nehamas (1990, 3–16).

27. For the dating and translation of *Dialexeis,* see Robinson (1979, 34–41). Conley (1985, 59–65) doubts the standard dating, but the absence of fourth-century terminology provides support for the traditional date of around 400 B.C.E.

28. For a survey of the literature and discussion of Protagoras' thesis, see Schiappa (1991, ch. 5).

ciated with sophistic theories or "definitions" of rhetoric:[29] "To put the matter generally, all things are seemly when done at the right time, but shameful when done at the wrong time" (*Dialexeis* 2.20). Chapter nine concerns memorization. Before suggesting ways of improving one's memory, the author claims that the ability to memorize is an important discovery: "It is useful for all purposes, for both Inquiry and Wisdom" (*es philosophian te kai sophian*).[30] What is noteworthy about both chapters is the complete lack of reference to political or public-speaking contexts. In light of the centrality of the topics of *kairos* and memory to (later) classical approaches to rhetoric, the absence of any rhetorical treatment of them in the *Dialexeis* implies that the disciplinary matrix connecting these concepts to persuasive speechmaking either had not emerged or was not yet fixed in Greek language or thought.[31]

The opening sentence of chapter eight of the *Dialexeis* depicts a single, all-purpose *technē* that the author commends to the audience: "I believe it belongs to the same man and to the same skill to be able to hold dialogue succinctly, to understand the truth of things, to plead one's court-cases correctly, to be able to make popular speeches, to understand argument-skills, and to teach about the nature of all things — how they are [their condition] and how they came to be" (*Dialexeis* 8.1).[32] Besides the audacious breadth of the abilities pictured by the author, the passage is noteworthy for the terminology it fails to use. Normally one would expect to find the word "dialectic" (*dialektikē*) to designate skill in dialogue, as well as *rhētorikē* and *philosophia* to refer to the other skills explicated. The lack of these terms is good evidence for the preplatonic, predisciplinary character of the treatise. Once clearly conceptualized and disciplinized, Rhetoric and Philosophy were seen as in tension because the goals of the two subjects, political success and truth, were, according to Plato, incompatible. The significance of chapter eight of *Dialexeis* is that no such incompatibility is evident. Far from it: success and true understanding are presented as two sides of the same coin. Compare the phrase here with Socrates' words as portrayed by Plato decades later: "A man must know the truth about all the particular things of which he speaks or writes, and be able to define everything separately" (*Phaedrus*, 277b).

Robinson characterizes the skill discussed in chapter eight of *Dialexeis* as *omnicompetence:* an ability to produce true and compelling discourse in a

29. See Kennedy (1963, 66–68); Race (1981, 197–213); Poulakos (1983a, 27–42).

30. Based on Robinson's and Untersteiner's (fasc. III) editions *Dialexeis* §9.1 (cf. DK 2: 416).

31. On the notion of *disciplinary matrix* see Kuhn (1970, 182).

32. For the Greek see DK 90.8.1 or chapter 2, note 6, above.

Fifth- and Fourth-Century Conceptualizations Contrasted

	Scope	Means	Ends	Context
Logos (as a predisciplinary focal term)	General: "Thinkers," speakers, and arguers	Various forms of argumentation, discussion, Q&A, and speeches	Success/ Truth	General: Both political and nonpolitical
Rhētorikē (as a disciplinary focal term)	Specific: *Rhētôr*	Formal speeches	Success	Political and specific: Deliberative, forensic, and epideictic settings
Philosophia (as a disciplinary focal term)	Specific: Philosopher	Dialectic (or scientific demonstration)	Truth	Nonpolitical and private settings

variety of circumstances (1979, 221–37; 1977). Such omnicompetence resonates with the scope and function of *logos* in Gorgias and sophistic training as portrayed by Aristophanes. Before discourse was fragmented into various disciplines in the fourth-century writings of Plato and Aristotle, fifth-century studies in and of *logos* supplied a multifaceted training for the mind, to paraphrase Isocrates, just as gymnastic training of the era provided rigorous training for the body.

The table above offers an illustrative contrast between the conceptualizations of *logos* and *rhētorikē* in the fifth and fourth centuries B.C.E. Any summary representation such as offered here is bound to oversimplify the similarities and differences among positions. Different Sophists articulated distinctive theories of *logos,* and Plato's and Aristotle's theories of Rhetoric were quite distinct. Nonetheless, it is my hope that this table usefully represents the Platonic-Aristotelian legacy of differentiating between Rhetoric and Philosophy as distinctive, rival disciplines.[33]

The preceding analysis is sufficient, I hope, to challenge the logic behind the claims of the standard account repeated at the beginning of this chapter:

Sophist : Success-Seeking Rhetoric : : Philosopher : Truth-Seeking Philosophy

33. As I make clear in chapter 10, Isocrates had a quite different disciplinary sense of *philosophia.*

Space does not permit a comprehensive redescription of the dominant view of the Older Sophists, so for the purposes of this chapter I will simply assert the existence of a counterview that portrays the Sophists as quite different from what Plato described (see Kerferd 1981b; de Romilly 1988). According to the revised view, the Sophists were not fundamentally different from the people now referred to as Philosophers. From the standpoint of method of inquiry, subject matters pursued, and even specific doctrines espoused, what the so-called presocratic philosophers, Socrates, the Sophists, and Plato had in common "was of greater importance than what separated them" (Havelock 1963, 290). All represented an "intellectualist movement" that broke from traditional modes of discourse and thinking. "If they were called 'philosophers,' it was not for their doctrines as such, but for the kind of vocabulary and syntax which they used and the unfamiliar psychic energies that they represented. Sophists, pre-Socratics, and Socrates had one fatal characteristic in common; they were trying to discover and to practise abstract thinking" (Havelock 1963, 285–86).

The most significant difference between those the ancient sources call Sophists and Philosophers seems to be the economic and social class with which each group is identified. As Ostwald has documented in detail, most writers from the fifth and early fourth centuries B.C.E. were conservative members of the upper classes. Their writings display a remarkably consistent bias against Athenian democracy in general, and the middle class from which most democratic leaders came (after Pericles) in particular (Ostwald 1986, 213–29). Accordingly, since the Sophists were often from the middle classes (or, worse yet, from an Athenian standpoint, were foreigners), they are seldom treated kindly in the literature of their time. Regardless of the reasons for traditional biases against the Sophists, the important points are that the standard view of the Sophists is being radically revised, and that part of that revision must include a reconsideration of what is meant by Sophistic Rhetoric. In what follows, I provide a brief account of two of the most important Sophists, Protagoras and Gorgias, in order to illustrate further the point that the standard view of the origins of rhetorical theory has oversimplified their contributions to Greek thought.

Protagoras and Gorgias

The term *logos* was one of the most overworked words of ancient Greek and is difficult to translate into English. Summarizing the predominant senses of *logos* found in the fifth century B.C.E., Kerferd has written: "[T]here are three main areas of its application or use, all related by an underlying conceptual unity. These are first of all the area of language and linguistic formulation, hence speech, discourse, description, statement, arguments (as expressed in words) and so on; secondly the area of thought and mental processes, hence thinking, reasoning, accounting for, explanation (cf. *orthos logos*), etc.; thirdly, the area of the world, that *about* which we are able to speak and to think, hence structural principles, formulae, natural laws and so on, provided that in each case they are regarded as actually present in and exhibited in the world-process" (1981b, 83).

The *logos* of sixth- and fifth-century thinkers is best understood as a rationalistic rival to traditional *mythos* — the religious worldview preserved in epic poetry: "Philosophy proper arose as a commentary upon and correction of the cosmic imagery of Homer and the cosmic architecture of Hesiod's *Theogony*" (Havelock 1983, 80). The epic poets in general and Homer in particular enjoyed a sort of institutional status in Greek society. The poetry of the time performed the functions now assigned to a variety of educational practices: religious instruction, moral training, history texts, and reference manuals (Havelock 1963, 29). Because the vast majority of the population did not read regularly, poetry was preserved communication that served as Greek culture's collective stored memory. Accordingly, poetry enjoyed a monopoly over education in general and "citizenship training" in particular (Havelock 1963, 43).

Havelock has documented in detail the role of those we now call presocratic philosophers in advancing abstract analysis over the mythic-poetic tradition (Havelock 1982, ch. 11; 1983). The evidence is clear that the Older Sophists performed the same role in the fifth century B.C.E., as did Plato in the fourth. In the dialogue *Protagoras,* Socrates and Protagoras engage in an analysis of a passage by the poet Simonides (338e–348a). Commentators have viewed Socrates' outrageous (mis-)interpretation of the passage as evidence of Plato's distrust of poetry and poetic interpretation (Guthrie 1975, 227; Taylor 1976, 141–48). As C. C. W. Taylor notes, the section also provides clues about Protagoras: "It seems likely that he saw the importance of literary criticism rather in developing the critical faculty and the exact use of language than in promoting the understanding and appreciation of poetry as an end in itself" (1976, 141). Protagoras points out a contradiction in Simonides' poem and claims that it is important to be able to evaluate poetry and give a *logos* when questioned (339a). Even allowing for some degree of distortion by Plato, it is clear that Protagoras has made a crucial analytical leap: from mere repetition of the culture's repository of wisdom to its critical analysis. His analysis was "meta-poetic" in the sense that poetry had become an *object* of study rather than being the medium through which the world was understood (as it was for the nonliterate).

Aristotle also provides evidence of Protagoras' critical approach to poetry. In *Sophistic Refutations* (173b) and in the *Rhetoric* (1407b6–7) Aristotle reports that Protagoras was concerned with the proper gender of words, and in the *Poetics* claims that Protagoras criticized the opening of Homer's *Iliad* for using the mode of "command" rather than "request" (1465b15). Ammonius quotes Protagoras critically analyzing another passage in the *Iliad* (DK 80A30). The *Gnomologium Vaticanum* records the following anecdote: "When a maker of verses cursed Protagoras because he would not approve of his poems, his answer was 'My good sir, I am better off enduring your abuse than enduring your poems' " (DK 80A25 trans. in Sprague 1972, 16).

In short, there is some evidence that Protagoras broke from the poetic tradition by making poetry a subject of critical analysis. Other presocratics had criticized Homer and Hesiod, but Protagoras' method of analysis was different and original. When Heraclitus criticized the poets for failing to recognize that day and night are One, it was a matter of his opinion (*doxa*) versus theirs (DK 22, B57; see Kahn 1979). After Parmenides describes the nature of "what-is," it is defended as being the result of divine revelation. In both instances *logos* is understood as rationalized *mythos,* and is set against a traditional *mythos.* With Protagoras *mythos* became an object of analysis, a text or *logos* that can be analyzed, criticized, and altered. Plato's account of Protagoras analyzing epic poetry is the earliest recorded instance of "textual criticism" and it apparently started a practice that was continued by other sophists at least through Isocrates' time (see *Panathenaicus* 18).

The extant fragments of Protagoras, when viewed as a whole, form a coherent view of humanity, discourse, and the world (Schiappa 1991). A summary of his more important fragments can demonstrate, albeit in cursory fashion, how his theorizing represented an advancement over mythic explanations of the world and contributed to the further development of rhetorical theory and practice. His most famous aphorism is "Of all things the measure is Humanity: Of that which is, that it is the case, of that which is not, that it is not the case" (DK 80 A1).[34] The aphorism was allegedly the opening line of a book that was motivated, in part, as a critique of Eleatic monism as espoused by Parmenides (see Gagarin 1968, 122; Austin 1986, 120; Guthrie 1971, 47; Kerferd 1981b, 92). Protagoras' point seems to have been that *humans* are the judge of what is or is not the case, not the gods or heroes of epic poetry, and not the divinely inspired philosophical poets like Parmenides. It is commonly accepted that Protagoras helped provide the theoretical justification for Per-

34. For thoughtful treatments of the Human-as-Measure fragment, see Guthrie (1971, 188–92); Untersteiner (1954, 77–91); Versenyi (1962, 178–84).

iclean democracy. Although the precise relationship between Pericles and Protagoras is far from certain, it is clearly the case that both Parmenides' and Protagoras' "philosophical" positions had strong ideological implications.[35] Accordingly, it is accurate to say that Protagoras' particular rationalization of the *mythos* is in keeping with the trends of Athenian democracy.

Protagoras' "two-*logoi*" fragment states that two opposing *logoi* are true concerning every experience. The thesis is an extension of contemporary theorizing about the nature of "things." By the fifth century, the predominant rationalistic (non-mythical) schemata for understanding nature were various theories of "opposites" (Kahn 1960, 119–65). Human health was understood by many fifth-century physicians as being an appropriate balance of opposites, such as dry and wet, hot and cold (see Jones 1923, 2:229). During the sixth and fifth centuries B.C.E. theories of opposites grew more sophisticated as the available analytical vocabulary and syntax evolved, and Protagoras' two-*logoi* statement contributed to that evolution. The two-*logoi* statement has proven difficult to interpret because the meaning of *logoi* mentioned is unclear. Did Protagoras simply mean that two competing speeches are possible about every "thing," or did he mean that each "thing" could be experienced in contrary fashion such that two opposing *accounts* could both be true? The answer must be both. The philological evidence from the fifth century B.C.E. suggests that *logos* covered equally the notion of objective states, courses of action, or ways of life, as well as speeches about the states and actions (Cole 1972). Accordingly, Protagoras' statement must be interpreted as a claim about the world as well as a claim about discourse.

The Protagorean fragment most conducive to interpretation as an incipient theory of rhetoric is his alleged "promise" recorded by Aristotle to "make the weaker argument stronger" (*Rhetoric* 1402a23). Traditionally the statement has been interpreted as representing "sophistry" at its worst, as reflected in Lane Cooper's translation "making the worse appear the better cause" (1932, 177). Accordingly, those who reduce Sophistic teaching to "mere" rhetoric tend to refer to Protagoras' promise as evidence of the unethical nature of their lessons. Such an interpretation of the fragment does much violence to the actual Greek and ignores much of what is known about the historical Protagoras. As mentioned earlier in this chapter, the superior interpretation is to read the "promise" in tandem with the two-*logoi* fragment. What Protagoras meant by making one *logos* stronger than its opposite was the substitution of a preferred (but weaker) *logos* for a less preferable (but temporarily dominant)

---

35. For Protagoras see Morrison (1941, 1–16); for Parmenides see Minar (1949, 41–53).

logos of the same "experience."[36] Again, *logos* carries a dual reference: to the end-condition a speaker seeks to change (from the weaker to the stronger) and to the means of producing such a change.

Over time the sense of *logos* as an end-condition would fade as increasing attention was given to *logos* as a means of effecting change. Nevertheless, it can be stated with confidence that Protagoras' theorizing about *logos* heralds an important beginning of the development of what would later be called rhetorical theory. Based strictly on his methods and doctrines it is difficult to distinguish between Protagoras and his predecessors. Both broke from the poetic-mythic tradition, and both sought a rationalistic account of the world and how to change it. "Philosophical" and "Sophistic" rhetoric have more in common than the traditional account acknowledges.

Protagoras' doctrines by no means exhaust fifth-century theorizing about *logos*. A second example of an incipient rhetorical theory of the fifth century B.C.E. is that of Gorgias' approach to *logos*. A brief summary is offered to illustrate further the need for individualistic studies that provide an alternative to the standard account of early Greek rhetorical theory.

The prevailing opinion concerning Gorgias is that he was not a particularly serious thinker, that his rhetorical style was excessively ornate, and that the portrayal found in Plato's dialogue of the same name is generally accurate. In the past thirty years, an alternative picture of Gorgias has begun to emerge that treats him as a serious thinker with legitimately "philosophical" interests. The difference between the two views can be attributed, in large measure, to the relationship one assumes between Gorgias and Rhetoric. Kennedy, reflecting the attitude that "rhetorical" interests logically precede the content of the Sophists' teachings, suggests that the new "philosophical approach to Gorgias . . . probably exaggerates his intellectual sophistication and credits him with an uncharacteristic power of conceptualization" (1980, 31).

This book sides with the position that Gorgias, like Protagoras, was a serious thinker who shared an interest in advancing *logos* over *mythos*. Plato and Theophrastus report that Gorgias subscribed to Empedoclean theories concerning the sun, optics, and color (DK 82 B4, 5, cf. A17, B31). Such interests clearly identify Gorgias with the new rationalism considered characteristic of the "philosophers" of his time. Charles H. Kahn has written two seminal works concerning the Greek verb *einai*, "to be" (1966, 1973). Kahn's extensive survey of the ancient Greek literature revealed that there were cer-

---

36. See O'Brien's translation of the weaker/stronger *logoi* fragment in Sprague (1972, 13); Cole (1972); Kerferd (1967, 506).

tain technical constructions of the verb "to be" that occurred very rarely in pre-Platonic writings. According to Kahn, at least one of the technical uses, the negative form of *einai,* was employed exclusively by "philosophers" (1973, 366–70). Significantly, both Protagoras' and Gorgias' extant fragments employ such a negative form of *einai.* Protagoras uses the negative construction of *einai* twice in his "man-measure" statement, and Gorgias authored an entire address on the subject of "On Not Being."

The argument advanced in Gorgias' *On Not Being* has long been the subject of controversy. Gorgias' argument was threefold: "(1) nothing is, (2) even if it is, it cannot be known to human beings, (3) even if it is and is knowable, it cannot be indicated and made meaningful to another person" (Kerferd 1981b, 93, based on DK 82, B3). Most commentators agree that the argument was prompted by the extreme monism embodied in Parmenides work "On Being," and that Gorgias was attempting to refute Parmenides' position by reducing it to absurdity. However, there is little agreement whether the argument should be considered "philosophical" or merely "rhetorical." As has been suggested previously, the dichotomy is anachronistic-a point that will be explored further in chapter eight. As has been amply documented by Kerferd, the address was concerned with theoretical controversies that were at the heart of the fifth-century intellectual movement (1981b, 93–99). Gorgias raised issues that would now be referred to as having to do with predication, meaning, and reference — issues that later became of vital importance to Plato. Accordingly, it makes little sense to dismiss the seriousness of Gorgias' addresses on the premise that a "mere" rhetorician would not have held serious theoretical positions.

Like Protagoras, Gorgias held an implicit theory of *logos* that can be usefully understood as an incipient rhetorical theory. Gorgias' theory of *logos* has been carefully analyzed by Segal (1962) and is discussed in more detail in chapter seven. According to Segal, the key to Gorgias' theory is a literal analogy between drugs and *logoi.* As a doctor's drugs affect the diseases and the life of the body, *logoi* alter the psyche and the emotions: "The processes of the psyche are thus treated as having a quasi-physical reality and, perhaps more significant, as being susceptible to the same kind of control and manipulation by a rational agent as the body by the drugs of the doctor" (1962, 104). The force of *logos* works directly on the psyche, having an immediate ability to change it from one state to another. Gorgias' conception of *logos* and the psyche has more in common with the materialism of Democritus than the idealism expressed in Plato's philosophy. For that reason, it, like other fifth-century writings concerning *logos,* rarely has been understood or appreciated.

Viewed in its historical context, Gorgias' writings can be respected as an early effort towards theorizing about subjects that remain difficult over two thousand years later.

The point of this chapter has been to call into question the traditional ways of differentiating between Philosophical and Sophistic Rhetorical Theory. I am certainly not claiming that there are no salient differences among the figures known as Sophists, Plato, and Aristotle. I merely want to problematize those parts of the standard account of the beginnings of Greek rhetorical theory that have been based on what I believe are misreadings of key fifth-century texts. At this point, all of the claims I have associated with the standard account have been challenged. In the chapters that follow, I do not seek to provide a full and complete counternarrative. While it possible to reconstruct the history of ancient rhetorical theory as "the growth of a single, great, traditional theory" (Kennedy 1963, 9), I strongly suspect that any such effort would similarly fall victim to oversimplifying the key figures involved and overgeneralizing from the available texts. Instead, my goal is to attempt to illustrate the utility of a different approach to the texts in question — an approach that focuses on *petits récits* rather than a grand narrative, and an approach that explores the process of theorizing and disciplining itself, rather than examining the texts of the time as end-products of a process already completed.

PART II

Gorgias and the Disciplining of Discourse
Three Studies

6

Gorgias' Compositional Style

Anyone with more than a casual interest in Gorgias eventually must come to terms with his unusual and infamous style. As with other provocative Sophistic texts, there is considerable disagreement over how Gorgias' style ought to be assessed. Barrett praises his style as "winsome and novel" (1987, 17), while Jacqueline de Romilly claims that the "remarkable" prose of Gorgias "made the glamour of elevated style available to all" (1975, 21). E. R. Dodds calls Gorgias "an indefatigable stylist, a man who polished painfully every sentence that he wrote," but concludes that his style is "affected and boring" (1959, 8–9). Cole blasts Gorgias' style as "arhetorical," without ethos, and full of "stiff formality" and "harshness to the ear" (1991a, 73). Eduard Norden blames Gorgias' style, in part, for the death of Greek tragedy (1958, 78), R. C. Jebb describes Gorgias as "an artist whose faults are to us peculiarly glaring" (1962 [1893], cxxiv), Larue Van Hook calls his style "inartistic in the extreme" (1913, 122), Kennedy refers to it as "highly artificial" (1989, 83), and J. D. Denniston wondered, bluntly, how he was able to "get away with it" (1952, 12).

In this chapter I want to revisit the issue of Gorgias' style in an effort to understand his contributions to early Greek prose composition.[1] In the pro-

---

1. Portions of this chapter previously appeared in *Pre/Text*, 12 (1991): 237–57. They are reprinted by permission of the publisher.

cess, I hope to show that Gorgias does not deserve the volume of vilification he has received. I develop my argument in five sections. First, I sample a selection of Gorgias' stylistic wares to describe their most distinctive features. Second, I summarize and particularize the criticisms that have been leveled against Gorgias by ancient as well as recent reviewers. Third, I defend Gorgias' style by repositioning it as an important and positive part of promoting and advancing performance-prose composition in early Greek literature. Fourth, I consider the question of whether Gorgias has an explicit theory of arrangement. Last, I discuss aspects of Gorgias' use of meter.

Disassembling Gorgias' Distinctive Style

Gorgias' style is difficult to convey in English. I begin by relating selected passages of *Helen* and the *Epitaphios;* first in Greek, then English.[2]

Κόσμος πόλει μὲν εὐανδρία, σώματι δὲ κάλλος, ψυχῆι δὲ σοφία, πράγματι δὲ ἀρετή, λόγωι δὲ ἀλήθεια. τὰ δὲ ἐναντία τούτων ἀκοσμία. ἄνδρα δὲ καὶ γυναῖκα καὶ λόγον καὶ ἔργον καὶ πόλιν καὶ πρᾶγμα χρὴ τὸ μὲν ἄξιον ἐπαίνου ἐπαίνωι τιμᾶν, τῶι δὲ ἀναξίωι μῶμον ἐπιθεῖναι. μίση γὰρ ἁμαρτία καὶ ἀμαθία μέμφεσθαί τε τὰ ἐπαινετὰ καὶ ἐπαινεῖν τὰ μωμητά. (*Helen* 1)

Becoming to a city is a goodly army; to a body beauty, to a soul wisdom, to an action excellence, to speech truth. But their opposites are unbecoming. Man and woman and speech and deed and city and event should be honored with praise if praiseworthy, but on the unworthy blame should be laid; for it is equal error and ignorance to blame the praiseworthy and to praise the blame-worthy. (adapted from Kennedy 1991, 284)

Εἰ δὲ βίαι ἡρπάσθη καὶ ἀνόμως ἐβιάσθη καὶ ἀδίκως ὑβρίσθη,
δῆλον ὅτι ὁ ἁρπάσας ἢ ὑβρίσας ἠδίκησεν,
ἡ δὲ ἁρπασθεῖσα ἢ ὑβρισθεῖσα ἐδυστύχησεν. (*Helen* 7)

But if by violence she was defeated
and unlawfully she was treated
and to her injustice was meted,
clearly her violator as a terrifier was importunate,
while she, translated and violated, was unfortunate. (Van Hook 1913)

ἐπειράθην καταλῦσαι μώμου ἀδικίαν
καὶ δόξης ἀμαθίαν,

2. Unless otherwise indicated, English translations of Greek are adaptations of those by Kennedy (1972b; 1991) of Gorgias, by Kennedy (1991) of Aristotle's *Rhetoric,* and of those available in the various Loeb editions in the case of other classical Greek authors. For Greek text for Gorgias see DK section 82 and Buchheim (1989).

ἐβουλήθην γράψαι τὸν λόγον
Ἑλένης μὲν ἐγκώμιον ἐμὸν δὲ παίγνιον. (*Helen* 21)

I have essayed to dispose of the injustice of defamation
and the folly of allegation;
I have prayed to compose a lucubration
for Helen's adulation and my own delectation. (Van Hook 1913)

τί γὰρ ἀπῆν τοῖς ἀνδράσι τούτοις ὧν δεῖ ἀνδράσι προσεῖναι;
τί δὲ καὶ προσῆν ὧν οὐ δεῖ προσεῖναι; εἰπεῖν δυναίμην ἃ βούλομαι,
βουλοίμην δ᾽ ἃ δεῖ, λαθὼν μὲν τὴν θείαν νέμεσιν,
φυγὼν δὲ τὸν ἀνθρώπινον φθόνον. (*Epitaphios* DK 82 B6)

What did these men lack that men should have?
    And what did they have that men should lack?
    May what I say be what I sought to say,
and what I sought to say what I ought to say —
    free from the wrath of gods,
    far from the envy of humanity. (Adapted from Cole 1991a, 71)

These passages, particularly if read aloud, give the reader some idea of the general effect of Gorgias' prose. An examination of the two texts (*Helen* and *Palamedes*) and one sizable fragment (*Epitaphios*) that are generally regarded as authentically by Gorgias identifies a number of stylistic features that are particularly prominent or interesting in Gorgias' prose. They are alliteration, asyndeton, antithesis, isocolon, parison, homoioteleuton, assorted types of assonance, epanalepsis, paronomasia, rhetorical questions, and the use of compound words, metaphors, and "poetic" terms. I end with a brief discussion of Gorgias' "periodic" approach to sentence construction. Throughout the remainder of this section I have transliterated Greek passages so that Gorgias' soundplay can be experienced by readers with or without knowledge of Greek.

Alliteration is found rarely in early Greek prose, yet it is apparent in drama and poetry. Though one finds alliteration in a few of the early writers of aphorisms, such as Heraclitus and Democritus, its use in Gorgias is noteworthy for its prevalence and conspicuousness. As Bromley Smith put it, Gorgias was almost "as fond of [alliteration] as an Anglo-Saxon poet" (1921b, 351). In *Helen* (4) we find the passage *pleistas de pleistois epithumias erōtos eneirgasato, heni de sōmati polla sōmata sunēgagen andrōn epi megalois mega phronountōn,* in which "first p predominates, then e, then s, then m" (Denniston 1952, 127). Later we find *dei de kai doxēi deixai tois akouousi* (8). In *Palamedes, pantōs ara kai pantēi panta prattein adunaton ēn moi* appears. Smith points out a series of alliterations in the short fragment that survives of the *Epitaphios* (1921b, 351). For example, in the short phrase *Ti gar apēn tois andrasi toutois hōn dei andrasi proseinai; ti de kai prosēn hōn ou dei proseinai,* Gorgias begins with an *a-t* combination, then shifts to an emphasis on *pro-*. There may be passages in Thucydides and Plato where alliteration is intended, but generally the use of alliteration in Gorgias must be considered uncommon in prose and thus conspicuous to its hearers (Denniston 1952, 126–29). Like the alliteration found in Greek proverbs, Gorgias' use of alliteration may been intended to make his discourse more memorable (Russo 1983).

Asyndeton is the omission of conjunctions between words, phrases, or clauses. In Greek literature the use of asyndeton is distributed oddly. It is rarely found in Thucydides, Isocrates, or Plato, but is used extensively by Demosthenes (Denniston 1952, 99). Asyndeton is used freely in Gorgias' *Palamedes,* but rarely in *Helen.* In the former one finds *hos ge sōizei patrida, tokeas, tēn pasan Hellada,* "one saves his parents, homeland, all of Greece," and *tōi nomōi, tēi dikēi, tois theois, tōi plēthei tōn anthrōpōn,* "the law, the just, the Gods, the whole of Humanity," while in the latter *andra kai gunaika kai logon kai ergon kai polin kai pragma,* "Man and woman and speech and deed and city and affairs," is found.[3] As Denniston notes, "the truth of the matter is that a great chain or series is of its essence impressive, whether connectives are inserted or omitted" (1954, xlv).

The use of a strongly antithetical asyndeton by Gorgias in *Palamedes* (32) may be unparalleled in Greek prose: *Tois eutuchousin ou phthoneros, tōn dustuchountōn oiktirmōn,* "[For I am] . . . to the fortunate unenvious, to the unfortunate merciful."[4] An example of two-limbed asyndeton with repetition occurs in *Palamedes* (22): *phrason toutois ton tropon, ton topon, pote, tou, pōs eides,* "tell these judges the manner, the place, the time, when, where, how you saw" (Denniston 1952, 108). Gorgias' asyndeton at the end of *Helen* provides an incisive summary of his speech: *apheilon tōn logōi duskleian gunaikos, enemeina tōi nomōi hon enthemēn en archēi tou logou. Epeirathēn katalusai mōmou adikian kai doxēs amathian, eboulēthēn grapsai ton logon Helenēs men egkōmion emon de paignion,* "I have by argument removed disgrace from a woman. I have abided by the rule I posed at the beginning of

3. Other examples can be found at *Palamedes* 13 and 19. For examples of asyndeton with adjectives see *Palamedes* 25 and 36; with verbs, *Palamedes* 11 and 22; with clauses, *Palamedes* 20.

4. Denniston (1952, 103–4); Gorgias' technique here may be parodied in Plato, *Symposium* 197d1–e5. Cf. also Gorgias in his funeral oration (DK 82 B6) with Isocrates, *Evagoras* 44–46.

my speech. I have tried to end unjust blame and ignorant opinion. I wished to write an account that would be Helen's encomium and my own plaything."[5]

Gorgias is most famous for his use of antithesis. Formally, antithesis occurs any time two contrasting ideas are conjoined. Isocolon refers to two clauses with an equal number of syllables, while parison refers to parallel constructions. Gorgias utilized all three of these figures, often in combination. An example of such symmetrical antithesis is found in John F. Kennedy's famous phrase: "Ask not what your country can do for you; ask what you can do for your country." Antitheses of all shapes and sizes are found in the texts of Gorgias. He notes in *Helen* (1) that things should be honored "with praise if praiseworthy, but on the unworthy blame should be laid," followed almost immediately with the claim that it is ignorance "to blame the praiseworthy and to praise the blameworthy" (*to men axion epainou epainōi timan, tōi de anaxiōi mōmon epitheinai: isē gar hamartia kai amathia memphesthai te ta epaineta kai epainein ta mōmēta*). A typical example from *Palamedes* is *ou tois sois kakois alla tois emois agathois*, "not through your vices but through my virtues" (27). The fragment from his *Epitaphios* begins with three consecutive symmetrical antitheses: "What did these men lack that men should have? And what did they have that men should lack? May what I say be what I sought to say, and what I sought to say what I ought to say." A quotation by Aristotle of one of Gorgias' sayings has been reconstructed as *dei tas spoudas tōn antidikōn gelōti ekluein, ta de geloia tais spoudais ekkrouein*: "One should end the seriousness of opponents with humor, and rend their humor with seriousness" (Cope 1877, 3:215–16, after Aristotle's *Rhetoric* 1419b4–6). Gorgias' prose is so filled with antithesis that it has been suggested that all of Gorgias' style is rooted in antithesis (Kennedy 1963, 65n, based on Drerup 1902, 258–61).

Though antithesis, isocolon, and parison are found in earlier prose, in Gorgias "they abound," and they often are augmented by *homoioteleuton,* the rhymed endings of clauses (Denniston 1952, 72). Homoioteleuton occurs in such constructions as *sphalera kai abebaios ousa sphalerais kai abebaiois* (*Helen* 11). The *Helen* ends with *eboulēthēn grapsai ton logon Helenēs men enkōmion emon de paignion,* which Van Hook translates (somewhat loosely) as "I have prayed to compose a lucubration for Helen's adulation and my own delectation." Smith identifies a special sort of homoioteleuton in Gorgias where a like ending of words is found at the *beginning* of clauses, such as

---

5. The use of asyndeton at or near the end of a speech can be found also in Isaeus (6.62, 9.37), Aeschines (1.196, 2.182), and Demosthenes (8.76, 21.226).

lathōn . . . phygōn, apeiroi . . . semnoi, and *hosioi . . . dikaioi* in the *Epitaphios* (1921b, 351).

Assonance refers to "resemblance or similarity in sound between vowel-sounds preceded and followed by differing consonant-sounds in words in proximity" (Lanham 18). The assonance found in Gorgias sometimes may be explained as the natural result of Greek syntax, but in most places the acoustical effect is clearly deliberate. He is fond of creating short wordplays, such as *epainou epainōi* (*Helen* 1) and *etarachthē kai etaraxe* (*Helen* 16). One also finds double rhymes, such as *para tois barbarois* (*Palamedes* 21) and *gnōmēn kai rhōmēn* (*Epitaphios*). Gorgias sometimes creates an "echo-effect" through the juxtaposition of related words in longer phrases, such as in the *Epitaphios: toigaroun autōn apothanontōn ho pothos ou sunapethanen, all' athanatos ouk en athanatois sōmasi zēi ou zōntōn,* "Dead though they be, our longing for them dies not; but deathless among bodies not deathless, it lives, though they live not"; *Helen: hosoi de hosous peri hosōn kai epeisan kai peithousi de,* "How many have persuaded and persuade still how many others about how many things?" (11); and *Palamedes: pantes panta horōsi kai pantes hupo pantōn horōntai. pantōs ara kai pantēi panta prattein adunaton ēn moi* "Everybody sees everything and everybody is seen by everyone. So in every way and at every point it was impossible for me to perpetrate these acts" (12).

A related technique is known as epanalepsis: the repetition of the same word (usually) after intervening matter. In the *Epitaphios,* for example, we find three words (*andrasi, hōn dei, proseinai*) each occurring twice in the first sentence. A variation is found midway through the *Epitaphios: hybristai eis tous hybristas, kosmioi eis tous kosmious, aphoboi eis tous aphobous, deinoi en tois deinois,* "insolent with the insolent, decent with the decent; fearless with the fearless, terrible among the terrible." According to Smith, epanalepsis helps the speaker to make clear his or her meaning: "By doubling the mental impression they rivet the idea in the mind of his [Gorgias'] auditors" (1921b, 355; see also Drerup 1902, 259–60).

So far the stylistic techniques examine function acoustically. That is, even if they enhance the "meaning" of the discourse, they are identifiable primarily through auditory reception. I turn now to figures that combine sense and sound to accomplish their ends. The first of these is paronomasia; the playing on the sounds and meanings of words (similar to the contemporary dictionary definition of punning). Paronomasia intended to be humorous in Greek prose is initially uncommon; in fact, in Heraclitus and Democritus punning is "regarded as a means of attaining truth" concerning the relationship between two "things" with similar sounding words (Denniston 1952, 136). Gorgias, by contrast, uses paronomasia "for the sole purpose of ear-tickling," a use that added to the novelty of his compositions even if such use was not wholly original.[6]

According to Philostratus in his *Lives of the Sophists,* "Chaerephon, carping at Gorgias' seriousness, said, 'Why, Gorgias, do beans inflate the belly but do not fan the fire?' Gorgias was not disturbed by the question and said, 'I leave this to *you* to consider; for my part I have long known that the earth grows hollow reeds for such ends" (proem = DK 82 A24).[7] Plutarch attributes the following double entendre to Gorgias: "Of a woman not the figure but the fame ought to be 'familiar' (*gnōrimon*) to the many" (*Bravery of Women* 242e = DK 82 B22). And the *Gnomologium Vaticanum* claims that "Gorgias said that orators were like frogs: for the latter made their cry in water and the former before the waterclock" (743.167 = DK 82 B30). These examples must be treated with care, as the sources are centuries removed from Gorgias. Nonetheless, they attribute to Gorgias a playfulness toward language that seems to be borne out when viewed with those texts regarded as authentic. Three more examples are cited by Denniston. First: *kallos, ho labousa kai ou lathousa esche* (*Helen* 4); "beauty, which getting (*labousa,* literally "taking") and not forgetting (*lathousa,* literally "escaping") she preserved." Second: *epi tēn archēn tou mellontos logou probēsomai, kai prothēsomai tas aitias* (*Helen* 5); the key being the wordplay of *probēsomai* and *prothēsomai,* both of which can refer to moving forward, and here meaning "proceed" and "propose." Third: *suneste gar moi, dio suniste tauta* (*Palamedes* 15). Here the wordplay involves *suneste* and *suniste;* the sense is "you are my *compadre,* so you *comprende.*" Finally, Aristotle relates the following anecdote: "Gorgias of Leontini, partly at a loss what to say, partly in irony, said that just as mortars are what is made by the mortar-makers (*holmopoiōn*), so also Larisians are what is made by the magistrates, for they are 'Lariso-makers' (*Larisopoious*)" (*Politics* 1275b26–30).

Gorgias skillfully uses rhetorical questions to guide the hearer through his reasoning. As Smith (rhetorically) asks: "What better way has ever been devised to draw attention, to ally the speaker with his [or her] audience, to make them responsive?" (1921b, 353). For example, the beginning of the *Epitaphios,* which is quoted above, begins with two consecutive questions. Further-

6. Denniston (1952,138) suggests that humorous punning "pretty certainly originated" with Gorgias' prose, but such a statement understates the prevalence of punning and riddles in Herodotus as well as in common language use.

7. W. C. Wright (1921, 11 note) explains the pun as follows: "The jest lies in the ambiguity of the meaning and also the application here of this word [*narthex*], which is originally 'hollow reed,' such as that used by Prometheus to steal fire from heaven, but was also the regular word for a rod for chastisement" (see also Kennedy 1972b, 39n).

more, *Helen* is filled with questions. Gorgias supposes that if Helen was forced against her will to run away to Troy, she should be held blameless. If she was kidnapped, "How should she not be pitied rather than pilloried?" (7). If she was persuaded by speech, "How many have persuaded and persuade still how many others about how many things by molding false speech?" Hence, "What is there to prevent the conclusion that Helen too, when still young, was carried off by speech just as if constrained by force?" (12). If she was swept away by passion, "If love, a god, prevails over the divine power of the gods, how could a lesser one be able to reject and refuse it?" (19). Gorgias concludes: How then can blame of Helen be thought just? (20). In short, the basic argumentative structure of *Helen* is punctuated through the use of questions, the answers to which lead to Gorgias' conclusion. *Palamedes* similarly uses a good number of questions; Kennedy's translatation interprets nearly seventy!

Gorgias' choice of words often is the subject of comment; in particular his use of compound words, metaphors, and poetic or elevated terminology. In Greek, as in German, it is easy to form compound words. Martin Heidegger's terms *Mitvorhandensein* and *Inderweltsein,* for example, translate as Being-present-at-hand-along-with and Being-in-the-World, respectively. A number of fifth-century Sophists were famous for creating new words; a practice often lampooned by Aristophanes (Denniston 1927). Gorgias in particular was not shy of coining compound words. From the *Epitaphios,* Smith identifies *eu-orgē-tos, en-oplios,* and *philo-kalos,*[8] while more exotic examples are identified by Aristotle: *ptōchomousokolokas,* "beggar-mused-flatterers," and *epiorkēsantas kat' euorkēsantos,* "forsworn-and-right-solemnly-sworn" (Kennedy 1991, 226).[9]

Though *Helen, Palamedes,* and the *Epitaphios* are not overly peopled with metaphors, it is for such figures that Gorgias was noted often by ancient commentators. Pseudo-Longinus quotes Gorgias as calling Xerxes "the Persian's Zeus," and two sources claim that he referred to vultures as "living tombs" (*On the Sublime* 3.2 = DK 82 B5a). Aristotle provides an example he explicitly attributes to Gorgias: "You have sown shamefully and have reaped

---

8. Smith (1921b, 355). See Liddell and Scott (1940), s.vv. εὐοργ-ησία, ἐνοπλ-ίζω, and φιλο-καλλωπιστής.

9. In Edward Meredith Cope's commentary on Aristotle's *Rhetoric* (1405b38–1406a1), he explains "beggar-mused-flatterers" as being "one who prostitutes his literature and intellectual accomplishments to flattery and sycophancy to make a living by them, 'making his Muse a beggar'," or perhaps "one whom poverty inspires" (1877, 3:37). The objections to "forsworn-and-right-solemnly-sworn" are that Gorgias exaggerates in the Greek with a superfluous *kata* and that he uses two words to express what could be said simply with one: *euorkein* (Cope 1877, 3:37–38).

badly."[10] Another phrase has been reconstructed by Friedrich Solmsen as "Trembling and wan are the writings, pale and bloodless the doings."[11] Like his predecessors in poetry and drama, Gorgias is reported to have used the names of gods metaphorically, such as Ares to signify courage (DK 82 B24) and Eros to signify passion (*Helen* 19). His reference to Logos as "a powerful lord" is well-known (*Helen* 8). The last words of Gorgias are reported by a very late source as being "Sleep already begins to hand me over to his brother Death" (DK 82 A15). So, even though the preserved texts are not overly burdened with metaphorical expressions, it is clear that metaphors were an important part of Gorgias' style.

Commentators ancient and modern have noticed that Gorgias on occasion uses *poetic* terms borrowed from Greek tragedy where plainer words normally would be expected. Blass (1887, 65) identifies the examples of *dissa* or *dissōn* instead of *duo* or *dittos* (*Epitaphios, Helen* 10, *Palamedes* 2, 5, 19), *tokeus* instead of *goneus* (*Epitaphios, Palamedes* 3, 19, 36), and *litai* for prayers (*Palamedes* 33, DK 82 B27). Smith adds the example of *nemesis* in the *Epitaphios* (1921b, 356). In each case the effect is to improve the euphony or to elevate the tone of the language used, or both — effects that are appropriate for performance texts (Smith 1921b; Zucker 1956).

The last aspect of Gorgias' composition style on which I want to comment is his method of sentence construction, which could be called *mini-periodic*. Ancient Greek literary critics identify two sorts of prose-writing: "the *lexis eiromenē*, in which the component parts are 'strung together' in co-ordination, and the *lexis katestrammenē*, the 'knit' or periodic style, in which long and highly organized sentences are built up by subordination of clauses" (Denniston 1952, 60). Though periodic writing is found fairly early in Greek literature, it is mostly associated with prose writers. The increase in periodic writing is a manifestation of the spread of literacy during the fifth and fourth centuries. In a "wholly" oral composition, only a style that emphasizes continuing the story would aid memory. In Homer, for example, one finds *kai* ("and") as the primary connective. As literate habits grew and changed, a greater variety of constructions encouraging subordination of phrases and ideas can be seen. Isocrates' non-forensic compositions are examples of the periodic style in the extreme.

Denniston claims that Gorgias' compositions make very little use of the

---

10. Aristotle, *Rhetoric* 1406b9–10, translated by Kennedy (1991, 228).

11. Based on Aristotle's *Rhetoric* 1406b9 and Demetrius *On Style* 116 (see Solmsen 1979, 69). Cited by Kennedy (1991, 228 note 53). Cf. Cope's comments and criticisms of both metaphors (1877, 3:45).

period; Gorgias "gets his effects by elaborate antitheses of small compass" (1952, 60). He argues that Gorgias' sentence structure more closely resembles oral-poetic styles than the more periodic prose of Plato or Isocrates. In contrast, Blass, Friedrich Zucker, and Smith all call the prose of Gorgias "periodic." Blass, for example, contends that Gorgias' sentence construction is, indeed, periodic, though the period is of the simplest possible sort (1887, 69).[12] Zucker maintains that Gorgias' texts represent a "periodicizing style of prose-art" (*periodisierenden Stil der Kunstprosa*) that, while constructing short sentences, nonetheless expresses different logical relations through subordinate conjunctions (1956, 3–7). Smith notes that the Gorgianic period is "often so short that it resembles a verse of poetry" (1921b, 348).

Though Gorgias' prose "resembles" poetry, it is not the *same* as poetry. Gorgias does not employ the sort of repetitive meters found in Greek poetry (Maas 1962, 23–24). In a sense, highly poetic English translations of Gorgias may mislead us here: "Unlike English poetry whose rhythm is largely the result of the arrangement of stressed and unstressed syllables, Greek verse is measured by predominantly quantitative standards"; that is, specific sequences of long and short syllables.[13] Early Greek prose is not like "everyday speech." It may, in fact, be "even further removed from everyday speech than poetry" (Nagy 1989, 8). Nonetheless, when analyzed using the standard tools of metrical analysis, Gorgias' prose is clearly distinct from typical Greek poetry (see below).

Before closing this section, it is worth noting that Gorgias' prose is, in many respects, very rationalistic and logical. For example, he argues using the apagogic method by which an advocate enumerates a series of possibilities and addresses each in turn (Kennedy 1963, 167–68). Also, Denniston's classic study of Greek particles documents the use of a number of logical connectives in Gorgias' texts that distinguish them from traditional poetry (1954, see 41, 104–5, 240–41, 351–52, 566–67). Like Parmenides' famous philosophical poem, Gorgias' prose demonstrates that early Greek authors felt no apparent conflict over producing highly polished and "poetical" literature that posits sophisticated arguments.

So far I have enumerated a series of characteristics of the composition style

12. Blass (1887, 69): "Sonst ist der Satzbau zwar, wie Demetrios sagt, periodisch, aber die Periode ist die allereinfachste."

13. James W. Halporn et al. (1980, 4). Paul Maas offers an appropriate warning about the difficulty of comparing contemporary poetry with ancient Greek poetry: "Scarcely any facet of the culture of the ancient world is so alien to us as its quantitative metric. . . . [Purely quantitative rhythm] has now vanished not only from the literature, but from the speech of Europe" (1962, 3).

of Gorgias. Their cumulative effect is discussed in the third section of this chapter. For the moment, it must suffice to describe the effect of Gorgias' prose as striking and almost musical. We have no record of anyone — poet or prose-writer — of his era who spoke quite like he did; the evidence indicates that his audiences were, indeed, struck by his novelty. I suspect that later commentators are struck in part because of the denseness of his technique: every sentence — every phrase — illustrates multiple figures. Whether one finds his artistry dazzling or gauche, there is no doubt that Gorgias' speeches were impressive performances. Smith calls Gorgias' prose *symphonic* "because when read aloud it recalls a piece of music; for it has the cadences, tonal effects, diminuendos and crescendos of a sonata" (1921b, 350).

A Catalog of Critiques of Gorgias' Style

In this section I outline the criticisms made against Gorgias' style. I begin by surveying the criticisms made in antiquity in roughly chronological order, then I summarize the criticisms made by contemporary commentators. In Gorgias' own heyday, we find virtually no comment about his style. Though there are two insults apparently offered against him by Aristophanes, neither directly or indirectly refers to his style (*Birds* 1694, *Wasps* 420). Though Plato parodies Gorgias' style in Agathon's speech in *Symposium* (194e4–197e5, 198c1–5), which was probably written around 380 B.C.E., neither there or elsewhere do we find a specific critique of his compositional techniques. Xenophon's *Symposium* (2.26), written about the same time, refers to the word "besprinkle" (*epipsakazōsin*) as a "Gorgianic expression" (*Gorgieiois rhēmasin*), but the tone is not particularly insulting.

The first set of specific, style-related criticisms made against Gorgias are found in book three of Aristotle's *Rhetoric,* which also is the first text we know of that makes a systematic study of style (Kennedy 1989, 185; Cole 1991a, 122). Aristotle repeatedly calls Gorgias' prose excessively poetic (1404a24–28). In particular, the metaphors and compound words cited previously are described as "far-fetched" and they are offered by Aristotle as examples of "frigidity" (1405b38–1406a1, 1406b8–11). He also cites the beginning of one of Gorgias' lost speeches as too abrupt: "Elis, happy city" (1416a3). Not all of Aristotle's references to Gorgias are hostile, however. For example, he quotes the introduction to one of Gorgias' speeches as a perfectly acceptable beginning of an epideictic address: "You are worthy of the admiration of many, O men of Greece" (1414b31–32). He cites with approval Gorgias' technique of amplification: "What Gorgias used to say — that he was never at a loss for words — is similar: if he is talking about Achilles, he praises [his father]

Peleus, then [his grandfather] Aecus, then the god [Aecus' father, Zeus]"
(1418a35–37). He claims that "Gorgias rightly said that one should spoil the
opponents' seriousness with laughter and their laughter with seriousness"
(1419b4–6). In a passage that gives us an idea of Aristotle's aesthetic sen-
sibilities, he claims that:

> Gorgias' exclamation to the swallow when she flew down and let go her
> droppings on him is in the best tragic manner: he said, "Shame on you,
> Philomela," for if a bird did it there was no shame, but [it would have been]
> shameful for a maiden. He thus rebuked the bird well by calling it what it once
> had been [Philomela transformed into a swallow, according to myth] rather
> than what it now was. (1406b15–19)

Aristotle later says that some poetic expressions are acceptable when put to
the service of "irony," as Gorgias did (1408b20).[14]

For the most part, criticism in later antiquity tends to repeat Aristotle's
negative assessments without mentioning his more positive comments. Noting
that if certain words "have similar case-endings, or if clauses are equally balanced, or if contrary ideas are opposed, the sentence becomes rhythmical by its
very nature, even if no rhythm is intended," Cicero claims that Gorgias was the
first to strive for "this sort of symmetry" (*Orator* 49.164–165, 167). Cicero
declares that Gorgias used such devices "immodestly" and with an excess of
poetic rhythm: "Gorgias is too fond of this style, and uses these 'embroideries'
[*festivitatibus*] too boldly" (*Orator* 52.175–176, cf. 12.39–40).

One of the most influential early literary critics was Dionysius of Halicarnassus; his evaluation of Gorgias' style was almost uniformly negative. Writing late in the first century B.C.E., Dionysius describes Gorgias' style as "vulgar" and "inflated" (*Lysias* 3). He claims in his essay on Isaeus that "Gorgias
of Leontini exceeds the bounds of moderation and frequently lapses into puer-
ility" (19). Dionysius calls Gorgias' style "artificial" and refers to antithesis
and balanced clauses in his speeches as "trashy devices" (*Demosthenes* 6, 25).
He suggests that Gorgianic figures "can arouse the utmost displeasure" (*Demosthenes* 5). Such parallelisms and word-play Dionysius deems "osten-
tatious" and "excessively" used by Gorgias (*Thucydides* 24).[15] Later in the
same essay he equates frigidity with "the Gorgianic style" (*Thucydides* 46). It
should be remembered that Dionysius makes these criticisms in the context of

---

14. Cope (1877, 3:81–82) believes this reference may be to Gorgias' irony reported in
Aristotle's *Politics* 1275b26; while Kennedy (1991, 237) points to Gorgias' mockery of
the swallow in *Rhetoric* 1406b15.

15. See also Dionysius' *Second Letter to Ammaeus* (2, 17) and his *Letter to Gnaeus
Pompeius* (2).

his preference for Atticism over Asianism—both in style and ideology (Kennedy 1963, 330–36).

Pseudo-Longinus pokes fun of Gorgias' metaphors as pretentious but otherwise does not comment on his style (*On the Sublime* 3.1). The precise date of the treatise is not known, but it is generally placed in the first century C.E. Similarly, the authorship and date of "Demetrius' " *On Style* are uncertain; W. Rhys Roberts suggests that it was written late in the first century C.E., though others would place it much earlier (1932, 271). Demetrius describes Gorgias' style as periodic, then criticizes him for using an excessively repetitive pattern of periods. He declares that such a style is unpersuasive and thus inappropriate for public speakers to use (12, 15). Later, however, he notes that Gorgias' symmetrical antithesis can, in fact, "tend to heighten expression" (29).

Modern criticism concerning Gorgias' style can be grouped into general and specific complaints. The general complaints can be summarized as claiming that Gorgias' prose style was excessively poetic and artificial. To the negative verdicts quoted at the beginning of this chapter, the following may be added: Denniston characterizes Gorgias' influence as "wholly bad. What he did was, in fact, to take certain qualities inherent in Greek expression, balance and antithesis, and exaggerate them to the point of absurdity" (1952, 10). Similarly, Kennedy suggests that Gorgias "flagrantly indulged" in the use of Gorgianic figures (1989, 184). Engelbert Drerup (1902, 257–58) lambasts Gorgias as a "laughable figure" (*lächerliche Figur*) whose excesses are "childish and tasteless" (*kindisch und geschmacklos*). He claims that Gorgias' excessively poetic style "chokes" on the affectations of the words and thoughts.[16] James A. Arieti and John M. Crossett claim that "Gorgias stands as the most famous and most spectacular representative of rhetoric[al style] in the bad sense" (1985, 21). John M. Robinson declares that Gorgias' style is "as repellent as it is artificial" (1973, 52). And Blass complains that Gorgias' style is excessively poetical and relies on artificial figures of speech (1887, 63–64).

In addition to the foregoing general comments, a series of specific criticisms can be identified. First, it is argued that his style was abrupt and harsh. Norden (1958, 64) and Drerup (1902, 262) complain that his sentences are excessively choppy ("*Zerhacktheit*"), and Zucker (1956, 3) calls it "staccato-like" (*staccatomäßig*). Blass deems the style uncomfortable because of the short and choppy phrases (1887, 70). And Denniston describes Gorgias' prose as "jerky bombast" (1952, 22).

Second, Gorgias is accused of sacrificing sense for sound—that is, for promoting euphony at the expense of clarity. W. H. Thompson complains that in

---

16. See Drerup (1902, 257): "die Poesie in die Künsteleien der Worte und Gedanken."

Gorgias' speeches "the assonances [are] tedious, and the sacrifice of sense to sound, perspicuity to point, [is] manifest throughout" (1871, 176). Similarly, Blass contends that Gorgias' use of antithesis was more for acoustical than conceptual purposes (1887, 71). Both Blass (1887, 70–71) and Norden (1958, 65) suggest that Gorgias violates the "natural" word order of the Greek language in order to construct his balanced phrases and rhymes.

Third, some critics complain simply that Gorgias' speeches are vacuous. Thompson declares that "the ideas are, with some exceptions, superficial" (1871, 176). Blass agrees by suggesting that the thoughts expressed in Gorgias' speeches are not as dignified as the form (1887, 70). Fourth and finally, some modern critics echo Aristotle's opinion that Gorgias' metaphors and compound words are sometimes "tasteless" or "far-fetched" (Smith 1921b, 357).

Gorgianic Style Reconsidered: Gorgias as Prose Rhapsode

As the preceding section documents, the outrageousness of Gorgias' prose is practically taken for granted; "the style of Gorgias" typically connotes excess, artifice, and ostentation. Even if we take such assessments as legitimate, it does not necessarily follow that Gorgias' style deserves the censure it has received. The tremendous popularity of Gorgias as a speaker in the late fifth century B.C.E. invites another look at the evidence. Plato and Aristotle certainly would not have spent the time they did criticizing Gorgias had he not been well-known and influential. Smith reasons from the available evidence that "there must have been something remarkable about these exhibitions [Gorgias' orations], else the honor of a golden statue at Delphi would not have been awarded to him" (1921b, 336; see DK 82 A7). Surely, Smith argues, "a man who could attract the multitudes and could draw a steady stream of pupils must have possessed something worthy of careful study" (1921b, 345).

The fact that the citizens of Leontini entrusted Gorgias with the role of ambassador suggests that his speaking skills were noteworthy and inoffensive. Leontini and Syracuse had been at odds for years, and in 427 B.C.E. Gorgias successfully persuaded the Athenians to assist Leontini against a recent military assault by Syracuse. It was this successful visit to Athens that prompted early assessments that Gorgias was an impressive and persuasive speaker. Diodorus Siculus was a Sicilian historian writing in the first century B.C.E. Diodorus claims that Gorgias was, "in power of speech, by far the most eminent of the men of his time. . . . [B]y the novelty of his style he amazed the Athenians, who were cultivated and fond of letters" (12.53 = DK 82 A4). It is sometimes argued that Gorgias would not have used his "epideictic" style in a deliberative setting, but there are two factors that make such an objection less than compelling. First, there is no clear evidence that, prior to Aristotle, there was a clear and distinct difference drawn between "epideictic" and "deliberative" genres. Second, some of the speeches found in deliberative settings in Thucydides are stylistically similar to those of Gorgias. If, as some scholars have argued, Thucydides' portrayals are at least partially accurate, the probability that Gorgias' style before the Assembly was similar to the written texts we possess is increased (Kennedy 1963, 47–51; Tompkins 1969).

Writing in the second century C.E., Pausanias repeats the claim that "Gorgias was famous" for his speeches at the Olympic games and for his embassy to Athens (6.17.7 = DK 82 A7). Philostratus, writing in the beginning of the third century C.E., tells us that Gorgias was admired by many — in Athens, in Thessaly, and in "all Greece" (*Epistle* 73 = DK 82 A35). Though some of the specific claims made by Philostratus are dubious, the evidence is quite clear that Gorgias was popular enough to speak throughout Greece and to amass a small fortune. Philostratus describes the *Epitaphios* as composed "with surpassing cleverness" and commends Gorgias as an example "of unexpected expression and of inspiration and of the grand style for great subjects and of detached phrases and transitions, by which speech becomes sweeter than it has been and more impressive, and he introduced poetic words for ornament and dignity" (*Lives of the Sophists* 1.9 = DK 82 A1).

When assessing the criticisms of Gorgias' style the *perspective* of his critics must be kept in mind. The well-educated of ancient Greece represent a privileged economic and social class (Ostwald 1986, 213). As written manuscripts were scarce and expensive, the only group with the interest and ability to own and, in turn, to write about them would have been the leisure class. Accordingly, their reactions cannot be taken as typical of the large audiences to which Gorgias spoke. Aristotle's comment about Gorgias' "poetic" style in the *Rhetoric* is telling: "Even now, the majority of the uneducated think such speakers speak most beautifully" (1404a26–28). At least part of the opprobrium heaped upon Gorgias is due to the snobbery of his genteel and "cultured" critics (cf. Trevett 1996).

By definition, those people we now identify as early "literary critics" were highly literate. Though a sort of basic literacy was fairly widespread among male Athenian citizens, what we might call "book-oriented" literacy was rare and usually the sign of being part of the intellectual elite (Robb 1994). Even by the middle of the fourth century B.C.E., the literacy rate for Attica was not likely to have been "much above 10–15%" (Harris 1989, 328). Accordingly, the bulk of Gorgias' audience probably was made up of people at best only partially literate compared to the sort of reading fluency attained by the *literati* (Swearingen 1986, 150–52). Once it is recognized that Gorgias' speeches were composed for oral performance for audiences with aural predilections, it is possible to reconcile the fact of his popularity with the severe treatment his works later received at the hands of critics.

The aesthetic experience of performing a text to oneself is very different from hearing a text performed by its creator in person. And it is only through such performances that Gorgias' style is experienced and interpreted: "The work is irreducible to its performances and yet graspable only through them or, rather, in them" (Dufrenne 1973, 27). The public performance gives the control of the auditory experience more to the speaker, adds a visual dimension to the performance, and creates greater excitement with the presence of an expectant audience (Dufrenne 1973, 37–41). Cole likens the difference between reading a speech aloud to oneself and hearing it performed publicly to the difference between "staying at home from an opera or concert in order to read the score" (1991a, 115). Clearly, what is aesthetically pleasurable in one context may not be in another. The aesthetic experience of Gorgias' style obviously would be significantly different for those attending his speeches from those reading it decades later. Written texts, which served as the basis of literary criticism, "changed the nature of the critical act" (Kennedy 1989, 88).

That different generations acquire different literary tastes should be obvious, but in Gorgias' case the evidence is direct. Aristotle notes that, even in his generation, poets and tragedians were moderating their style in order to sound less "poetic" and more colloquial (*Rhetoric* 1404a24–35). Diodorus reports that Gorgias "was the first to use extravagant figures of speech . . . that *at the time* were thought worthy of acceptance because of the novelty of the method, but *now* seem tiresome and often appear ridiculous and excessively contrived" (12.53.4 = DK 82 A4, emphasis added). Kennedy concedes that "in his own age the style of Gorgias did not seem in poor taste. There was then a general desire to create a literary prose. . . . There was further a zest for sound among the Greeks, seen equally in the puns of the dramatists. In the Renaissance a new literary prose in the vernacular languages turned with enthusiasm to a style as flamboyant as that of Gorgias" (1963, 66; see also 1989, 184). Similarly, Erling B. Holtsmark notes that "it is correct to assume that the conceits of his stylistic puerilities found great favor with the contemporary Athenians, living, as they did, in a fundamentally oral culture" (in Bryant 1968, 51).

Connors has offered a defense of Gorgias that situates him as a master of oral technique in an age when performers of epic poetry could mesmerize their audiences. Drawing heavily on the work of Havelock, Connors suggests that preliterate cultures display an "oral state of mind." Such a consciousness is "passive, communally oriented," and "non-critical"; hence it is open to powerful manipulation by poets and rhapsodes (1986, 40). He claims that "Gorgias was the most successful manipulator of oral consciousness whose work the ancient world has left us" (1986, 47). By drawing upon the techniques of the poets, Gorgias could leave his audiences literally spellbound; a state "which involved the whole unconscious mind and probably the central nervous system, a total loss of objectivity as the audience gives itself up to identification with the speaker and his goals" (1986, 48). As literacy spread, cognitive changes took place such that literate people were no longer affected by rhythmic discourse (mostly poetry) in the same way. Connors explains the later criticisms of Gorgias' style, beginning with that by Aristotle, as being the result of a "literate" mindset and a bookish sense of taste (1986, 46–49). Aristotle is rightly called "the father of literary criticism," not the father of oral performance criticism (Oudemans and Lardinois 1987, 215).

Though Connors is correct to reposition Gorgias as an oral performer with a mostly nonliterate audience, his portrayal of the effects of Gorgias' speeches needs to be attenuated. Havelock's portrayal of the "hypnotic" effects of the performance of certain epic poetry presumes that the hearers are, in effect, reciting the story as well (1963, 152). The "hypnotic" psychological effects are identified by Havelock only with those full-fledged recitals that included instruments, song, and dance (1963, 145–60). Accordingly, even if one fully accepts Havelock's account of the psychology of the poetic performance, it would not fit Gorgias' performances since they had no persistent meter, were not accompanied by instrumentation or dance, and were not recited by the audience along with Gorgias.

Nonetheless, Gorgias' close relationship to the traditions of Greek poetry are clear. Helen and Palamedes are figures straight out of Homer. Prior to Gorgias, the encomium was a genre of poetry; none had been composed in prose. Kennedy suggests that one can detect the antecedents of performance prose in lyric poetry: the "so-called Gorgianic figures" were prose analogies to re-create certain "effects of poetic sound and rhythm" (1989, 184). Those figures now called "Gorgianic" actually were not so much "invented" as "adapted" by Gorgias; all can be found in earlier poetry. Gorgias was "the first writer of Greek *prose* to exploit consciously the use of rhyming clauses" (Denniston 1952, 10, emphasis added). In particular, "the use of short, symmetrical rhyming clauses" and the use of "similarly derived words in close juxtaposition" are characteristic devices in Greek poetry as well as in the texts of Gorgias (Denniston 1952, 11). Gorgias is even reported to have appeared in the purple robes normally worn by rhapsodes — professional performers of poetry (DK 82 A9).

Accordingly, I propose that Gorgias be understood as a *prose rhapsode*. By calling Gorgias a rhapsode I wish to emphasize the fact that his speeches were composed to be performed and to underscore his debt to the oral poetic tradition. Gorgias' poetic style is said by Diodorus to have "stunned" (*exeplēxe*) the Athenians: "It may be no coincidence that the same verb (*ekplēttō*) is used by Plato to describe the impression made by the rhapsode Io on his audience" (Verdenius 1981, 119–20; cf. *Ion* 535b2). At the same time I want to draw attention to Gorgias' important contributions to the development of Greek prose composition. After all, Gorgias may have been one of the earliest prose writers to utilize the Attic dialect. As Blass puts it, we are "in the dark" as to how much Attic prose there may have been prior to Gorgias (1887, 55).[17] Indeed, Gorgias is credited by Thomas Duncan as being "the creator of a new artistic medium, Attic prose" (1938, 402, 415; see also Blass 1887, 55–56). The earliest known prose-writer, Pherecydes, wrote in Ionic (Jacoby 1947). Herodotus, the earliest prose author for whom we have a large amount of text, also wrote in Ionic. Parmenides' famous poem, written in epic hexameters, was written mostly in Homeric Greek with some Ionic. Though Attic Greek was common in fifth-century drama, Gorgias' compositions played an important and "decisive" role in the development of an art of written prose in the Attic dialect (and, indeed, in prose in general) that eventually would become of common Hellenic value.[18]

Having been composed in the Attic dialect, rather than in Sicilian Doric or in the Ionic one might expect from a Leontinian, Gorgias' speeches were ideal for oral performance: "The Attic 'dialect' was the least provincial of all, avoiding the extreme harshness of the Doric and the softness of the Ionic, and tended to be more and more the language of cultivated Greeks."[19] Accordingly, his choice of Attic ought to be considered an important facet of Gorgias' prose aesthetic (Duncan 1938, 409; Blass 1887, 55–56). Even Blass, who at times sharply criticizes aspects of Gorgias' style, acknowledges his systematic devotion to eloquence and his pioneering accomplishments in prose composition (1887, 66, 71, 82).

The Criticisms Reconsidered

How does repositioning Gorgias as a prose rhapsode answer the criticisms of Gorgias' style identified above? To the general complaint that his

17. His Attic was not "pure," however. *Helen* contains certain Ionisms, such as *kreisson* and *hesson,* and *Palamedes* mixes *dissōn* and *pessous* with *prattein* and *kreittonas* (cf. Blass 1887, 56).

18. Blass (1887, 56): "Aber der Aufschwung der attischen Kunstprosa und überhaubt der Kunstprosa ist jedenfalls auf Gorgias zurückzuführen." See also Kennedy (1989, 184–85).

19. George Norlin (1928–29, 2: 348–49n); cf. Isocrates 15.296 and Cole (1991a, 74–75). Of course, Attic later became the "common," or *koinē,* dialect for all Greeks.

compositions appear artificial and excessively poetic, the response must be that such matters of taste are historically and socially contingent; they are affected in part by the social penetration of technology (in this case, writing), in part by performance conditions (read in private settings versus public performance by Gorgias himself), and by each auditor's acquired preferences. That the earliest literary prose would be heavily "poetic" is not surprising. As Gregory Nagy observes, "prose assumes the prior existence of poetry" (1989, 8). The earliest Greek prose, which was automatically performance prose, is rooted in the concrete practices and self-understanding of performance poetry: "Poetic diction, the use of metaphor, patterns of sound, and rhythm are qualities which helped make prose literary to the Greeks" (Kennedy 1989, 184). Literary prose gained popularity by being pleasurable to the audience, by "inducing some of the emotional force of poetry" (Kennedy 1989, 184, see also 82).

As Mikel Dufrenne asks: "Since there are as many interpretations as performances, which is the right one?" His answer is that "they can all be valid" given that aesthetic experience is, in part, historically contingent (1973, 40). Thus, though we cannot declare Aristotle's (and others') negative verdicts "invalid," we can and ought to see them as the result of only one, relatively narrow point of view. As Kathleen Hall Jamieson has shown (1988), changing technology even in the past fifty years has altered dramatically our sense of what constitutes oratorical eloquence. Gorgias' speeches belong to a different generation and genre than the classical writings that, in comparison, make his prose style appear extreme. To condemn his style is to fail to understand its place in literary history.

What then about the specific complaints made? The first charge identified was that his style is excessively choppy. The most important reply, which has been discussed already, is that such aesthetic assessments are largely a matter of learned taste. Additionally, Gorgias' phrasing can be explained as an appropriate aid to memory. During Gorgias' lifetime, most knowledge and discussion of what we would call "literary texts" was based wholly on oral transmission and memorization (Thomas 1989, 20–21). Defending the shortness of Gorgias' periods, Smith argues that such sentences are more easily recalled by those attending a performance (1921b, 348). Similarly, Barnes argues that "when books are rare, when they come in rolls, when they lack page-numbers and indexes, when they are written for an audience rather than a readership, authors have all the more reason to cultivate a memorable style" (1983, 91). Furthermore, if Aristotle's claim that Gorgias required his students to learn speeches by heart, then his compact antithetical style would make their lessons easier (*Sophistical Refutations* 183b–184a).

The second specific criticism was that Gorgias sacrifices sense for sound.

Such a criticism fails on several counts. To begin with, I know of no evidence that the meaning of any particular passage is obscure as a result of Gorgias' preference for euphony. While it is true that there are disagreements over how certain of Gorgias' texts ought to be interpreted, those disagreements are no more pronounced than those over the texts of Plato or Aristotle. Most hermeneutical difficulties related to Gorgias have more to do with manuscript or philosophical disagreements than with his syntax or word choice. Further, as Barrett has argued, Gorgias' arguments are enhanced by his use of antithesis, parison, and isocola, not encumbered: "Through form, Gorgias built in agitation and competition of reasons; form contributed to substance. . . . [The] elements of language were inseparable from the fundamental structure of his reasoning. Neither can be reviewed in isolation" (1987, 17–18).

Finally, the distinctiveness of Gorgias' style may have enhanced his ability to make his case. As Chaïm Perelman and Lucie Olbrechts-Tyteca point out, all figuration can function argumentatively; one of the most important functions is to create *presence* (1969, 115–26). Barrett suggests that the very novelty of Gorgias' style "enhanced its attractiveness, as noted in the visual and graphic quality in his discourse. Style is a large contributor to this effect" (1987, 18). Furthermore, we should keep in mind that "the Greeks were inclined to regard the beautiful form of a speech as guaranteeing the truth of its contents, just as they were apt to regard corporeal beauty as a sign of mental superiority" (Verdenius 1981, 122). Accordingly, it is reasonable to assume that Gorgias believed the more aesthetically pleasing his performance, the greater his chances for successful advocacy.

To the related complaint, that Gorgias violates the "natural" word order of the Greek language, two responses should suffice. First, the intentional departure from "ordinary word order" known as *hyperbaton* is a perfectly acceptable means of creating presence (Lanham 1968, 56). Second, Dover's important study of Greek word order suggests that, with respect to texts from the classical era, "natural" or "normal" word order is largely a myth: "Greek literature, by attaching value to variety of form, maintained a resistence to that drift towards syntactical uniformity which has been the fate of other languages" (1960, 68).[20]

The third specific complaint identified earlier was that Gorgias' ideas are vacuous. It must suffice for the moment to refer to the remainder of this book as a refutation of such an allegation. The final specific complaint identified was that Gorgias' metaphors and compound words were far-fetched. Duncan defends Gorgias' metaphors against his ancient detractors on two grounds: first,

20. See also de Groot (1918, 138–39) and now Dik (1995).

they appear rarely, "in fact, a close study might show metaphor employed more in Demosthenes than in Gorgias" (1938, 414). We might hypothesize that Gorgianic examples were "safe" to use since there quickly became a consensus among the ancient critics that Gorgias' style was excessive. Second, Duncan notes that the metaphors seem tame enough, hence there is no reason to slavishly follow Aristotle's or Pseudo-Longinus' taste. After all, few would complain of such phrases as "pale and bloodless affairs" or "you have sown shame and reaped misfortune" (1938, 414). Like other fifth-century prose artists, Gorgias stretched the linguistic tools he inherited to their limit through metaphor and creation of new words. If some of his word-play struck his audience as provocative, I suspect Gorgias was delighted.

Did Gorgias Have a Theory of Arrangement?

Mark A. Smeltzer (1996) recently argued that Gorgias' texts *Helen* and *Palamedes* prove that Gorgias possessed and taught a specific theory of arrangment.[21] Smeltzer is correct to observe that most treatments of Gorgias emphasize the philosophical *or* the stylistic dimensions of Gorgias' texts with insufficient attention to how the two interact and coalesce at the level of "the pragmatics of his speech making" (1996, 156). Both Smeltzer and I agree with Richard Enos's suggestion that "Rhetoric's origin as a formal discipline is best understood as an evolution of compositional techniques" (1993, 42). Nonetheless, I must question Smeltzer's central claims. Smeltzer finds in Gorgias' speeches a "theory of arrangement" at work that has two interlocking components: Gorgias follows a canonical quadripartite division of rhetorical speeches; and, across and within these divisions, Gorgias organizes his arguments into three-step argument units consisting of the claim, proof of the claim, and restatement of the claim (1996, 157). I offer four counterclaims: the four-part pattern Smeltzer identifies is apparent neither in Gorgias' texts nor in other fifth-century B.C.E. texts; the three-step argument units Smeltzer identifies are characteristic of "ring composition" rather than an explicit theory of composition; recognizable patterns of composition do not constitute proof of a theory at work; and writing about the history of rhetoric would be enhanced by recognizing the concept of "undeclared" theory.

For Gorgias' use of the canonical four divisions (introduction, narrative, argument, and conclusion), Smeltzer offers three arguments: he invokes the Corax and Tisias legend; he cites external evidence to suggest that such divisions were prevalent during Gorgias' lifetime; and he claims that Gorgias' two

21. This section was written with Wilfred E. Major.

speeches also reflect these divisions. While the division of rhetorical speeches into four components was standard for much of Greco-Roman history, Smeltzer's arguments that the division was standard as early as Gorgias' day do not hold. Smeltzer begins by referring to Gorgias' fellow Sicilians (Syracusans to be precise) Corax and Tisias, who supposedly developed the four-part theory of arrangement for speeches during the mid-fifth century B.C.E. Recent scholarship challenges the Corax and Tisias legend, however (see chapter 3). The point is not that the legend is necessarily all wrong, but simply that there is enough doubt about the Corax and Tisias legend that reference to it cannot support claims about the arrangement of fifth-century B.C.E. texts.

Smeltzer cites examples of surviving speeches that demonstrate the prevalence of the canonical divisions during the late fifth and early fourth centuries B.C.E.: Antiphon's *Against a Stepmother* and Lysias' *Wounding with Intent to Kill* (cf. Freeman, 1946, 86, 97). According to Smeltzer, these two speeches, dating to the 410s and 390s, respectively, reflect the standard partitioning into introduction, narration, argument, and conclusion. Using these speeches to establish the norm for oratory in Gorgias' lifetime, however, drastically oversimplifies and overstates the case. These two speeches neither prove Smeltzer's claim nor fairly represent the practice of Athenian speechmaking as far as we can now judge (see Ober 1989, 341–49 for a useful checklist of surviving speeches and dates). Of the six complete speeches attributed to Antiphon, *Against a Stepmother* (Maidment 1953, 1: 14–31) is the only one to feature a narration, and it is a diminutive one at best. The other speeches, including the *Tetralogies,* are generic exemplars of court speeches and lack distinct narrative components. Because separating narration from the argument proper is a hallmark of classical rhetoric, the presence of a distinct narrative component is a useful sign of the presence of formal rhetorical training. Antiphon is notoriously weak when it comes to this crucial area, as are other successful orators of the time for whom we have textual remains. Lysias' *Wounding with Intent to Kill,* better known as *Against Simon* (Lamb 1957, 70–93), is indeed a well-ordered speech, but is exceptional among the thirty-four speeches attributed to Lysias. Indeed, the attribution of authorship of these speeches to Lysias is far more vexed than even those to Antiphon. Dover (1968b) shows that, with present evidence and methods, only one of the speeches (*Against Eratosthenes*) can be assigned to Lysias without reservation. Most speeches again lack a recognizable narrative component. Some are well organized but do not follow the canonical four divisions. Others are very short or reveal no coherent organization whatsoever.

At best, the known speeches that can be plausibly attributed to Gorgias' lifetime suggest that only in his advanced years (the 390s to 380s, when Gorgias was over ninety) did speeches with the canonical divisions appear and even then examples are sparse. Formal speeches in fifth-century drama such as those found in Euripides (Lloyd 1992, 24–28) and Aristophanes (Murphy 1938; Major 1996, 4–19), and in fifth-century historical writings such as Thucydides (Stadter 1973) corroborate this progression. It would be surprising, then, if Gorgias' two surviving speeches, *Helen* and *Palamedes,* followed the canonical quadripartite division. To be precise, they do not because, like so many other speeches of the time, they lack a clear narrative component — as Smeltzer admits openly (1996, 159). As Cole notes, "sharp separation of narrative from proof makes its first appearance in the dicanic speeches of Isocrates," and not before (1991a, 170n). Smeltzer argues that Gorgias omits narration in *Helen* because his audience already knew the details of the myth. His audience's knowledge of the myth, however, would not have been so uniform and consistent that narrative was unnecessary, since multiple and mutually exclusive versions of the myth existed (Groten 1955). The topic of Helen's guilt or innocence was a lively one and *Helen* is but Gorgias' contribution to the debate. In fact, as Gorgias proceeds through the "proofs" of Helen's innocence, he incorporates bits of various rivaling versions of the Helen myth known at that time. That is, Gorgias conflates the narrative with the argument. As for the *Palamedes,* Smeltzer admits that "no actual narrative statements are made" (1996, 159). Thus neither of Gorgias' speeches "adhere to the four-part scheme" as claimed by Smeltzer (1996, 159). None of this is to say that Gorgias did not carefully arrange his speeches or that structural patterns do not emerge. Where such patterns exist, they do not necessarily constitute evidence of a distinct and self-consciously held "theory" of arrangement put into practice, as argued below. The theoretical innovation of naming the four parts of the forensic oration cannot be evidenced prior to the middle of the fourth century B.C.E. (Cole 1991a, 82–85, 130–35).

Smeltzer also contends that Gorgias organizes his arguments into three-step argument units consisting of the claim, proof of the claim, and restatement of the claim. To support his argument, Smeltzer relies on internal analysis of the speeches themselves. However, an alternative perspective on speech composition and patterning during the fifth and fourth centuries B.C.E. may better explain the three-step unit and analogous structures in other speeches of the period. The pattern of beginning and ending with the same idea is common in archaic Greek composition, already found in full flower in the earliest Homeric poems. Under the rubric of "ring composition" scholars have documented its prevalence in ancient poetry from epics and hymns of the eighth century B.C.E. to the choral odes of the fifth (Edwards 1991, 44–48; Otterlo 1944). The pattern persists in the early prose of the fifth century, too (Reid

1997, 72–80), such as in the historical writings of Herodotus and in the *Constitution of Athens* by the so-called Old Oligarch (found with the spurious works attributed to Xenophon).

Applied to a persuasive speech, ring composition takes the more specific form of claim–proof–restatement-of-claim that Smeltzer identifies. Argumentative speeches of this form appear as early as Homer and persist through Plato.[22] Viewed in this way, Gorgias is following a traditional, archaic pattern of arrangement. That Gorgias should borrow such a pattern from poetry is consistent with his well-documented use of poetic rhythms and verbal structures. "Borrowing" is perhaps misleading: Gorgias is helping to forge a new type of intellectual expression, prose, out of the then predominant vehicle for cultural expression, poetry. Simply put, Gorgias adapts what he knows.

Gorgias may not have lived long enough to see the quadripartite division of speeches become productive in Greek oratory. Plato is the first author who explicitly discusses the four components of a speech by name (Cole 1991a, 130–32). Importantly, he does so in response to the variety of components and arrangements propagated by various Sophists and the lack of meaningful progression in such arrangements (*Phaedrus* 266d5–267d4). The plurality implied here matches the findings of this brief review of extant speeches from the period. Plato, of course, finds fault with the practice and precepts put forth by the Sophists and orators mentioned (including Lysias, at 235a).

Prior to the formalization of rhetorical study in the fourth century B.C.E., these compositional practices are more likely a result of imitation and evolving oral patterns of composition than a conscious "theory" at work. Smeltzer makes a type of inference all too common among scholars revisiting the texts of the Sophists; namely, the inference that an observable pattern of behavior (compositional or otherwise) constitutes proof of a distinct "theory" at work. Smeltzer refers to Gorgias' "theory" or "theorizing" no less than six times and finds it "difficult to argue that something so obvious [as Gorgias' arrangement] was not the product of theorizing about the correct way to make a speech" (1996, 164). But such a type of inference ignores the wealth of historical examples where practice outstrips theory. Think of the variety of Greek artistic and technical endeavors that reached excellence in the fifth century B.C.E., such as sculpture, architecture, comedy, and tragedy. Now think of Plato's and Aristotle's theoretical treatises on such topics a number of decades later. The point is that humans can get quite good at doing various things long before developing abstract theories and specialized vocabularies about what it is that

22. For examples see Edwards 1991, 47; Reid 1997, 72–80; Kennedy 1980, 249; Worthington 1992, 1996.

we are doing. Prior to the emergence of anything like competing "theories" of topics ranging from catharsis to physics, Greeks were practicing both quite well even without a technical vocabulary to describe what they were doing. The same is true with respect to language. As children we learn how to compose sentences, ask questions, make arguments, and tell stories long before we learn to articulate the formal rules of language-use or to acquire the technical names associated with grammar, logic, or narrative theory. To put it another way, our language use is "rule governed" long before we can articulate and describe those rules. In Greek history, the grammar of the language had evolved into something quite sophisticated long before Protagoras and other Sophists came along to name the parts of speech (Levin 1983). Accordingly, it should not surprise us that oratory as a practice became fairly sophisticated through a process of imitation and evolution well before a technical vocabulary developed and before self-consciously held "theories" emerged.

The historiographical point of significance here is that our own technical vocabulary to describe the origins of rhetoric as a discipline is not very sophisticated or self-reflexive. What we need is a more nuanced way to describe the development of theory and theorizing. We should not leave the choice of describing Gorgias with terms implying a false dichotomy of theoretical versus atheoretical. At a minimum, we need to identify at least three steps to the emergence of rhetorical theory of the type found full-blown in the texts of the fourth century B.C.E. *Nontheoretical texts* describes texts where patterns and implicit rules may be found but no evidence of discussion or reflection on such rules. All writers operate with at least an informal sort of self-conscious aesthetic about what "sounds right," but this does not mean they all "theorize" about discourse. *Undeclared theory* may be a useful way of describing texts in which patterns emerge and there is some evidence of reflection about composition — such as the emergence of a rudimentary technical vocabulary — but insufficient evidence to attribute a distinct and self-consciously held "theory" to the author. It is possible to cull an "inferred" or "implied" theory or set of rules out of such texts, but without adequate evidence it is potentially anachronistic and misleading to call it a theory of rhetoric (or in this case, a theory of arrangement). The phrase *rhetorical theory* can be limited to texts containing explicit discussion of rules and principles of rhetoric which may or may not influence the compositional practices of others. Clear examples of each would include Homer's epics as nontheoretical; Gorgias' texts for an undeclared theory of arrangement (though Gorgias articulates an *explicit* account of *logos*); and Aristotle's *Rhetoric* for rhetorical theory. Based on the preceding distinctions, Smeltzer has presented a good case for an undeclared theory of arrangement in Gorgias' *Helen* and *Palamedes*. Because we do not know how much Gorgias theorized about arrangement, it makes more sense to describe his composition patterns as an implicit or inferred theory or set of rules. Between the nontheoretical texts of Homer and the formal rhetorical theory of Plato and Aristotle are a set of texts that we can best read as undeclared theory—in which patterns emerge and there is some evidence of reflection about composition but insufficient evidence to attribute a distinct and self-consciously held "theory" to the author. Gorgias theorized explicitly about *logos*. But there is no evidence he theorized in a similarly explicit way about arrangement; even if an undeclared theory of arrangement can be found in *Helen* and *Palamedes,* that "theory" can be found in most other texts of the period as well.

Excursus: Gorgianic Meter

Further comment on the meter found in Gorgias' prose may be helpful as a means of distinguishing among the rhythm found in his prose, that of other prose-writers, and that found in Greek poetry. It is my goal in this section to illustrate why Gorgias' prose sometimes is called "poetic" while not constituting poetry, per se. As mentioned before, the rhythm found in Greek verse is measured by sequences of long and short elements. In general, a long element is a syllable containing a long vowel or a syllable with a short vowel followed by two consonants. All other syllables are considered short. In metrical analysis, long syllables are indicated with "–" and short syllables with "◡." The meter of Greek poetry is defined by the specific pattern of short and long syllables found in each "foot," or unit of the meter being used. Accordingly, the unit – ◡ – is known as cretic meter; – ◡ ◡ – is known as choriamb, and so forth (see Halporn et al. 1980). Homer uses one type of verse, the dactylic hexameter, which is made up of six dactyls (– – or – ◡ ◡). The first line of the *Iliad* and *Odyssey* can be represented, or "scanned" as follows:

Μῆνιν ἄειδε θεά, Πηληιάδεω Ἀχιλῆος (*Iliad* 1.1)

    – ◡   ◡–◡   ◡– – –◡◡ –   ◡◡ – –.

Ἄνδρα μοι ἔννεπε, Μοῦσα, πολύτροπον, ὃς μάλα πολλὰ (*Odyssey* 1.1)

  –◡   ◡ –◡◡   –◡   ◡–◡◡   – ◡◡ – –.

Greek poetry can be categorized metrically by the repetitive use of specific patterns of long and short syllables.[23] In contrast to Greek poetry, prose compositions are free to vary the meter from phrase to phrase, sentence to sentence. Gorgias, in the first recorded definitional statement to distinguish be-

---

23. There is, I should note, more room for aesthetic variation than the two above examples imply, but such variation is not relevant to my current purpose.

tween prose and poetry, proclaimed that "All poetry I regard and name as speech (*logos*) having meter" (*Helen* 9). Prose, it is implied, is speech without a meter. This is not to say that prose is wholly unrhythmic. Rather, the prose-writer has far greater freedom to alter the rhythm than does the ancient Greek poet (see Dionysius of Halicarnassus, *On Literary Composition* 25). Book 3, Chapter 8 of Aristotle's *Rhetoric* suggests that for prose speech "the form of the language should be neither metrical nor unrhythmical" (1408b21–22); that is, prose ought to develop its own sense of rhythm that is not as repetitive as poetry but is nonetheless carefully crafted for effect: "Thus, speech should have rhythm but not meter; for the latter will be a poem" (1408b30–31).

What sort of rhythm does Gorgias' prose reveal? Norden's scansion of a brief passage of *Helen* (2) provides a useful starting point from which to consider Gorgias' prose rhythm (1: 64):

ἐγὼ δὲ βούλομαι
υ‒́ υ ‒υ‒

λογισμ όν τινα τῶι λόγωι δούς
υ‒́ ‒́ υυ ‒ υ‒ ‒

τὴν μὲν κακῶς ἀκούουσαν
‒ ‒́ υ‒ υ‒‒́‒

παῦσαι τῆς αἰτίας ‖
‒́‒ ‒́υ̣‒́

τοὺς δὲ μεμφομένους
‒́ υ ‒υυ‒

ψευδομένους ἐπιδεῖξαι
‒́ υυ‒ υυ‒‒

καὶ δεῖξαι τἀληθὲς
‒́ ‒ ‒ ‒υ

καὶ παῦσαι τῆς ἀμαθίας
‒́ ‒ ‒ ‒ ‒ υυυ‒

Certain individual phrases (or colas) clearly are rhythmic. For example, the first phrase is one longum short of being hemiambic and the phrase ψευδομένους ἐπιδεῖξαι is made up of two dactyls and one spondee. But the passage as a whole fails to repeat a pattern that could be recognized as poetry. The combination of some rhythm, some rhyme, and occasional use of "poetic" or elevated words by Gorgias makes his prose "poetic" (that is, metrical) but it is clearly not verse as the Greeks understood it. Furthermore, in this brief passage we do not even find the sort of recurring rhythmic patterns that are in the later prose of writers such as Lysias, Demosthenes, and Plato (Blass 1906).

It is worth noting that critics condemn Gorgias' style for very different reasons. As noted previously, Dionysius of Halicarnassus objects that Gorgias' technique was too obvious and thus appeared artificial and contrived. But this does not mean that he objects to any poetic artifice put to the service of prose; he merely demands more subtlety from the author. In his *On Literary Composition* (18), Dionysius describes the following lines from Thucydides account (2.35.1) of Pericles' *Epitaphios:*

Οἱ μὲν |πολλοὶ | τῶν ἐν- | θάδε ἤ- | δη εἰ- | ρηκότων
– – | – – | – – | ∪∪– | – – |– ∪ –

ἐπαινοῦ- | σι τὸν προσ- | θέντα τῶι | νόμωι τὸν | λόγον τόν- | δε,
∪ – – | ∪ – – | – ∪ – | ∪ – – | ∪ – – | ∪

ὡς καλὸν | ἐπὶ τοῖς | ἐκ τῶν | πολέμων | θαπτομέ- | νοις ἀγο- | ρεύεσ- |
– ∪ – | ∪∪ – | – – | ∪∪ – | – ∪∪ | – ∪∪ | – – |

θαι αὐ- | τόν.
– – | ∪

Dionysius (in Usher 1974, 2: 134) notes with approval Thucydides' use of a series of poetic feet: spondee (– –), anapest (∪ ∪ –), cretic (– ∪ –), bacchiac (∪– –), and dactyl (–∪∪). Ironically, Gorgias is criticized for using overly poetic language at times, but with respect to his rhythm he is criticized for not being poetic *enough;* that is, partially because he does not rely exclusively on traditional poetic meters or what was subsequently identified as appropriate prose rhythms, he is accused of writing in a "choppy" and "jerky" style.

Rather than contrasting Gorgias' meter with traditional Greek poetry or with later prose writers, a more salient and interesting issue is how Gorgias' style compares to his contemporary prose authors. A useful comparison has been made by Drerup (1902, 225–74) between the surviving portion of Gorgias' *Epitaphios* and a passage by Thrasymachus as reported by Dionysius (*Demosthenes* 3 = DK 85 B1).[24] Drerup's punctuation suggests that Gorgias' cola are generally much shorter than those of Thrasymachus — about half the length.[25] Because Thrasymachus' phrasing requires less frequent stops, his meter has been described by later oral readers of Greek prose as smoother and

24. For comparisons between Gorgias and Thrasymachus, see also Denniston (1952, 14–15) and Blass (1887, 1: 244–62).

25. Since we are uncertain as to the precise time values of different sorts of short syllables (Maas 1962, 36–38), I computed the length of each colon in two ways. If each long syllable is counted as 1.0 and each short syllable as 0.5, then the average number of syllables per colon in Gorgias is about 6.5. The average for Thrasymachus is almost 11.5, which is only 1.5 syllables short of being twice the length of Gorgias' cola. Counting *every* syllable as 1.0, Gorgias' average is still only a little over 8 compared to 14.5 in Thrasymachus. My colleague André Lardinois pointed out to me that though Homer's hexameter lines are typically 12–18 syllables, they are broken up in the middle with a caesura, making Gorgias' cola similar in length to those of Homer.

less choppy than that of Gorgias. Because we do not know how either speaker sounded in person when performing their prose, we cannot say whether the audiences of the fifth century were bothered by such a difference. The available evidence suggests that they were not. Both styles were successful with their audiences, even if Gorgias' lost favor with later literary critics.

Both writers draw upon poetic meters without relying on them. In Gorgias' case, his primary interest seems to be to construct striking antitheses with striking sound effects. The meter is a natural consequence rather than being an end in itself. In the case of Thrasymachus, the rhythm is more clearly the result of "art-wise" (*kunstmäßiger*) composition; for this reason he, rather than Gorgias, has been called the inventor of "prosaic rhythm" (Drerup 1902, 246). With meter as with other facets of his composition style, Gorgias is found to be not poetic enough to be judged favorably by the standards of poesy, while at the same time being *too* poetic compared to later prose to be judged favorably by the standards of literary prose. Such is the price Gorgias' reputation has paid for being genuinely unique.

7

Rereading Gorgias' Helen

Gorgias' *Encomium of Helen* (hereafter *Helen*) is a text that has earned a central place in the revival of interest in Sophistic and Neosophistic rhetorical studies in the late twentieth century. Based on its composition style alone, the speech has been the object of considerable controversy.[1] Descriptions and assessments of the theoretical content of the text are equally diverse. Scholars find evidence in the text of a psychological theory of *logos* (Segal 1962), a magical account of discourse (de Romilly 1975), an incipient "postmodern" theory of epistemology (Enos 1976; Gronbeck 1972; Untersteiner 1954), a thinly veiled defense of the art of Rhetoric (Poulakos 1983b; Wardy 1996), and a nonrepresentational theory of language and meaning (Mourelatos 1985; Kerferd 1984). Despite the great interest the text has generated, there is remarkably little agreement even over the most rudimentary interpretive issues concerning the text, such as the genre to which it belongs, the role it played in fifth-century B.C.E. rhetorical practice, and its theoretical significance. Resolution of all of these issues is unnecessary and perhaps even undesirable. None-

---

1. Scholars as diverse as Dodds (1959, 9), Cole (1991a, 73), Jebb (1893, cxxiv), and Van Hook (1945, 122) condemn Gorgias' stylistic "excesses" while scholars such as Barrett (1987), de Romilly (1975), Crowley (1989), and myself (see chapter 6) praise his artistry and creativity.

theless, I believe that recent developments in the historiography of the Sophists opens a space from which to consider and visit the text anew.

This chapter offers a predisciplinary historical description of Gorgias' famous speech. I call the description "predisciplinary" to indicate the belief that the texts of fifth-century Greek writers, especially those by the figures commonly referred to as the Older Sophists, ought to be approached with the awareness that certain "disciplines" were not yet formalized either in theory or in practice. In particular, the dichotomy often used to distinguish between Philosophical and Rhetorical discourse is simply not evident in the texts of the fifth century that describe Sophistic education. As maintained earlier, fifth-century texts concerning *logos* — such as Gorgias' *Helen* — differ substantially from fourth-century texts concerning Rhetoric (*rhētorikē*) — such as Plato's *Gorgias,* Alkidamas' *On Those Writing Written Speeches,* the *Rhetoric to Alexander,* and Aristotle's *Rhetoric.* Prior to the fourth century, one rarely finds a distinction between the art or skill of producing discourse that seeks "truth" and the art or skill of producing discourse that seeks persuasion. Accordingly, a predisciplinary description attempts to avoid the vocabulary and assumptions about discourse theories and rhetorical practice imported from the fourth century when analyzing fifth-century texts.

It is my contention that certain persistent questions about Gorgias' *Helen* obtain different answers once the speech is repositioned as a predisciplinary text. In this chapter I will revisit three questions: What is the speech's purpose? What are its contributions to fifth-century discourse practices? What are its contributions to fifth-century theory? I offer five arguments: identifying Gorgias' *Helen* as an "epideictic" speech is a somewhat misleading characterization; the speech is not a veiled defense of the Art of Rhetoric; Gorgias may have inaugurated the prose genre of the encomion; Gorgias advanced fifth-century B.C.E. "rationalism" by enacting certain innovations in prose composition; the *Helen*'s most significant "theoretical" contribution is to offer a secular account of the workings of *logos* — an account that functioned as an exemplar for later theorists.

What Is the Speech's Purpose?

Because the speech makes no reference to contemporary events, there is no confident way to date the text with precision; estimates range from before 415 to 393 B.C.E. (Blass 1887, 1: 72–75). The speech is written in the Attic dialect, a choice that suggests the text was designed for oral performance in a variety of venues (Norlin 1928, 2: 348–49n; see also Cole 1991a, 74–75).

The stated goal of the speech is to exonerate the legendary Helen of the

charge of deserting her husband, Menelaus, and running away with Paris—
the act precipitating the famous Trojan War. The topic was a familiar one, as
arguments back and forth about Helen's culpability can be found throughout
early Greek literature.[2] Some have supposed that Gorgias' account may have
been an answer to Euripides' or vice versa, but as D. M. MacDowell argues,
"There is no resemblance in details, and no strong reason to link Gorgias' discussion of Helen with anyone else's" (1982, 12; see also Blass 1887, 1:56–57).

Gorgias begins with a clear statement of purpose: his task is to remove,
through reasoning (*logismos*), the unjust blame that Helen has received (1–2).
After providing a brief account of her birth, personal qualities, and marriage
(3–5), Gorgias posits a list of four possible causes behind Helen's departure to
Troy: chance and the gods, physical force, persuasion by *logos,* or passion (6).
He then addresses the four causes in turn, arguing that each is such a powerful
force that Helen should not be blamed for her behavior. The amount of space
he spends on each cause is noteworthy: Gods and chance are dealt with in one
paragraph (6), as is force (7), while *logos* is addressed in seven (8–14) and
passion in five (15–19). He then concludes by summarizing the causes and
suggesting that he has accomplished his purpose (20–21).

Beyond Gorgias' stated agenda, for what purpose was the discourse composed and performed? Most commentators categorize the *Helen* as epideictic
rhetoric. The verb *epideiknunai* is typically translated as "to display" or "to
show," and *epideixis* denotes a particular exhibition or demonstration. Since
ancient writers refer to *Helen* as an epideictic address, it is commonly assumed
that the purpose of *Helen* was primarily to show off Gorgias' oratorical abilities. Segal calls it a "mythological showpiece of rhetoric" and an "epideictic
encomium" (1962, 100), John Robinson dubs it a "display piece" (1973, 53),
Poulakos says that Gorgias in the *Helen* "indulges in the delights afforded by
epideictic rhetoric" (1986, 301), and Van Hook deems it an "epideictic . . .
tour de force" (1945, 54). Jarratt classifies the *Helen* as "epideictic" and
says that Gorgias "exploits the latitude offered by a rhetorical performance"
(1991, 59). Scott Consigny argues that all of Gorgias' speeches are categorized
properly as epideictic and that Gorgias "uses the epideictic primarily to advertise his own rhetorical skills" (1992, 291). The purpose of Gorgias' display of

2. Frank J. Groten's study (1955) of various treatments of the Helen legend in Greek
literature makes it clear that Gorgias was not the first to argue that Helen was blameless.
Furthermore, the many previous sympathetic treatments of Helen call into question the
claim that Gorgias' *Helen* was an unprecedented effort to "radically reconstruct" history
to "dislodge a mythic source for misogynism" (Jarratt 1991, 74). For a reading that
argues Gorgias' *Helen* "reiterates in oratorical discourse the general trend toward further
subjugation of women" in ancient Greece, see Biesecker (1990, 77).

oratorical prowess, most commentators believe, was to attract more students of Rhetoric.

A description of *Helen* as predisciplinary problematizes, though does not necessarily reject, such a conclusion. To begin with, it is not at all clear that Gorgias' extant texts ought to be limited by the apparently mutually exclusive choice of Philosophy or Rhetoric. Certainly in the past the *Helen* has been appropriated in just such a limiting fashion. Though often cited in histories of rhetoric, the *Helen* is rarely, if ever, mentioned in histories of Greek philosophy. As argued earlier, categorizing texts from the fifth century B.C.E. exclusively as Rhetoric or Philosophy often risks anachronism. The question is, what were Gorgias' speeches supposed to accomplish? Were they "display" speeches intended solely to entertain? Were they intended to be, at least in some instances, efforts to theorize about issues later labeled "philosophical"? Interpretations of the text that privilege one feature of the text over the other can neglect the obvious answer that Gorgias' texts—like anyone else's—potentially serve multiple functions. Locating the text as predisciplinary gives us reason to hesitate before describing and assessing it with specific, disciplinary criteria.

For example, I believe that it is inappropriate to confine *Helen* to the Aristotelian genre of epideictic rhetoric. Even though one can refer to a performance of *Helen* by Gorgias as an *epideixis,* and despite the morphological link between *epideixis* and *epideiktikē,* identifying Gorgias' *Helen* as an "epideictic" speech is somewhat misleading. Assignment of fifth-century texts to a specific genre of discourse may presume a greater degree of genre-related compositional expectations than were the case during Gorgias' career. Aristotle's well-known threefold taxonomy of Rhetoric was not codified until his lectures, given decades after Gorgias' death (Kennedy 1991, 299–305). Accordingly, one problem with characterizing *Helen* as epideictic is that a discrete genre of epideictic rhetoric is not clearly identified as such until well into the fourth century B.C.E. Aristotle's conceptual formulation of epideictic rhetoric is almost certainly original. The earliest extant use of the word *epideiktikē* is in Plato's *Sophist* (224b5), where it is used to describe "the art of display" that helps to define the profession of the Sophists. The *Sophist* was one of Plato's later dialogues, however, and the prior absence of the word suggests that it is prompted by fourth-century Sophists and has been applied only with hindsight to those of the previous century. *Epideiktikē* might have been yet another example of Plato's original construction of an *-ikē* word to designate a specific art or skill (Ammann 1953; Chantraine 1956, 97–151).

Cole contends that the word "epideictic" is part of a later developed standard terminology that has its roots in the "preanalytic stage" of the history of rhetoric. He suggests that what marks a speech as an *epideixis* is that it is written to be presented rather than that it has the quality of "showing off."

> Epideictic oratory will then be, in origin, what *epideixis* is in Xenophon's account of Prodicus: not the showing off of one's talents, but the displaying or revealing (orally) of what was already in existence beforehand—in the form of a prememorized piece. . . . And its ultimate use as a designation for ceremonial rather than judicial or political oratory will be a natural result of the fact that ceremonial occasions were the only ones at which recitation of a written (or prememorized) text would have been considered acceptable by a fifth-century audience. (1991a, 89)

Cole's claim may be supported by the following speculative morphological argument. I noted earlier that *epideiknunai* is typically translated as "to display" or "to show." I should add that the same is true of shorter verb *deiknunai*. Other meanings include "to bring to light" and "to show forth." The noun *deikēlon* can designate a specific exhibition. The meaning of the preposition *epi-* varies; it lacks the sort of core meaning that some prefixes have. Its sense depends on context and case; possible meanings include: upon, at, toward, and against. The question becomes: Why was the preposition *epi-* compounded with *deiknunai* to create *epideiknunai*? It is difficult to say. Even in English, one can find prefixes that at one point might have conveyed an active sense of position or motion, but that later became a dormant appendage: One can *cede* or *concede* a position. One can *limit* or *delimit*. One can *splay* or *display* a banner. We may conjecture plausibly that originally *epideiknunai* designated a special sort of "showing." It is possible that, with respect to discourse, it had to be written in order for it to be some *thing* that could be "displayed" or re-presented. If Cole's argument is correct, then what later would be called epideictic speech originated with the recounting or recitation of an "exhibit" or "specimen" of written prose discourse.

Whether Cole is correct or not about the original sense of *epideixis* before the formalization of Rhetoric in the fourth century, the redescription of Gorgias' *Helen* as prediscipplinary leads to important insights. The most obvious implication is that there simply were not the same sort of formal, generic expectations for prose compositions of the fifth century that are found a century later. Gorgias would not have felt any tension between writing a theoretical "versus" an epideictic speech, because no one had yet felt a particular need to distinguish prose texts on the basis of instructional versus entertainment aspirations. An *epideixis*—or "demonstration"—could strive for both. While there is no doubt that he intended his distinctive style to entertain, there is no reason to doubt that he also wanted to instruct—just like other early Greek writers, including "philosophers" such as Parmenides, Empedocles, and Heraclitus. Gorgias adapted and transformed poetic styles and genres of composition and in the process created texts that now appear to us as rhetorical "hybrids." Gorgias' innovation was not so much stretching a given set of prose genres as much as taking certain poetic forms and creating texts that embody certain rhetorical goals and forms of composition that soon would be separated by later prose writers. Isocrates' comment (*Helen* 14–15 in Van Hook 1945, 67) about the competing needs of *apologia* and *encomia* would have struck Gorgias as strange.

Michael F. Carter (1991) argues that epideictic rhetoric played an important ritualistic function in ancient Greek culture. The funeral oration (*epitaphios*), in particular, is credited with creating an "extraordinary," transcendent knowledge for its participants, generating a strong sense of community, and guiding behavior toward accepted norms. Similarly Perelman and Olbrechts-Tyteca suggest that the function of epideictic rhetoric is not to change beliefs or attitudes but to "increase the adherence to values held in common by the audience and speaker" (1959, 52). There is no evidence that any of these objectives are pursued by Gorgias through the *Helen,* at least not in the sense the objectives are explained by Carter or Perelman and Olbrechts-Tyteca. And there is no evidence that *Helen* was ever given in anything approaching a setting that would be conducive to performing ritualistic functions. Rather than concluding that Gorgias is somehow a "failed" epideictic speaker, as Blass suggests (1887, 1:68), a description of *Helen* as predisciplinary challenges the assumption that — prior to epideictic's formalization by Aristotle — an address such as *Helen* would have been expected to increase adherence to community values or perform ritualistic functions.

A further consequence of redescribing the speech as predisciplinary is that historical interpretations of *Helen* that presume Rhetoric was a discrete discipline or clearly demarcated body of literature are anachronistic. The clearest example of such an interpretation is that by John Poulakos, who argues that the Helen portrayed in Gorgias' speech is actually "the personification of rhetoric" (1983b, 4). Recalling that Gorgias is said to have alluded to an analogy between Penelope and *philosophia,* and noting that both *rhētorikē* and *philosophia* are feminine nouns, Poulakos suggests that Gorgias, "although talking about Helen, is really referring to rhetoric" (1983b, 10). Advocating an analogical reading of Helen as Rhetoric based on "historical and textual grounds," he notes that "both are attractive, both are unfaithful, and both have a bad reputation" (1983b, 4–5).

Poulakos' reading is dubious history on three counts. First, the available evidence suggests that the Greek word for Rhetoric — *rhētorikē* — had not yet been coined when Gorgias wrote *Helen* (as discussed in chapter 1). Or, even if *rhētorikē* was in use, it would have been so novel at the time as to make pretext unnecessary and the allusion unsuccessful. Second, Poulakos' "historical explanation" of the need for pretext on behalf of Gorgias is weak. He claims that "Gorgias must have been aware of the Athenian practices of intolerance; frequent banishments and condemnations, the burning of books in public, and excommunications by exile must have dictated that he approach his task indirectly" (1983b, 7). Such a characterization grossly exaggerates Athenian "intolerance" and presumes that certain poorly attested legends, such as the burning of Protagoras' books, are true (see Dover 1976; Stone 1988, 231–47; Schiappa 1991, 144–45). Third, if there had been an urgent need for pretext, Gorgias' speech certainly would have failed. Poulakos cites the names of Aristophanes' plays *Frogs, Wasps,* and *Birds* as examples of the artistic masking of purpose, but there was no mistaking the playwright's message as anything other than a lambasting of specific politicians and policies (Dover, 1972). The powerful leader Cleon, for example, was ridiculed by Aristophanes even though — perhaps even because — Cleon was sitting in the audience! Likewise, the power of speech is an explicit and developed theme of *Helen.* If there had been intolerant censors lurking about in Athens, it is highly unlikely that they would have considered Gorgias "harmless and nonthreatening" simply because he omitted the word "rhetoric." After all, Critias the Tyrant's alleged ban on discourse instruction is described by Xenophon as a prohibition of *logōn technē,* not *rhētorikē (Memorabilia* 1.2.31).

Poulakos, of course, is not the only one who has read *Helen* as being primarily about Rhetoric.[3] Verdenius suggests that Gorgias conceptualized an "art of rhetoric" and that in composing *Helen* the analogy between rhetoric and poetry "clearly preponderates in his mind" (1981, 116–17). And de Romilly believes that Helen's defense is a pretext for a defense of Gorgias' Art: "Under the vindication of Helen pierces a cry of pride of the Master of Rhetoric."[4] Such descriptions are underdetermined by the text; they overemphasize and overparticularize one set of purposes and contributions of the text, while they underestimate other possible agendas.

3. To be fair, after Poulakos offers explicitly "historical" grounds for his reading, he retreats in his conclusion to the position that *Helen* "may be read" as a defense of rhetoric, regardless of whether the Helen/Rhetoric analogy "even crossed his [Gorgias'] mind" (1983b).

4. "Sous la justification d'Hélène perce un cri de fierté du maître de rhétorique" (de Romilly 1988, 103). Janet Lloyd translates this as "Under the guise of justifying Helen, the master of rhetoric proclaims his pride in his skills" (de Romilly 1992a, 67). See also de Romilly (1988, 108), Gomperz (1912, 36–37), and Wardy (1996).

Practical Contributions of Gorgias' Helen

Once the disciplinary expectations and nomenclature of classical rhetorical theory are set aside, Gorgias' role as an innovator in prose composition is
more easily discernible. There are no extant examples of a prose composition
being called an *encomium* prior to Gorgias' *Helen* (Blass 1887, 1:72; Duncan
1938, 405). It is not until after Gorgias' death in the fourth century B.C.E. that
one finds texts such as the *Rhetoric to Alexander* describing "rules for the
genre" (Dover 1980, 12). As Dover notes, "*enkōmion* and *enkōmiazein* are
freely used in the fourth century of formal praise in prose or verse, but in fifth-
century usage *enkōmion* is especially a poem celebrating someone's victory"
(1968a, 237). Such use is found in Pindar, Hesiod, and Aristophanes, but not
in any prose writer.[5] Though it is possible that "encomium" was added to the
formal title at some later date, Gorgias explicitly calls his discourse "an encomium of Helen" in the final sentence of the speech — a self-reference suggesting that Gorgias was aware of the relationship between his speech and the
poetic tradition. The most probable inference is that Gorgias helped to inaugurate a tradition of prose *encomia* that was infamous less than a century later,
when we learn in Plato's *Symposium* (177a–c) that speeches of praise had been
composed on subjects as diverse as Heracles and salt. It does not really matter
that we would now classify Gorgias' speech as *apologia* or a rhetorical "hy-
brid" rather than as an encomium. It is not unusual for writers to contribute to
the formulation of canons and genres in ways that they did not, and could not,
anticipate.

Gorgias' *Helen* is also noteworthy for being an early and masterful example
of the apagogic method of argument by which an advocate enumerates a series
of possibilities and addresses each in turn. Kennedy's description merits quotation in its entirety:

> After a brief introduction in which Gorgias seeks to justify the choice of
> subject — it is right to praise the praiseworthy and defend the maligned — he
> states (6) that Helen must have yielded to Paris either through fate or the
> wishes of the Gods, or else she was ravaged by force or persuaded by words or
> maddened by love. No other possibilities are presumed to exist. Each of those
> enumerated is examined in turn and it is demonstrated by what Aristotle
> would call enthymeme or example within the limits of probability that in each
> case Helen cannot be blamed for her action. The most interesting discussion is
> that of persuasion by words (8 ff.), where Gorgias develops an analysis of psy-

5. See Aristophanes, *Clouds* line 1205 (Rogers 1924, 2:374); Hesiod, *Works and Days*
line 344 (Evelyn-White 1936, 28); Pindar, *Olympian* 2.47, 10.77, 13.29; *Pythian* 10.53;
and *Nemean* 1.7 (Sandys 1937).

chological effects. The speech ends with a brief conclusion echoing the statements of the introduction. In four and a half pages Gorgias has given a vivid, even unforgettable, example of the same logical method which he employed in his famous discussion of being. He refers to the little work as a *logismos* or "reasoning" in section two, and this seems entirely appropriate. . . . It is playful in mood, but it also has a serious purpose in demonstrating a method of logical proof. (1963, 167–68)

It is easy to fixate on Gorgias' exotic style and his "magical" use of language and, as a result, neglect his more "rationalistic" side. Such neglect is a mistake. There is a clear parallel in ancient Greek discourse between the transition from poetic to prose styles and the gradual proliferation of modes of reasoning. Because many texts of this era tend to combine elements of "rationalistic" prose and "mythic" poetry, there is a tendency to see such a "mixed" style as a fault of the writer rather than evidence of rapid changes in modes of composition. For example, Parmenides tried to put the meter of Homeric poetry (epic hexameter) to the service of philosophical analysis. Though some commentators praise Parmenides' abilities to express himself in verse, others argue that the vocabulary and syntax of poetry were very much in tension with his goals and that Parmenides had to struggle to adapt his ideas to an unsuitable medium.[6] Gorgias was similarly situated in and influenced by an oral-poetic culture. Gorgias' unique prose was transforming the uses to which prose discourse was being put, thereby contributing to what is often called the transition from *mythos* to *logos* (Nestle 1966).

Gorgias says in his introduction that "I wish to offer reasoning by particular arguments to free the accused of blame, to reveal that her critics are lying, and to show the truth and to halt the ignorance" (2).[7] It is significant that Gorgias identifies "reasoning" (*logismos*) as his method. *Logismos* is not a very common word in fifth-century texts. A typical early use is Democritus' advice to "Drive out by reasoning the unmastered pain of a numbed soul" (in Barnes 1987, 283). Aristophanes uses the word only once — to make fun of rational argumentation in the plays of Euripides (*Frogs* 973 in Rogers 1924). The word

6. Barnes (1982, 155) complains that "It is hard to excuse Parmenides' choice of verse as a medium for his philosophy. The exigencies of metre and poetical style regularly produce an almost impenetrable obscurity." The most thorough discussions of Parmenides' composition style is in Mourelatos (1970, 1–46, 264–68). See also David Gallop (1984, 4–5), Coxon (1986, 7–8), and Havelock (1982, 220–60; 1983).

7. ἐγὼ δὲ βούλομαι λογισμόν τινα τῶι λόγωι δοὺς τὴν μὲν κακῶς ἀκούουσαν παῦσαι τῆς αἰτίας, τοὺς δὲ μεμφομένους ψευδομένους πιδείξας καὶ δείξας τἀληθὲς [ἢ] παῦσαι τῆς ἀμαθίας (DK 1951–52, 2:288–89). All passages quoted from Gorgias' *Helen* are based on Kennedy's most recent translation (1991, 284–88) with slight alterations by the author.

occurs sixteen times in the works attributed to Hippocrates, where it usually has the sense of careful analysis (see, e.g. *On the Art* 11). Though Herodotus never uses the word, Thucydides employs it thirteen times — always to connote calculation, logical decision-making, or reflection.[8] Gorgias' self-conscious identification of his method as "reasoning" positions his text as contributing to the pursuit of what we would now call rational argumentation. Though his style is notably poetic, it is also notably rationalistic for its time.

By calling the speech "rationalistic" I do not mean to imply that Gorgias was a "rationalist" in the sense implied by the word in modernist philosophies. There are all sorts of "rationalities" that are performed in different ways at different times in different cultures (MacIntyre 1988; Rorty 1992b). Though Gorgias' manner of composition may strike some readers as "irrational" or "nonrational" compared to Aristotle's prose, for example, the more relevant comparison is between the sorts of compositions produced immediately prior to Gorgias and in his own generation. In so doing, we will come closer to understanding the Other sort of rationality found uniquely in the texts of Gorgias. Specifically, Gorgias' speech contains a number of literate characteristics that mark it as an example of fifth-century "rationalism"; that is, for its time the *Helen*'s "argumentation is didactic, obvious, and academic" (Barrett 1987, 17). His arrangement of arguments is "remarkably orderly and well-signposted"; his introductory forecast, clear transitions, and summarizing conclusion could serve as a model for persuasive speeches today (MacDowell 1982, 17). C. Jan Swearingen contrasts the beginning of *Helen* with the mythologized narrative that begins Parmenides' famous poem, and concludes that the two reveal "vastly different" styles of composition:

> Gorgias' text exemplifies several "literate" features: definition of attributes, contrasts, and opposites; explicit statement of authorial/rhetorical purpose; and explicit identification of Gorgias as the composer and originator of the defense. There is no trace of even a vestigially formulaic attribution to the Muse or a god, except perhaps in the repetition of the story of Zeus as Helen's real father. But most of all, observe how Gorgias' argument is clearly marked *as an argument*, with metalinguistic terms and phrases that define structural and logical relationships among its statements. (1986, 149)

Furthermore, style and content are interrelated in Gorgias' text and complementary in a manner unlike Parmenides' poem. Barrett notes that his use of the apagogic method "was clearly a stimulator of listener involvement and response. It insisted on a battle among ideas, on an agonistic clash promoting

---

8. See sections 2.11.7; 1.40.3; 2.40.5; 3.20.3; 3.83.2; 4.10.1; 4.92.2; 4.108.4; 4.122.3; 5.68.2; 6.34.4; 6.34.6; 8.57.2 (Smith 1919–23).

excitement. Thus in *Helen,* Gorgias structured an 'adversary' relationship among ideas in testing arguments. . . . Through form, Gorgias built in agitation and competition of reasons; form contributed to substance" (1987, 17).

Finally, it should be noted that Gorgias identifies himself as a writer — a self-identification that is very rare and unusual for a fifth-century author. Gorgias ends his speech with the words: "I wished to write a speech as Helen's encomium and my own recreation" (21). One is far more likely to encounter verbs of saying and hearing when sixth- and fifth-century texts describe the role of the author/speaker. It is exclusively in the texts and fragments of a small number of "philosophers" such as Diogenes of Apollonia that one finds statements like "as will have been shown clearly in this written composition (*suggraphēi*)" (DK 64B4). Gorgias' self-conscious identification of himself as the author of the text is remarkable for its time. Furthermore, his combination of an epic theme, a highly poetic style, systematic reasoning, and self-conscious writing provides reason to doubt "great divide" theories that pit oral/mythological "versus" literate/rationalistic styles and mindsets as wholly distinct. Such schemata simply do not work when one examines the texts of various Sophists (Jarratt 1991, 31–61).

The practical contributions of Gorgias' *Helen* can be summarized best by describing them as advancing the art of written prose in general, and argumentative composition in particular. Though the subject matter is ostensibly mythical, the modus operandi of the discourse supplements the qualities of traditional, oral-poetic composition with such humanistic-rationalistic practices as the apagogic method of argument. Finally, it is possible that Gorgias helped to inaugurate the practice of composing encomium in prose.

Theoretical Contributions: Explicit and Implicit

My intent in this section is not to provide a detailed commentary on the text, which already has been done admirably by MacDowell (1982), Thomas Buchheim (1989), and others. Nor will I attempt the sort of extended argument that outlines and defends a specific Gorgianic theory of this or that based on Gorgias' extant texts. Instead, in this section I focus on the portion of the text that is of most interest to historians of rhetorical theory — the discussion of *logos* in paragraphs 8 through 14. *Logos* is a notoriously polysemous term in ancient Greek. Throughout this section I leave *logos* untranslated so as to avoid overly modernistic or reductionistic renderings. In most fifth-century Sophistic texts the term is meant quite broadly, as with the current term "discourse." Because the term is often set in opposition to *mythos,* "reasoned speech" is not too far off the mark. Some scholars suggest that for Gorgias *logos* simply means expression in prose (Duncan 1938, 407).

Specifically, I address several hermeneutic practices that have obscured some of the ways Gorgias' *Helen* affected the content and practice of later theorizing. I want to identify those features of classical-era theoretical texts that can be described as paradigmatic, that is, that function as exemplary (in Kuhn's sense) for later theorists. Kuhn describes "exemplars" as shared examples: practical, concrete "problem solutions" — the methods or procedures of which are imitated by others (1977, 298). The virtue of such an approach is that it emphasizes that theorizing is a form of praxis. Gorgias' *Helen* is not only a set of interesting concepts, but it is also a way of conceptualizing. His text not only provides us with another chapter in the history of thought, but in the fifth century B.C.E. it enacted a novel means of thinking. In short, in addition to asking the question "What did Gorgias *say?*," we need to ask "What did his speech *do?*" Advancing new ways of thinking about the world is at least as important as the content of the specific theories we might associate with specific figures. It well may be the case that Gorgias' most important theoretical contribution is his act of theorizing rather than any particular theoretical statement, per se.

Though Gorgias' speech is filled with statements that we now find theoretically provocative, propositions of the form "Gorgias had a theory of X" are potentially misleading. There is a tendency to read even a few sentences about a concept by an early Greek writer as indicating that the writer "held a theory" about it. So, for example, Duncan titles his article "Gorgias' Theories of Art" and suggests that he held "theories of style" as well as a theory of catharsis (1938, 406–8, 412). Enos (1976, 35, 45) and Richard A. Engnell (1973, 175) contend — in separate articles — that Gorgias developed "theories of rhetoric." Verdenius says that Gorgias held a "theory of knowledge" (1981, 116), and Bruce E. Gronbeck (1972) believes Gorgias defended a specific "theory of language" consistent with contemporary existential phenomenology.

Such statements are potentially misleading in two ways. First, they overestimate the maturity of theory development by implying more coherence and completeness than can be demonstrated with the available evidence. The term "theory" has many meanings, of course, but it seems reasonable to stipulate that a "theory" is made up of a constellation of beliefs that attempts to solve some specific intellectual problem or explain particular phenomena. It probably exaggerates the degree of development of a person's thought to impute to him or her a full-blown "theory of X" on the basis of one or two sentences that predicate certain qualities about a given X. Accordingly, it is more appropriate at times simply to identify a statement as a belief or even hypothesis rather than as a theory.

Second and more important, the attribution of a number of theories to ancient writers on the basis of isolated or few statements mischaracterizes the process of intellectual investigation in ancient Greece during the sixth and fifth centuries. By the late fourth century, the scientific and philosophical vocabulary, syntax, and available models of studies had developed to the point that one can identify competing "schools of thought" about various "theories" in more or less distinct "disciplines." Aristotle's accounts of earlier philosophy give us the impression that such was the case fully two centuries earlier. However, as the important work of Cherniss (1935) and Havelock (1983) has demonstrated, Aristotle's "history" is both inconsistent and misleading. Aristotle presumes that the conceptual categories and patterns of explanation available to him and his students were also available to his predecessors. In the search to find historical anticipations of his theories, Aristotle often radically retranslates earlier thinkers' notions into his own vocabulary. As Havelock argues, something important is lost in the translation: "Such vocabulary subtly distorts the story of early Greek thought by presenting it as an intellectual game dealing with problems already given and present to the mind, rather than as a groping after a new language in which the existence of such problems will slowly emerge" (1983, 57). One of the major tasks of earlier thinkers was to develop the analytical tools necessary for "philosophical" or "scientific" investigation to take place. As Solmsen suggests in his study of the fifth-century Greek "Enlightenment," the most important advancements may not "necessarily take the form of doctrines" or "programs of reform" but rather were experiments in ways of thinking about things (1975, 4). In particular, what we call in hindsight the birth of Western philosophical thinking is the effort to describe the world with generalizations that privilege secular explanations of causes (Guthrie 1962, 26–38).

In short, we underestimate the significance of the earlier writers' efforts to come to grips with the process of theorizing itself by overestimating the sophistication of such early "theories." If predisciplinary theoretical efforts are treated as if the authors were educated in methods and language developed much later, then their role in transforming intellectual practices is missed.

In the case of Gorgias, one of the most important theoretical contributions of the *Helen* is that it engaged in relatively systematic, secular, physical explanation and description. Gorgias provides a serious account of the workings of *logos* and the psyche. With respect to *logos,* Gorgias enumerates its qualities, describes its effects, and explains how it works. The *Helen* is the earliest surviving extended discussion of *logos* and certainly the most sophisticated of his time. Prior to Gorgias, all we have are a few fragmentary aphorisms by theorists such as Heraclitus and Protagoras that simply posit declarations about *logos*. Gorgias begins the relevant section of *Helen* by making a similar type of declaration: "*Logos* is a powerful lord that with the smallest and most invisible body accomplishes most godlike works. It can banish fear and remove grief and instill pleasure and enhance pity. I shall show how this is so" (8). But then Gorgias goes on to do what no one prior to him (that we know of) did: explain how *logos* works.

To explain the power of *logos*, Gorgias compares its effect with that of poetry: "All poetry I regard and name as *logos* having meter. On those who hear it come fearful shuddering and tearful pity and grievous longing as the psyche, through *logos*, experiences some experience of its own at others' good fortune and ill fortune" (9). Aside from providing what we might now call a psychological account of the effects of oral discourse (Segal 1962), the passage is remarkable for containing a potentially unprecedented propositional form: a definition. While the practice of defining terms has its recorded start in the dialogues of Plato (Schiappa 1993, 406), the statement "all poetry I regard and name as *logos* having meter" clearly ought to count as a stipulative definition. Gorgias' *Helen* may be our earliest example of the practice of explicating precisely what a particular word means in one's own discourse. That Gorgias defined a word is, itself, a significant advance in the practice of theorizing.

The succeeding sentences have been the basis for various commentators' descriptions of Gorgias as a defender of an "irrational" or "nonrational" account of language: "Divine sweetness transmitted through speech is inductive of pleasure, reductive of pain. Thus by entering into the opinion of the psyche the force of incantation is wont to beguile and persuade and alter it by witchcraft, and the two arts of witchcraft and magic are errors of the psyche and deceivers of opinion" (10). Enos, among others, describes Gorgias as articulating a "nonrational epistemology" and says that Gorgias "did not stress rational methods for attaining krisis but, rather, used nonrational, stylistic procedures for gaining the assent of listeners" (1993, 85, 88). However, as noted earlier, such characterizations underestimate the "rational" aspects of Gorgias' texts. Furthermore, as Solmsen argues, accounts such as Gorgias' are better understood as attempts to rationalize language and thought "on a purely secular basis, with no need for divine causation" (1975, 5). Unlike storytellers who depend on the Muses for mystical inspiration, Gorgias' account implies that speakers have a "self-conscious relation" to their speech (Jarratt 1991, 57). As de Romilly points out, Gorgias "was deliberately shifting magic into something rational" (1975, 20). In *Helen*, Gorgias proceeds to provide a rational explanation of why such "magic" works: "If everyone, on every subject, had memory of the past and knowledge of the present and foresight of the future, *logos* would not do what it does, but as things are it is easy neither to remember the past nor consider the present nor predict the future; so that on most subjects most people take opinion as counselor to the psyche. But opinion, being slippery and insecure, casts those relying on it into slippery and insecure fortune" (11).

Gorgias then spends the equivalent of two paragraphs arguing that Helen is blameless because *logos* is so powerful that its use amounts to the use of force (in Greek, *bia*). First, he identifies *logos* as the powerful vehicle of *peithō*, persuasion: "What is there to prevent the conclusion that Helen too, when still young, was carried off by *logos* just as if constrained by force? Her mind was swept away by persuasion, and persuasion has the same power as necessity (*anagkē*), although it may bring shame. For *logos*, by persuading the psyche that it persuaded, constrained her both to obey what was said and to approve what was done. The persuader, as user of force, did wrong; the persuaded, forced by *logos*, is unreasonably blamed" (12). Second, he proves just how powerful *logos* can be by providing a series of examples of how easily humans are persuaded by competing *logoi*:

> To understand that persuasion, joining with *logos*, is wont to stamp the psyche as it wishes one must study, first, the arguments of the astronomers who, substituting opinion for opinion, removing one and instilling another, make what is incredible and unclear things appear true to the eyes of opinion; second, the forceful contests of argumentation, where one side of the argument, written with skill but not spoken with truth, pleases a large audience and persuades; third, the debates of rival philosophers, in which swiftness of thought is also exhibited, making belief in an opinion easily changed. (13)

The key contribution made here is the act of raising a provocative theoretical question: When does persuasion amount to force? The question is both unusual and interesting because Greek literature prior to Gorgias usually treated persuasion and force, *peithō* and *bia*, as antithetical. As John T. Kirby puts it, "I will try to persuade you, but, failing that, I will force you. Such a disjunction is rooted in our most fundamental concepts of civilization. The wild beasts settle their disputes by *bia*; it is a mark of our humanity, we feel, that we can use persuasion to effect change, that we are not limited to the use of coercion" (1990, 215). Kirby suggests that "the *peithō/bia* axis is at the basis of some of our most ancient literary and rhetorical formulations" (1990, 216; see also Buxton 1982, 58–63). From the standpoint of intellectual history, it is arguably the case that Gorgias' questioning of a taken-for-granted dichotomy is a more important step in developing new modes of inquiry than any particular claim Gorgias makes about *logos, peithō,* or *bia.*

In the process of describing the persuasive/forceful workings of *logos,* Gorgias develops an analogy that proved to be influential: "The power of *logos* has the same effect on the condition of the psyche as the power of drugs to the nature of the body; for just as different drugs dispel different secretions from the body, and some bring an end to disease and others to life, so also in the case of *logos* — some bring pain, others pleasure, some bring fear, others instill courage in the hearers, and some drug and bewitch the psyche with a kind of evil persuasion" (14). De Romilly contends that "Gorgias' magic is technical. He wants to emulate the power of the magician by a scientific analysis of language and its influence. He is the theoretician of the magic spell of words" (1975, 16). Gorgias theorizes in this case by drawing the analogy to the increasingly secular, "rational," and "scientific" art of medicine (1975, 20). The analogy functioned paradigmatically in the sense that both Plato's *Gorgias* and Aristotle's *Rhetoric* later sought to explain the art of persuasion by comparing it to the developing art of medicine. Gorgias' effort at analogy may seem simplistic by contrast to the relatively sophisticated vocabulary and theories of Aristotle or the late dialogues of Plato, but the analysis provided by such later theorists would not have been possible without the efforts of intellectuals such as Gorgias.

Based on the passages in *Helen* that discuss *logos* and passages in other Gorgianic texts, theorists have likened claims in Gorgias' texts to contemporary aesthetic, psychological, and speech-act theories of language. Such readings have produced conflicting accounts of Gorgias' description of *logos* among which I will not try to arbitrate. There are at least five distinct categories of readings: psychological (Segal), magical (de Romilly 1975), epistemological (Enos 1976; Gronbeck 1972; Untersteiner 1954), dramatistic (Verdenius 1981; Rosenmeyer 1955), and sematological (Mourelatos 1985; Kerferd 1984). Each reading tends to tease out of selected phrases a distinct theory of *logos,* language, rhetoric, and so on. As interesting and helpful as these treatments are, I think the "content" of Gorgias' account is remarkably straightforward and stands on its own. Though it is useful to interpret and reposition Gorgias' account into contemporary terminology, *Helen* also deserves to be understood, insofar as it is possible, in its original context, and appreciated for what it contributed to its own generation of intellectuals. Once so positioned, we may find its most profound influence is not a particular "idea," per se, but a metaphor picked up by a later author, or a problem he poses. In terms of the history of rhetorical theory, we must remember that the writing of systematic or theoretical treatises was exceedingly rare prior to the mid-fourth century. The scope and complexity of Gorgias' analysis is impressive when compared to his contemporaries and predecessors, even if it seems crudely metaphorical compared to some of his successors.

On Paignion: *Gorgias* Helen 21

The closing words of Gorgias's *Helen* are: *Eboulēthēn graphai ton logon Helenēs men enkōmion emon de paignion.* The final word, *paignion,* is typically translated as "trifle," "recreation," or "diversion"; the most literal translation would be "plaything." Various commentators have seized upon the word as proof that one should not read the speech too seriously or as a key heuristic for interpreting the text (Duncan 1938, 404; Verdenius 1981, 125). D. M. MacDowell wonders if calling his speech a *paignion* implies that Gorgias does not really believe what he has said: "one may imagine the twinkle in Gorgias's eye as he reveals in the very last word that he regards the whole paradoxical composition as a game" (1982, 16, 43). Poulakos argues that the speech was not intended as "model" speech for students because no one would end such a speech "with a comment that might be interpreted by one's listeners as telling them 'You've been had' " (1983, 3). Kennedy suggests that with this word "Gorgias plays at undercutting a serious purpose in the speech" (1991, 288n). J. M. Robinson concludes that the word means that we do not even know how "we are to take the work" (1973, 52). Heinrich Gomperz even uses the appearance of the word *paignion* in *Helen* to interpret *other* works by Gorgias as examples of joke-speech (*Scherzrede*) — most notably the treatise *On Not Being:* "Die Schrift über die Natur war ein paignion" (1912, 33–35).

Such readings use the appearance of the word *paignion* to confirm the characterization of Gorgias as not "really" serious thinker and not a "true" philosopher. The case has already been made that we ought to set aside this sort of assessment as anachronistic and ill-founded (Casertano 1986; Segal 1962). The work Gorgias does in the *Helen* is serious in the sense that it is an important composition that contributed to the development of prose discourse and intellectual inquiry. It is not a plaything in the sense an innocuous ditty might be — such as an encomium for Mickey Mouse. Accordingly, we should be wary of readings that overemphasize the significance of this one word as a heuristic key to the entire speech.

How, then, do we explain the choice of the word *paignion* by someone obviously quite careful in his writing? I think the question needs to be "unasked" or at least downplayed. Unlike many ancient texts, the speech appears to be complete. There is plenty of textual material with which to work without overemphasizing the significance of the last word. After all, one might speculate that Gorgias' choice of *paignion* was merely a matter of acoustical preference, since *paignion* is a useful word to complete the melodious phrase *men enkōmion emon de paignion*. It would have been a crowd-pleasing euphony with which to end the performance — one can almost imagine Gorgias taking a bow upon speaking the final word. Furthermore, there is no need for a choice here between treating the speech as either "serious" or merely "playful." The text serves multiple functions.

Over half a century after Gorgias' *Helen*, Plato provided the first definition of the word *paignion* in the process of describing a whole class of art: "So this one name will be applied properly to all the members of this class; for none of them is practiced for any serious purpose, but all of them purely for play."[9] We have no reason to believe that Gorgias would have agreed with such a one-dimensional description of his work. Or, if he had, he would have insisted that all verbal arts be so designated.

In sum, it is both unnecessary and inappropriate to place disproportionate weight upon this single word for the purposes of interpreting the speech. If the manuscript had, at some point in time, lost this last word, the speech's importance would not have been changed one whit.

Gorgias' teachings surely belong to the history of the development of rhetorical theory and practice, but Gorgias' precise place in that history is more complex than most treatments suggest. Gorgias wrote and spoke a generation before Rhetoric was recognized as a distinct "discipline" upon the coining and popularizing of the word *rhētorikē*. His discussion of *logos* is more precisely characterized as a set of beliefs about discourse in general than as a "theory of rhetoric" in the classical sense of the phrase. Nonetheless, it is obvious that Gorgias significantly influenced the early theoretical articulation of the discipline of Rhetoric by theorizing about the workings of persuasive discourse. Enos suggests that "Rhetoric's origin as a formal discipline is best understood as an evolution of compositional techniques" (1993, 42). If so, then the *Helen* demonstrates that Gorgias played a significant role in that origin. Though, strictly speaking, Gorgias' *Helen* should not be labeled an "epideictic" speech in the Aristotelian sense of the word, Gorgias advanced fifth-century B.C.E. "rationalism" by enacting certain innovations in prose composition; these include the apagogic method of argument, identifying his means of persuasion as "reasoning" (*logismos*), identifying himself as the writer of the speech,

9. Plato, *Statesman* 288c8–10 (cf. 288c6). Translation adapted from Fowler (1925, 115).

probably inaugurating the prose genre of *encomia,* and by offering a secular account of the workings of *logos*. There are many ways of making Gorgias' *Helen* meaningful by reading it as a historical text and as source of inspiration for contemporary Neosophistic theorists. As an addition to such readings, describing the *Helen* as predisciplinary underscores the text's historical significance, I hope, by situating it in the context of fifth-century Greek compositional and theoretical practices and by avoiding the imposition of fourth-century categories and expectations.

8

Rhetoric and Philosophy in On Not Being

*Denying Be-ing, he says [it is] nothing; and if [it] is, it is unknowable;
and if it is and [is] knowable, it cannot be made evident to others.*
Οὐκ εἶναί φησιν οὐδέν· εἰ δ'ἔστιν, ἄγνωστον εἶναι· εἰ δὲ καὶ ἔστι καὶ
γνωστόν, ἀλλ᾽ οὐ δηλωτὸν ἄλλοις
(On Melissus, Xenophanes, and Gorgias 979a12–13)

In this chapter I outline the different schools of interpretation of Gorgias' lost text known as *On Not Being or On Nature (Peri tou mē ontos ē peri
phuseōs)* with respect to the key word *esti* as a prolegomenon to a detailed
account of Gorgias' arguments. In this chapter, I simply want to make the
important point that it is impossible to translate, let alone describe, Gorgias'
arguments without imposing a particular interpretation. The syntax is ambiguous and one cannot translate the ever-present *esti* without importing a preference for one reading or another. Accordingly, it seems reasonable to alert
readers to a range of possible interpretations before providing an exegesis that
is unavoidably partisan.

The chapter is divided into five parts. I first discuss the extant versions of *On
Not Being* in order to identify some of the preliminary difficultes facing the
modern interpreter. Second, I describe the disciplinary assumptions made
about the philosophical and rhetorical dimensions of *On Not Being* that have

informed many past interpretations. Third, in order to provide an understanding of the context in which *On Not Being* originally was composed, I describe some of the arguments made about "being" in the surviving texts of Parmenides, Melissus, and Zeno. Fourth, in light of the different interpretive traditions associated with the texts of the Eleatics, I offer alternative approaches to intepreting the "being" in Gorgias' *On Not Being* that are less influenced by the Philosophy/Rhetoric framework through which the text is usually approached. Finally, I offer a brief formalization of part of Gorgias' argument in order to illustrate how the text functions simultaneously in rhetorically and philosophically interesting ways.

The Texts

On Not Being is the oldest of Gorgias' texts for which we have information and is said to have been given at the eighty-fourth Olympiad, around 444 B.C.E. (DK 82 A10). The original text of Gorgias' *On Not Being* is lost. What survives amount to two paraphrases, one by Sextus Empiricus and one in the anonymous treatise *On Melissus, Xenophanes, and Gorgias.*[1] The two paraphrases use some of the same arguments, but there are sufficient differences in vocabulary and the lines of arguments developed that it is likely that each of the two authors developed his analyses without the other's before him. Where each originally encountered Gorgias' treatise is unknown. We do not know, for example, whether either had access to copies of Gorgias' original treatise, but it is unlikely. It may be the case that Gorgias never "published" and circulated his treatise in the same way *Helen* and *Palamedes* were distributed. The tripartite organization of Gorgias' position is easily remembered, as are most of the supporting arguments. Their similarity to argumentative moves made by well-known Eleatics would have made it easier to transmit Gorgias' position orally. In any event, what we have now may be re-creations of re-creations of Gorgias' speech allegedly given ca. 444 B.C.E. Accordingly, in the discussion that follows I will not dwell on matters of fine detail, since such disputes suppose that Sextus and the author of *On Melissus, Xenophanes, and Gorgias* were far more precise in their rendering of the original Gorgianic presentation than can be proven.

For many years the vast majority of commentators have considered Sextus' treatment to be the more accurate of the two texts (see, e.g., Barnes 1982;

---

1. For Sextus' text see *Adversus mathematicos* 7.65–87 in DK 82 B3, Mutschmann and Mau (1961) or Bury (1935, 34–44); translated in Kennedy (1972b) and Bury (1935, 35–45). For MXG in Greek see Bekker (1831, 2: 974a1–980b21) or Hett (1936, 496–507); translated in Hett and in Barnes (1984, 2: 1539–51). See also Buchheim (1989).

Mazzara 1982). Sextus was a Skeptic writing in the third century C.E. whose main task was to "expose the folly of every form of positive doctrine" (Bury 1933, 1: vii). The watchword of Skepticism was "suspend judgment," since the Skeptics of Sextus' time believed that one could never positively confirm the possibility of knowledge. His treatment of Gorgias is entirely consistent with his general purpose. For example, he makes passing reference to Gorgias three times in *Outlines of Pyrrhonism*.[2] A typical passage reads: "Now those who claim that we should attend to the intellect only in our judgment of things will . . . be unable to show that the existence of intellect is apprehensible. For when Gorgias, in denying that anything exists, denies also the existence of intellect, while some declare that it has real existence, how will they decide this contradiction?" (2.57 in Bury 1933, 1: 188–89). Sextus' paraphrase of *On Not Being* appears in a treatise in which he discusses those thinkers who "abolish the criterion" of truth.[3] Because Sextus is reporting Gorgias' argument rather than criticizing it, his summary can be taken as a fairly "faithful" rendition of Gorgias' argument as Sextus understood it. It is likely that he has fleshed out certain points in his own fashion and in general clothed Gorgias in Skeptic garb. Fortunately, knowing Sextus' purposes puts us in a position to make informed estimates of how much distortion may be taking place in his paraphrase.

Of late, there has been great interest in reassessing the independent value of *On Melissus, Xenophanes, and Gorgias* for interpreting Gorgias' arguments. A growing number of scholars contend that the reconstruction of Gorgias' argument found in *On Melissus, Xenophanes, and Gorgias* ought to receive at least equal attention to that by Sextus.[4] The author of *On Melissus, Xenophanes, and Gorgias* is unknown, though the appearance of certain Stoic technical terms suggests that it was written sometime in the first two centuries C.E. The treatise was once attributed wrongly to Aristotle, and it is usually found in comprehensive collections of his work. The surviving manuscripts of *On Melissus, Xenophanes, and Gorgias,* unfortunately, have significant lacunae and inconsistencies; one scholar declares "the text is sometimes almost

2. See 2.57.4; 2.59.4; 2.64.4. The work is also cited as *Pyrrhoniae hypotyposes*.

3. The treatise is alternatively labelled as *Adversus mathematicos* (Book 7), *Adversus dogmaticos* (Book 1), and *Adversus logicos* (Book 1). In all versions the sections paraphrasing Gorgias' ONB are numbered 65–87.

4. Verdenius claims, "It may now be taken for granted that as far as historical reliability is concerned this source [MXG] is far superior to Sextus" (1964, 75 n. 4). See also Calogero (1932, 157–222), Gigon (1936, 186–213), Untersteiner (1954, 166 n. 26), Kerferd (1981b, 96), and Mansfeld (1985, 243–71). The most in-depth treatment of MXG is that by Barbara Cassin (1980).

unintelligible" (Mansfeld 1988, 256). Recent attempts to produce a trustworthy text are far from securing universal acceptance.[5] Mansfeld has made a case that *On Melissus, Xenophanes, and Gorgias* may be the work of a "Pyrrhonizing Aristotelian" (1988). Specifically, Mansfeld identifies Stoic and other later sorts of terminology that could not have been Gorgias' own words, and he suggests that the author reformulated parts of Gorgias' arguments in a Pyrrhonist way: "The bones of Gorgias' argumentation in MXG chs. 5–6 (and in the parallel passage in Sextus) are of undoubtable and venerable antiquity. What can hardly be doubted either is that these bones have so to speak been a bit modernized at their junctures and that more definite oscillating motions have been imparted to the latter in order to flesh out the skeleton with a semblance of life" (1988, 265).

Some have expressed doubts about the authenticity of the ascription of *On Not Being* to Gorgias in light of the fact that neither Plato or Aristotle mention it explicitly, but Isocrates' clear references to this text are decisive evidence in favor of its authenticity. In *Helen* (3) Isocrates asks, "For how could one surpass Gorgias, who dared to say that 'that-which-is is not'?" And in *Antidosis* (268), Isocrates refers to speculative thinkers who try to describe the "sum of all things": "Empedocles [said] that it is is made up of four, with strife and love operating among them; Ion, of not more than three; Alcmaeon, of only two; Parmenides and Melissus, of one; and Gorgias, of none at all" (Norlin 1929, 2: 332–35).

Interpreting the Text: Disciplinary Presuppositions

No other text by Gorgias has evoked the kind of intense and contradictory responses by modern scholars that *On Not Being* has. As Jonathan Barnes notes: "Some scholars make Gorgias a profound thinker, a nihilist and a sceptic; others treat *What is Not* as a serious and witty *reductio* of Eleatic metaphysics; others again take it for a rhetorical *tour de force*" (1982, 173). For present purposes, the various interpretations of *On Not Being* can be grouped usefully into two schools of readings: *On Not Being* as "pure" rhetoric and *On Not Being* as "pure" philosophy. At one extreme is John M. Robinson's declaration that the work is devoid of philosophical significance. It is the work of a "clever mimic" of philosophy and is not "the real thing, nor is it even very much like the real thing" (1973, 60). Robinson accepts Plato's

5. Kerferd (1955) considered Diels' 1900 text the best. Kerferd's suggested emendations have been adopted by relatively few other scholars. Concerning Cassin's 1980 text, Mansfeld (1988, 239) suggests that "the Greek text is based on the editorial principles of the Lille school (always prefer the manuscripts, however garbled)."

depiction of Gorgias in the dialogue of the same name as mostly accurate, and Plato views Gorgias "neither as a serious thinker nor as having any pretensions to being so regarded" (1973, 49). In a similar vein, Kennedy suggests that a "philosophical" approach to Gorgias' *On Not Being* "probably exaggerates his intellectual sophistication and credits him with an uncharacteristic power of conceptualization." Gorgias "imitated" the philosophers, but what was really important to him was his "rhetoric" (1980, 31). According to the "pure" rhetoric reading, *On Not Being* is display oratory designed to dazzle and delight its audience, but *On Not Being* is not discourse intended to further the ends of "real" philosophy. In fact, Gorgias is believed by some to be parodying philosophers and making fun of Parmenides and Eleatic philosophers in particular. So, Guthrie notes that "it is all, of course, engaging nonsense," and suggests that the "main weight of his irony fell upon the Eleatics" (1971, 197 note, see also 199, 270–71). Similarly, Blass says the point of *On Not Being* was to show the uselessness of philosophical analysis (1887, 49).[6]

At the other extreme are scholars who regard *On Not Being* as pure and serious philosophy. Kerferd argues that "there is nothing humorous about the treatise and no indication that it was ever intended to be so." Because the arguments in *On Not Being* are difficult to follow, Kerferd suggests that it would not have amused audiences; thus, "the view that it was purely a rhetorical exercise" is not plausible (1955, 3).

I have deliberately cited the most extreme postures taken toward *On Not Being* in order to highlight an important underlying presupposition informing the rationale of each school of interpretation: the age-old conflict between the disciplines of Rhetoric and Philosophy. The Rhetoric/Philosophy dichotomy is deeply ingrained in most contemporary thought; further, we have been coached to see each primarily *in contrast to* the other. Despite a good deal of effort in contemporary scholarship to overcome this ancient dualism, most investigations into ancient Greek thought still embrace it. Since Gorgias in *Helen* and *Palamedes* is so "obviously" a rhetorician, it is unimaginable to many that he also could have been a "real" philosopher. In this matter we have been misled by the writings of the fourth century B.C.E., and by Plato and Aristotle in particular. The dichotomous worldview they provide was not shared by all Greek intellectuals of their time, and it radically transformed the more holistic and integrative intellectual practices that can be identified from the previous century. In particular, the "disciplines" of Rhetoric and Philosophy were neither named nor recognized *as* discrete and competitive disciplines until the writings of Plato.

6. "Die Nutzlosigkeit des philosophischen Grübelns."

Plato would have us choose one or the other: If our goal is to seek success in persuasion without regard to the truth, then our discourse is Rhetorical. If our goal is to seek the truth without regard to success in persuasion, then our discourse is Philosophical. One might be either a Rhetorician or a Philosopher, but one cannot be both. At the time Gorgias presented *On Not Being,* however, no such forced choice was perceived. Prior to Plato, the texts regarding discourse (*logos*) do not reflect such a dichotomy. To learn to speak effectively required one to think critically and to use language "correctly." During most of Gorgias' life, and certainly during the period he composed *On Not Being,* the "art of discourse," or *logōn technē,* would have referred generally to learning to argue well. That *logōn technē* includes instruction in what would later be confined to the rubric Philosophy is made evident by the fact that Xenophon uses the phrase to describe Socrates' teaching and his practice of holding discussion (*Memorabilia* 1.2.31–34). In other words, Gorgias' text can be read as predisciplinary. We can appreciate Gorgias' playfulness without denying the philosophical seriousness of *On Not Being* one bit, and we can imagine Gorgias presenting *On Not Being* at the Olympiad ca. 444 without assuming that he compromised the integrity of his arguments in order merely to please the crowd. In short, we need not impose choices on Gorgias that he would not have considered necessary.

How, then, are we to make sense of *On Not Being?* Read "cold" and without context, Gorgias' claims appear patently absurd. How on earth could anyone argue that "nothing exists"? Along with other scholars, I assume that Gorgias' *On Not Being* initially was motivated by certain Eleatic arguments made popular by Parmenides and his fifth-century successors. To understand the argumentative context in which *On Not Being* appeared therefore compels us to interpret Parmenides' famous poem and the subsequent development of Parmenides' philosophy in Melissus and Zeno.

Parmenides, Melissus, and Zeno

Parmenides' poem no longer survives intact.[7] The extant fragments are estimated to represent about one-quarter to one-third of the original. The poem uses epic hexameter, draws heavily from Homer for its vocabulary, and is cast in narrative form.[8] The poem is believed to begin as follows: "The mares that carry me kept conveying me as far as ever my spirit reached, once they had

7. For reconstructions in Greek and English see Tarán (1965), Gallop (1984), Coxon (1986), and Austin (1986, 155–73). See also Curd 1998.

8. On the composition style of Parmenides' poem, see Mourelatos (1970, 1–46, 264–68), Gallop (1984, 4–5), Coxon (1986, 7–11), and Havelock (1982, 220–60; 1983).

taken and set me on the goddess' way of much importance, which carries through every stage straight onwards a man of understanding."[9] The narrator is led to the Goddess, who welcomes him and says he must "learn everything" (*panta puthesthai*). The fundamental question for Parmenides is how human beings reach an understanding (*noos*) of truth or reality (*alētheia*). The Goddess proceeds to tell him her story (*mythos*) about the only ways of Inquiry available. The first is described by the expression *hopōs estin te kai hōs ouk esti mē einai*, which can be translated as "that [it] is and that [it] cannot not be." The subject is left unexpressed (a practice not uncommon in Greek),[10] so the sense of the sentence is that once one predicates being, one cannot predicate not-being of the same "thing." The second and unacceptable way of inquiry is described by Parmenides with the expression *hōs ouk estin*, "that which is not," which is qualified as *hōs chreōn esti mē einai*, "is not and needs must not-be." Charles Kahn notes that this generic-negative construction is exceedingly rare in Greek and is used exclusively by "philosophers." There is nothing incorrect about the construction, only that it is filled with logical puzzles (1973, 366–67).

Accordingly, the two competing formulae can be described as "*is* and is-not for not-being," and "*is not* and must needs not-be" (cf. Coxon 1986, 19). These two options are presented as the only choices, and are considered by Parmenides to be mutually exclusive. He argues that the second way of thinking, "is not," is concerned literally with no-thing and leads nowhere. Inquiry should pursue the first way of thinking, that is, "by asking what can and must be made the subject of an unconditional 'is'" (Coxon 1986, 20). The result of pursuing the path of "is not" is described by Parmenides (B6) as leading to confusion and contradiction: "First I bar you from this route of inquiry, but also from the one on which mortals wander, knowing nothing, double-headed. For helplessness in their breasts steers a mind set adrift. They are tossed about, as much deaf as blind, an undiscerning horde, by whom being and not-being are considered the same and not the same — and the route of all is backward-turning" (adapted from Austin 1986, 161).

Though the extant text is fragmentary, Parmenides apparently supports his case through a series of arguments that: first, present the hearer with an apparently incompatible pair of options (either X or not-X); second, rules out one option as impossible (not not-X); and third, concludes that the remaining

---

9. Translation adapted from Coxon (1986, 43–44). The text reads: Ἵπποι, ταί με φέρουσιν, ὅσον τ' ἐπὶ θυμὸς ἱκάνοι πέμπον, ἐπεί μ' ἐς ὁδὸν βῆσαν πολύφημον ἄγουσαι δαίμονος, ἣ κατὰ πάντ' ἄ⟨ν⟩τη⟨ν⟩ φέρει εἰδότα φῶτα.

10. See the examples provided in Coxon (1986, 175–76).

option is the only one that makes sense (∴ X). For example, Parmenides claims that "Being is ungenerated and imperishable, entire, unique, unmoved, and perfect."[11] To support the notion that Being is ungenerated, for example, Parmenides suggests the alternative is impossible: "For what birth would you seek for it? Which way, from what did it grow? Nor will I allow you to say or think 'out of what-is-not.' For it cannot be said or thought that it is not. And what need urged it on to grow later or earlier, starting from nothing? So it must either be completely or not at all" (B8, tr. Austin 1986, 163). As Barnes points out, Parmenides is providing a *reductio:* Parmenides' contention, that whatever *is* exists and cannot not exist, must be true because the contrary leads to absurdity (1982, 174–75; and see below).

Obviously, the most difficult element of Parmenides' poem to interpret is also its most central—the concept of being. There are a number of possible meanings of *esti,* or "is," in Parmenides poem. It can be read existentially (is = "exists"), or as a copula (linking subject and predicate, as in "the rose is red"), or veridically (is = "is true"), or in some combination of these senses. The issue is important because interpretations of Gorgias' *On Not Being* also turn on how one understands "being" in his text. Furthermore, as will be illustrated below, there is reason to believe that Gorgias' use of *esti* probably paralleled Parmenides' use.

Often readers of Greek ascertain which sense of *esti* is meant by the accentuation provided: ἔστι meaning existence or possibility, and ἐστί indicating a copulative sense.[12] However, early manuscripts did not indicate accent marks and there are now serious doubts as to whether the semantic distinctions drawn above were maintained before Plato and Aristotle (Mourelatos 1970, xix–xx). Accenting differences, therefore, tend to reflect the interpretations of later copyists and commentators, or are the result of specific syntactic variables.[13] In either case, they cannot be taken as reliable indicators of the meaning of *esti* in Parmenides or Gorgias.

Until fairly recently, the dominant reading of Parmenides' "being" was existential. Benjamin Fuller (1945), for example, sees the poem as defending "the Real." Contrary to those who see Reality as in everchanging change and "be-

---

11. Fragment 8 as translated by Coxon (1986, 60). Parmenides sometimes turns Being into a substantive with the noun-expression *Eon.*

12. Some commentators suggest that Parmenides fails to distinguish between the use of "is" to indicate existence and "is" as a copula. Calogero (1932) contends that Parmenides has mistakenly confused the existential and copulative senses, while Furth (1968) argues that the poem can be given a plausible reading with either sense.

13. Kahn (1973, 420–34). See also Mourelatos (1970, xx) and Havelock (1978, 356–57).

coming," Parmenides proves that Being "is One." All change is an illusion (Fuller 1945, 61–65). Similarly, Burnet reads Parmenides as defending a monistic physical theory: "What *is,* is a finite, spherical, motionless corporeal *plenum,* and there is nothing beyond it. The appearances of multiplicity and motion, empty space and time, are illusions" (1930, 182). In a related vein, his text is read as a prescription about the nature of inquiry: "Parmenides claims that in any enquiry there are two and only two logically coherent possibilities, which are exclusive — that the subject of the enquiry exists or that it does not exist" (Kirk, Raven, and Schofield, 1983, 241). Gallop points out that "on this interpretation, when the goddess points out to her listener that he could neither know or point out what-is-not, she is precluding reference in thought or speech to the non-existent" (1984, 8). Similarly, Barnes summarizes Parmenides' basic thesis as "whatever we inquire into exists, and cannot not exist" (1982, 163).

The existential reading has been critiqued extensively in light of changes in our understanding of the functions of the Greek verb *einai,* "to be." Due in large measure to two studies by Kahn (1966; 1973), a growing number of commentators now believe that a strict, existential sense of "to be" is not apparent in early Greek usage (Havelock 1978; Mourelatos 1970). Three recent, full-length studies accept the notion that Parmenides is concerned primarily with inquiry and emphasize a linguistic and epistemological interpretation over an ontological reading. A. H. Coxon suggests that "it is mistaken to understand his conception of being as 'existential'" (1986, 175). Parmenides is concerned with delimiting the appropriate scope of inquiry, and is interested in *esti,* the verb for *is,* "given its essential rōle in 'asserting and thinking'" (1986, 20). Alexander Mourelatos, citing Kahn's work, defends a "veridical" reading of Parmenides' *esti* (see esp. chapter 2 and appendix II, 1970). He argues that Parmenides is not concerned with Reality or Existence as such but with distinguishing two modes of discourse and thought, a positive mode (X is-Y) and a negative mode (X is-not-Y). Parmenides rejects the second and embraces the first as the only legitimate route for inquiry. Austin portrays the poem as an early exploration into the logic of the copula. There is a logical difference between saying, for example, that "someone *is* not-at-home" and saying that "some *isn't* at home." The first statement makes a positive assertion, but the second says someone "is not," which Parmenides felt led to absurdity. Furthermore, Austin sees the poem as anticipating, though not explicitly articulating, what later is named the law of non-contradiction. Parmenides rejects most (but not all) constructions of the form *ouk esti* as incomprehensible, particularly when *ouk esti* could imply contradictory sentences of the form X is-Y *and* X is-not-Y (1986).

Parmenides "had an enormous influence" on subsequent Greek intellectualizing (Kirk, Raven, and Schofield 1983, 241). By Gorgias' time, it is reasonable to assume that most educated people had heard some form of Parmenides' position — either read from a copy of Parmenides' poem or passed on by word of mouth. The basic themes developed in the poem continued to be advanced and developed in the fifth century B.C.E. by Melissus and Zeno. Melissus repeats some of the same argumentative moves made by Parmenides, but he does so in prose and provides a more detailed case than that extant by his predecessor. His argument for the ungenerated nature of Being is as follows: "It always was whatever it was and it always will be. For if it came-to-be, it is necessarily [the case] that before it came-into-being it was-nothing. Now if it was-nothing, in no way could anything come-to-be from nothing."[14] Like Parmenides, Melissus argues that most people do not understand the way things are since they willingly embrace contradictory notions: "We say that we see and hear and understand correctly: Yet we believe that the warm becomes cold, and the cold warm; and the hard soft, and soft hard; and the living dies, and the living come-to-be from what is not-live; and that all these things have changed."[15]

It is believed that Zeno's famous paradoxes were offered as proofs that motion is an illusion. Most of Zeno's sayings come down to us in the form of oral paraphrases. The "only unquestionably authentic fragment of Zeno which has come down to us intact" (Kirk, Raven, and Schofield 1983, 266) is clearly Parmenidean in spirit, and, like most of Melissus' fragments, relies on subject-less constructions of *esti*:

> If *estin* [is] many, it is necessary that "they" are as many as they are and no more or and no fewer. But if they are as many as they are, they will be limited.
>
> If *estin* [is] many, that-which-is is unlimited. For there are always others between that-which-is, and again others between that. And thus that-which-is is unlimited. (Adapted from Kirk, Raven, and Schofield 1983, 266 and Barnes 1987, 154)[16]

As important as Parmenides' poem is, I think it unlikely that Gorgias would

---

14. Simplicius, *Commentary on the Physics* 162 = DK 30 B1, translation adapted from Kirk, Raven, and Schofield (1983, 393).

15. Simplicius, *Commentary on the Heavens* 558 = DK 30 B8, translation adapted from Kirk, Raven, and Schofield (1983, 399).

16. εἰ πολλά ἐστιν, ἀνάγκη τοσαῦτα εἶναι ὅσα ἐστὶ καὶ οὔτε πλείονα αὐτῶν οὔτε ἐλάττονα. εἰ δὲ τοσαῦτά ἐστιν ὅσα ἐστί, πεπερασμένα ἂν εἴη.

εἰ πολλά ἐστιν, ἄπειρα τὰ ὄντα ἐστιν· ἀεὶ γὰρ ἕτερα μεταξὺ τῶν ὄντων ἐστί, καὶ πάλιν ἐκείνων ἕτερα μεταξύ. καὶ οὕτως ἄπειρα τὰ ὄντα ἐστί (DK 29 B3).

have composed his treatise had Melissus and Zeno, closer to being his contemporaries, not carried on the argument. The two preserved titles of Gorgias' treatise *On Nature (Peri Phuseōs)* or *On Not Being (Peri tou mē Ontos)* mirror nicely the preserved titles of Melissus' book *On Nature (Peri Phuseōs)* or *On Being (Peri tou Ontos)*; though, it must be admitted, we cannot be sure that such titles were supplied by the authors (see Kirk, Raven, and Schofield 1983 392n; Schmalzriedt 1970). Furthermore, Zeno and Melissus took certain of Parmenides' positions to such extremes that refutations and parodies were almost inevitable. Melissus argued that what-is is unchangeable and motionless, hence the conflicting beliefs of virtually all people are wrong. Furthermore, Melissus is quoted as saying, "That which is Nothing cannot exist" (B7.7). In short, it is likely that the context in which *On Not Being* was composed was heavily influenced by Eleatic arguments about being.

Alternative Approaches to Gorgias' On Not Being

With the discourse of Parmenides, Melissus, and Zeno in mind, I turn to Gorgias' paraphrased treatise. Sextus paraphrases Gorgias' arguments as claiming first "that nothing 'is'; second, that if 'it is,' [it is] inapprehensible to humans; third, that if apprehensible, [it is] still inexpressible and unexplainable to someone nearby."[17] The *On Melissus, Xenophanes, and Gorgias* begins by summarizing three similar arguments attributed to Gorgias: "Denying Be-ing, he says [it is] nothing; and if [it] *is*, it is unknowable; and if it *is* and [is] knowable, it cannot be made evident to others" (*On Melissus, Xenophanes, and Gorgias* 979a12–13).

All three of Gorgias' arguments directly correspond to positions advanced by Parmenides and his followers. Gorgias' first claim that "nothing is" directly flouts Parmenides' insistence on *hōs estin* (fr. 8.2) and his proscription against *hōs ouk estin*. Gorgias' assertion that "[it] is unknowable" or "inapprehensible" directly confronts Parmenides' statement that "the same thing is for knowing as is for being"[18] and "the same thing is for understanding as is cause of that which is understood."[19] And Gorgias' argument that "it" cannot be communicated directly challenges Parmenides' assertion that he can have "trustworthy discourse and thought about Truth."[20]

---

17. ὅτι οὐδὲν ἔστιν, δεύτερον ὅτι εἰ καὶ ἔστιν, ἀκατάληπτον ἀνθρώπωι, τρίτον ὅτι εἰ καὶ καταληπτόν, ἀλλὰ τοί γε ἀνέξοιστον καὶ ἀνερμήνευτον τῶι πέλας.

18. τὸ γὰρ αὐτὸ νοεῖν ἐστίν τε καὶ εἶναι (fr. 3), adapted from Coxon (1986, 54–55).

19. ταὐτὸν δ' ἐστὶ νοεῖν τε καὶ οὕνεκέν ἐστι νόημα (fr. 8.34), adapted from Coxon (1986, 70–71) and Austin (1986, 164–65).

20. πιστὸν λόγον ἠδὲ νόημα ἀμφὶς ἀληθείης (fr. 8.50–51).

As was the case with Parmenides' poem, the interpretation turns on whether to read the negative use of *esti* existentially, veridically, copulatively, or in some combination of the three. While Parmenides champions *esti* and opposes *ouk esti,* Gorgias appears to do precisely the opposite and hence the two must be deciphered together. I do not believe that classical scholarship has yet solved the riddles of Parmenides' and Gorgias' texts, so I will describe what I take to be the most plausible readings. I will refer to two groups of readings as the "existential" and the "predicative" readings.

Obviously, if one reads Parmenides as concerned with an existential sense of "is," then Gorgias' treatise can be read accordingly. But even if we accept an existential reading, at least three versions can be identified, which I call the radical nihilist, the "pure be-ing," and the object-of-inquiry interpretations. The oldest and most simplistic existential reading is to classify Gorgias as a radical nihilist who claimed, literally, that nothing exists. Most scholars who would classify *On Not Being* as a "joke" or "parody" tend to assume an existential reading. Blass, for example, describes Gorgias' position as "radical nihilism" (1887, 48). Bromley Smith, though he takes the treatise seriously, also claims that Gorgias is a nihilist and contrasts his views to Protagoras' skepticism (1921b, 344). In general, the nihilist-existential reading has been the least accepted in the past fifty years of scholarship on Parmenides and Gorgias. It is clearly the most counterintuitive reading possible and it is the most difficult to square with the more positive positions set forth in Gorgias' other texts. Even those contemporary commentators who want to read Gorgias as radically as possible usually elaborate upon the simple declarations of "nothing exists" as meaning "exists *absolutely*" or "things-in-themselves do not exist meaningfully." It should be noted, however, that such elaborations typically import philosophical concepts that simply cannot be found in Parmenides' or Gorgias' era or that no longer classify Gorgias as a nihilist. Accordingly, I suggest that the "radical nihilist" position be set aside as untenable.

The second existential interpretation can be described as the "pure be-ing" reading. According to such a reading, the point of Parmenides' poem is to articulate the route of pure be-ing, which is beyond the comprehension of most mortals who must make do with the "impure" world of seeming and becoming. Gorgias' *On Not Being* can be read, therefore, not as a nihilistic denial of reality but as a refutation of Parmenides' description of pure be-ing. Recalling Barnes's paraphrase of Parmenides route as a claim that "whatever we inquire into exists, and cannot not exist," the emphasis can be put on either objects-of-inquiry ("whatever we inquire into," abbreviated as x) or the nature of "exists" (abbreviated as E). Given the proposition xE, one may seek to problematize either x or E. The pure be-ing reading focuses on E, while the object-of-inquiry reading focuses on x.

Kahn notes that even when used as a verb of existence, *esti* does not precisely match the semantic value of "exists" in English (1966, 255–56). Parmenides' *esti* is even more eternal than the Gods of Olympus, since according
to myth they were all born at one time or another. Similarly, Melissus argues
that "[it] always was whatever [it] was and [it] always will be. For if [it] came-
to-be, necessarily before [it] came-to-be [it] was nothing. Now if [it] was
nothing, in no way could anything come-to-be from nothing."[21] Kahn observes that the Latin *exsistere* actually comes closer to the meaning of the
Greek verb for becoming—*gignesthai*—than to *einai*. So, for example, even
though it is correct to say in English, "I exist," I could *not* make such a
statement if I were to follow Parmenides' program strictly, because I was born
and will pass away.

At the same time, Parmenides' be-ing is not Absolute Being—if by "Absolute Being" we mean God. We typically think of God as a Super Being; as a
noun rather than as a verb. Mary Daly hyphenates Be-ing in her feminist
theological writings to redescribe God so as to change "the conception/per-
ception of god from 'the Supreme Being' to Be-ing. The Naming of Be-ing as
Verb—as intransitive Verb that does not require an 'object'—expresses an
Other way of understanding ultimate/intimate reality" (1985, xvii). Daly's
notion of Be-ing, it seems to me, resonates nicely with Parmenides' object-less
but ultimate, eternal, and unchanging *esti*.

Gorgias' arguments in support of the proposition that "Nothing exists"
involve the Eleatic sense of "existence," not ours. Parmenides' and Melissus'
"is" is *pure* be-ing in the sense of being ungenerated and unperishing, unchanging, stable, and forever. And it is just this "pure" sense of *esti* that
Gorgias is attacking. When *On Melissus, Xenophanes, and Gorgias* describes
Gorgias' first argument as *Ouk einai phēsin ouden*, it can be interpreted/trans-
lated as "denying Pure Be-ing, he says [it is] nothing."

The third existential interpretation can be described as the "object-of-
inquiry" reading. As noted before, the object-of-inquiry reading focuses on the
status of *x* while holding E constant (while the pure-being reading holds *x*
constant while problematizing E). Another difference between the object-of-
inquiry and the pure be-ing interpretation is that the former makes room for a
veridical reading of *esti*. That is, "is" can be understood as implying "is true"
or "is the case," and such constructions as *hōs esti* and *hōs ouk esti* refer to
"that which is the case" and "that which is not the case." Accordingly, the
object-of-inquiry reading assumes that Parmenides takes *esti* as a relatively

---

21. DK 30 B1 = Simplicius, *Commentary on the Physics* 162.24: ἀεὶ ἦν ὅ τι ἦν καὶ ἀεὶ
ἔσται. εἰ γὰρ ἐγένετο, ἀναγκαῖόν ἐστι πρὶν γενέσθαι εἶναι μηδέν· εἰ τοίνυν μηδὲν ἦν,
οὐδαμὰ ἂν γένοιτο οὐδὲν ἐκ μηδενός. See also DK 30 B2 and B4.

unproblematic concept, and is, instead, concerned with identifying the class of objects of which "is" can be predicated. The correct route of inquiry begins "by asking what can and must be made the subject of an unconditional 'is'" (Coxon 1986, 20). Gorgias' *On Not Being* is therefore read as turning Parmenides' position upside-down by declaring that *Nothing* can be made the subject of an unconditional "is."

"Nothing," in this context, is ambiguous. It can mean no-thing, in which case Gorgias is arguing that *not-a-single-thing* fits Parmenides' needs, or it can mean Nothingness or Non-Being, in which case Parmenides' route is reduced to absurdity. Put formally, one can argue that the set to which Parmenides refers is empty, as in $x = \varnothing$ or $z(E)$; or one can argue that the set to which Parmenides refers includes "Nothingness," as in $\sim E \in x, \therefore \sim E(E)$. The difference is a matter of emphasis. One can say either that "Nothing *exists*" (*no*-thing is-the-case in Parmenides' sense) or that "*Nothing* exists" (Nothingness *is* in precisely Parmenides' sense).

So far I have been describing three versions of the "existential" reading of *On Not Being*. I turn now to the "predicative" reading. Just as studies of Parmenides have turned away from purely ontological readings and toward linguistic readings that focus on the use of "is" as copula and predicate, so too have studies of Gorgias. The most influential of the predicative readings is that by Kerferd. He argues that Gorgias is not concerned with "existence" or "Being and Not-Being" but rather "how far the verb 'to be' can be used of phenomena without contradictions resulting" (1955, 23). Parmenides' poem is read as rejecting certain negative modes of expression because they imply contradiction. Any method of discussion that allows propositions of the form X is-Y and X is-not-Y is considered "two-headed" by Parmenides, so most uses of the phrase *ouk esti* must be rejected. Kerferd argues that Gorgias' *On Not Being* was intended to prove that the so-called positive route of Parmenides also leads to contradiction. By using a chain of reasoning remarkably similar to that used by Parmenides, Melissus, and Zeno, Gorgias demonstrates that it is possible to reach an opposite conclusion. In short, there "is no way in which the verb 'to be' can be applied to a subject without contradictions" (1981b, 96). In support of his detailed reading of *On Not Being* Kerferd notes that later intellectuals argued in favor of abandoning the verb "to be" or to confining its usage strictly. Antisthenes is thought to have argued that one could use "is" only to assert a relationship of identity: "It is not admissable to say 'man is good,' but only 'man is man' and 'good is good'" (Guthrie 1971, 209). Aristotle (*Physics* 185b) attributes similar mistrust of "is" as copula to Lycophron: "The more recent of previous philosophers were disturbed by the thought of making the same thing one and many. For this reason some abolished the word 'is,' as Lycophron did, while others altered the form of the expression, saying not 'the man is white' but 'the man has-been-whitened' [*leleukōtai*, one word in Greek], not 'is walking' but 'walks,' lest by adding 'is' they should make the one many, as if 'one' or 'being' had only one sense" (Guthrie 1971, 216).

Similarly, Simplicius (*Physics* 91) later reports that Lycophron omitted the verb "is," saying "white Socrates" (*Sōkratēs leukos*) instead of "Socrates is white" (*Sōkratēs leukos estin*). Stilpo the Megarian and certain Eretrians are other later philosophers who advocated limiting the use of "is" to mark identity, probably a full century after Gorgias.[22] According to Kerferd, Lycophron was a "disciple of Gorgias in other matters and the abolition of the copula would have been an extremely appropriate step for him to take if he also subscribed to Gorgias' doctrine that its retention is bound to lead to contradictions" (1955, 25).

In this chapter so far I have outlined the different schools of interpretation of *On Not Being* and I have avoided a detailed account of all of Gorgias' arguments. That task is better pursued elsewhere. I hope to have illustrated the important point that it is impossible to translate or describe Gorgias' arguments without imposing a particular interpretation. With respect to *On Melissus, Xenophanes, and Gorgias,* it is impossible even to reconstruct the Greek text without making numerous assumptions about Gorgias' meaning (Kerferd 1955). The differences among the various existential and predicative interpretations of *On Not Being* are significant but subtle. It is unlikely that the vast majority of Gorgias' hearers would have noted the distinctions I have drawn, but I am willing to wager that Gorgias himself could have distinguished between the existential and predicative interpretations if given the appropriate vocabulary and opportunity. It is possible, but unprovable, that Gorgias was aware of the variety of interpretations of Parmenides' position and deliberately fashioned an argument that was equally polysemous. It is not necessary to ponder his intentions, fortunately, because the very ambiguity of Parmenides' subjectless *esti* required the hearers of *On Not Being* to supply parallel semantic content to make sense of his similarly subjectless *ouk esti*.[23] In other words, despite the variety of interpretations possible, Gorgias could assume with confidence that *On Not Being* always would be read against Parmenides, Melissus, and Zeno.

---

22. For Stilpo see Plutarch, *Adversus Colotem* (in *Moralia*) 1119c–d, for the Eretrians see Simplicius, *Physics* 91, 28; for a discussion of both see Guthrie (1971, 217–19).

23. Though Kerferd claims that "the extent to which Gorgias is discussing the position of Parmenides is itself problematic" (1955, 7).

Intertextual Argument as Both Philosophy and Rhetoric

What follows is an effort to formalize some of the arguments found in the second part of the surviving reconstructions of Gorgias' *On Not Being*.[24] The effort was motivated by two factors. First, as mentioned above, it is claimed that the arguments were advanced as a reply, serious or otherwise, to those set forth by Parmenides and later Eleatics. Formalization provides a valuable tool with which to note the precise similarities and differences among the argumentative moves of Parmenides, Melissus, Zeno, and Gorgias. Second, I believe that Gorgias' arguments warrant study at the level of precision that formalization enables. Barnes formalizes portions of Parmenides' argument as "a necessary preliminary to any examination of Parmenides' metaphysics." He claims that "if we are to treat his argument with the respect it deserves, we must be prepared to analyse its components with a rigour that Parmenides himself was not equipped to supply" (1982, 1:165). Gorgias' arguments warrant similar close analysis.[25]

The formalization suggests that if Gorgias' argument is viewed in isolation, it is relatively unpersuasive and formally invalid. However, if read with a recognition of intertextual linkages with Parmenides' arguments, quite a different verdict is possible. Gorgias' argument gains rhetorical and philosophical strength the more closely it is read as a response to Parmenides' texts. Accordingly, it is inappropriate to consider Gorgias' argument, as is typically the case, as mere rhetorical display *as opposed to* "legitimate" philosophy.

Jonathan Barnes's formalization (1982, 1:165–75) of portions of Parmenides' arguments against the "path of ignorance" provides a convenient model to follow. By limiting focus to a fairly short argument from each author's larger work we are able to gain in precision what is temporarily given up in scope. Thus, it is my hope that the current effort serves as a prolegomenon to future comparative formalizations. Furthermore, relying on Barnes's translation of Sextus' version of Gorgias' arguments as well as Barnes's method of formalizing Parmenides allows a fair comparison that is not the result of partisan adjustments either to the translated text or to the process of formalizing Gorgias' argument. Barnes's translation of the relevant passage in Sextus is as follows:

24. This section was written with Stacey Hoffman, who also did the formalization of the argument.

25. Mazzara (1982) and Newiger (1973) provide close readings of Gorgias' argumentation, but neither begins the sort of structural comparison between Parmenides and Gorgias that formalization allows.

(77) [It must next be shown that even if anything exists[26] it is unknowable and unthinkable by {hu}mankind.] If what is thought of [says Gorgias] is not existent, then what exists is not thought of. [And that is reasonable; for just as, if being white belongs to what is thought of, then being thought of belongs to what is white, so if not being existent belongs to what is thought of, of necessity not being thought of will belong to what exists. (78) Hence, "If what is thought of is not existent, then what exists is not thought of" is sound and preserves validity.] But what is thought of [for we must take this first] is not existent, as we shall establish. What exists, therefore, is not thought of. Now that what is thought of is not existent is evident: (79) for if what is thought of is existent, then everything that is thought of exists—and that in the way in which one thinks of them. But that is not sensible. For it is not the case that if anyone thinks of a man flying or chariots running over the sea, a man thereby flies or chariots run over the sea. Hence it is not the case that what is thought of is existent. (80) In addition, if what is thought of exists, what does not exist will not be thought of. For opposites belong to opposites, and what does not exist is opposite to what exists. And for this reason if being thought of belongs to what exists, then not being thought of will certainly belong to what does not exist. But this is absurd; for Scylla and Chimaera and many non-existent things are thought of. What exists, therefore, is not thought of. (1982, 1:173–74)

Barnes (1982, 1:174–75) presents Parmenides as providing a *reductio;* his contention, that whatever we inquire into exists and cannot not exist, must be true because the contrary leads to absurdity. Similarly, as presented in Sextus' version of *On Not Being*, Gorgias' argument against the existence of thought-about objects is a *reductio*. Following Barnes, let us consider a thinker, *a,* and an object of thought, *O.* Now suppose, says Gorgias, that "what is thought of is existent" (§79, see also §80).

(1)   ($\forall x$) (if anyone can think of x, then x exists).

Then, in the case of our thinker:

(2)   if *a* can think of *o,* then *o* exists.

That is, whatever anyone can think of must exist. But this is obviously false, Gorgias continues, for we often think of nonexistent things, such as chariots that run over the sea (§79, cf. the Scylla and Chimaera example in §80). Suppose our thinker, *a,* considers such chariots, *c:*

---

26. For the purposes of this exercise, the controversy over *esti* may be set aside temporarily by giving *esti* the same logical status as a variable when formalizing both sets of arguments, thus making the semantic content of *esti* a moot point.

(3)   *a* thinks of *c*.

Then, from (2) and (3), we can infer:

(4)   *c* exists.

But we all know that there are no such chariots:

(5)   *c* does not exist.

Thus, (4) and (5) yield a contradiction that justifies a rejection of the initial assumption, (1).

At first blush, (1) appears to be a premise of straw, posited merely for Gorgias to show his rhetorical virtuosity. At no point does Gorgias *argue* for (1); it is merely plucked out of thin air. Or is it? I believe that Gorgias is responding to a well-known thesis. Specifically, Parmenides is credited with claiming that "the same thing is for knowing as is for being"[27] Barnes renders this as:

(P1)   ($\forall x$) (*x* can be thought of if and only if *x* can exist).

And from Parmenides' claim that "but nothing is not"[28] or "nothing is not for being" Barnes infers:

(P2)   ($\forall x$) (if *x* does not exist, *x* cannot exist).

Furthermore, Parmenides also claimed that "what is for saying and for thinking of must be,"[29] from which Barnes infers:

(P3)   If *a* can mention *o* or *a* can think of *o*, then *o* exists.

Such claims, combined with such statements by Parmenides as "the same thing is for thinking as is for-the-sake-of (or cause-of-that-for) which there is thought"[30] imply an identity relationship between things-thought-about and things-that-are. Thus, as shown below, (1) and (2) are readily inferred from premises already aired by Parmenides.[31] Accordingly, the prima facie plausability of (1) can be refused only at the cost of rejecting important parts of

27. τὸ γὰρ αὐτὸ νοεῖν ἐστίν τε καὶ εἶναι (fr. 3), adapted from Coxon (1986, 54–55). See also §80 of Parmenides' *adv Math:* "being thought of belongs to what exists."

28. μηδὲν δ' οὐκ ἔστιν (fr. 6), trans. Barnes (1982, 1:166, n.1).

29. χρή τό λέγειν τε νοεῖν τ' ἐὸν ἔμμεναι (fr. 6), trans. Barnes (1982, 1:158, n.1).

30. ταὐτὸν δ' ἐστὶ νοεῖν τε καὶ οὕνεκέν ἐστι νόημα (fr. 8.34), adapted from Austin (1986, 164–65) and Coxon (1986, 70–71, see also 209). Though Barnes's translation is quite different, he agrees with the inference that this line implies "any thinkable item carries an implicit rider of the form 'O exists'" (1982, 1:207n).

31. The first two steps in the proof correspond to premises 6 and 7 in Barnes' formalization (1982, 1: 174).

Parmenides' argument. Such a move gives Gorgias considerable rhetorical flexability: if one accepts (1), then the *reductio* may procede; if one rejects (1), then the plausibility of Parmenides' case is jeopardized. Gorgias' argument gets off the ground only if its hearers recognize the intextual link to Parmenides in (1); a result that increases the odds that Gorgias composed at least this portion of *On Not Being* with Parmenides explicitly in mind. Robinson's claim that Gorgias lacks "the slightest understanding even of what [Parmenides'] issues are" clearly fails to give Gorgias his due (1973, 59).

Gorgias' argument may be formalized as follows ("Txy" abbreviates "x thinks of y" and "Ey" abbreviates "y exists"):

[1]	$(\forall x)\,(\forall y)\,(\Diamond Txy \leftrightarrow \Diamond Ey)$	A	(P1)
[2]	$(\forall y)\,(\sim Ey \rightarrow \sim \Diamond Ey)$	A	(P2)
[3]	$(\forall y)\,(\Diamond Ey \rightarrow Ey)$	2, T	
[4]	$(\forall x)\,(\forall y)\,(\Diamond Txy \leftrightarrow \Diamond Ey)$	1, $\leftrightarrow$ I	(1, P3)
[5]	Tac	A	(3)
[6]	$\Diamond Tac$	5, $\Diamond$ I	
[7]	$(\forall y)\,(\Diamond Tay \rightarrow \Diamond Ey)$	4 UE	
[8]	$\Diamond Tac \rightarrow \Diamond Ec$	7 UE	(2)
[9]	$\Diamond Ec \rightarrow Ec$	3 UE	
[10]	$\Diamond Tac \rightarrow Ec$	8, 9 HS	
[11]	$\sim Ec$	A	(5)
[12]	Ec	6, 10 MPP	(4)
[13]	$Ec\ \&\ \sim Ec$	11, 12 & I	
[14]	$\sim (\forall x)\,(\forall y)\,(\Diamond Txy \rightarrow \Diamond Ey)$	4, 13 RAA	

Robinson argues that claims such as "Gorgias turned Eleatic logic upside-down" are "largely specious" and that Gorgias' reasoning in this section of *On Not Being* does not clash with Parmenides (1973, 59). Yet the formalization suggests that Gorgias' argument is very similar to that advanced by Parmenides and is directly relevant to (P1), (P2), and (P3). It is hard to imagine that such similarity is accidental. With respect to Kerferd's claim that "the extent to which Gorgias is discussing the position of Parmenides is itself problematic," the above analysis further supports the position that Gorgias meant his treatise to be understood as an answer to Parmenides (1955, 7).

But is Gorgias' argument valid? Again, the interaction with Parmenides' position is instructive. Gorgias' argument does not prove precisely what he claims it does. Though it is doubtful that Gorgias would recognize the difference between internal and external negation, it is clear to us, at least, that [14] does not state that "what is thought of is nonexistent" (§78). Just because one can imagine one object that is nonexistent does not mean that all objects of thought are nonexistent. But, interestingly enough, [14] *does* refute the stronger Parmenidean statement [1], which states that an object can be thought of if and only if that object can exist (see Barnes 1982, 165n). Once again, Gorgias' argument gains rhetorical and logical force as well as philosophical interest the more closely it is juxtaposed to Parmenides.

Robinson has declared that Gorgias' *On Not Being* is devoid of philosophical significance. It is the work of a "clever mimic" of philosophy and is not "the real thing, nor is it even very much like the real thing" (1973, 60). In a similar vein, Kennedy suggests that a "philosophical" approach to Gorgias "probably exaggerates his intellectual sophistication and credits him with an uncharacteristic power of conceptualization" (1980, 31). It is my hope that this formalization will embolden future work on Gorgias' treatise that shares the conviction that such verdicts are unfair and that, along with Kerferd, we ought to treat *On Not Being* as a work of careful argumentation and of not inconsiderable philosophical significance.

PART III

Fourth-Century Disciplinary Efforts
Three Studies

9

Early Use of the Terms Rhētoreia *and* Rhētoreuein

Historian and philosopher of science Thomas S. Kuhn argues that to comprehend the history of past theories one must internalize the technical vocabulary of such theories: "To understand some body of past scientific belief, the historian must acquire a lexicon that here and there differs systematically from the one current in his [or her] own day. Only by using that older lexicon can he or she accurately render certain of the statements that are basic to the science under scrutiny" (1989, 9). As obvious as Kuhn's admonition may be to students of classical texts, one can document clear instances of where sixth- and fifth-century B.C.E. texts and fragments have been analyzed primarily through the lens of *fourth*-century B.C.E. lexicons — primarily those of Plato and Aristotle (Cherniss 1935; Havelock 1983). A persistent theme of this book is that the standard accounts of the origins of classical Greek rhetorical theory have not paid sufficient attention to the dramatic differences between the vocabularies employed by writers of the fifth and fourth centuries B.C.E.

This chapter extends the investigation of the development of the specialized vocabulary of rhetorical theory by examining the earliest extant uses of *rhētoreia* (ῥητορεία, "oratory") and *rhētoreuein* (ῥητορεύειν, "to orate"). The question explored is whether, and in what ways, did the development of additional disciplinary terms such as *rhētoreia* alter the ways in which discourse was conceptualized and taught. This chapter proffers two claims specifically about classical-era usage. First, both noun- and verb-forms are surprisingly late in their development, the earliest appearances being in the works of Isocrates and Plato.[1] Second, fourth-century usage of *rhētoreia,* in particular, includes an interesting assortment of meanings. The semantic field of the term is broader than is suggested by many translations and by the relevant entry in the standard *Greek-English Lexicon* (Liddell and Scott, 1940). The chapter concludes with a tentative answer to the question of whether the introduction of *rhētoreia* and *rhētoreuein* altered the way in which discourse was conceptualized or taught.

Rhētoreia

The Homeric poems refer to *rhētēr* only once, in the famous phrase where Phoenix reminds Achilles that he has taught him "to be a teller of tales and a doer of deeds"; *muthōn te rhētēr emenai prēktēra te ergōn (Iliad* 9.443) The earliest extant instance of *rhētōr* is a legal inscription dated about 445 B.C.E.[2] *Rhētōr* and its variants are found only on occasion in authors such as Aristophanes, Euripides, and Thucydides, and earlier fifth-century authors such as Aeschylus, Sophocles, and Herodotus never use it. As Hansen and others document, *rhētōr* emerged in the later fifth century as a term denoting a special class of politicians who spoke often in the courts or the assembly.[3] Outside of Plato's writings, the term was used consistently in a narrow, quasi-technical sense that could be given positive or negative connotations (Arthurs 1993).

We have record of no author prior to Isocrates and Plato using such constructions as *rhētoreia* and *rhētoreuein.* Of course, it is possible that such terms were in use but simply were not preserved in writing. A more plausible and interesting explanation is that *rhētoreia* and *rhētoreuein* were, like *rhētorikē,* fourth-century neologisms coined in the wake of growing reflection about the teaching of discourse and the training of orators.

According to Liddell and Scott (1940), *rhētoreia* simply means "oratory" or "piece of oratory, set speech." As an *-eia* noun, oratory refers to a quality or condition resulting, in this case, from a practice in which one engages — that of the *rhētōr.* For example:

> (1) Plato, *Politicus* 303e10–304a2: τούτων δ᾽ ἐστί που στρατηγία καὶ δικαστική, καὶ ὅση βασιλικῇ κοινωνοῦσα ῥητορεία, πείθουσα τὸ δίκαιον, συνδιακυβερνᾷ τὰς ἐν ταῖς πόλεσι πράξεις. Herein are included the art of the general and that of the judge and all which *Oratory* shares with the art of the

1. According to a search of *Thesaurus Linguae Graecae* pilot CD-ROM version C with *Pandora* version 2.3.

2. Wilcox (1942, 127); Tod (1985, 88–90); Meiggs and Lewis (1969, 128–33).

3. Hansen (1981, 1983a); Ober (1989, 104–27); Sinclair (1988, 136–37).

ruler, because it persuades to justice, and thereby helps to steer the ship of state. (Adapted from Fowler 1925, 167–69)

Oratory as an abstract noun can denote an object-class. A "piece of oratory" or "oration" is a quality/condition of a product or performance created by an orator. For example:

(2) Aristotle, *Rhetoric* 1356b18–23: φανερὸν δὲ καὶ ὅτι ἑκάτερον ἔχει ἀγαθὸν τὸ εἶδος τῆς ῥητορείας . . . εἰσὶ γὰρ αἱ μὲν παραδειγματώδεις ῥητορεῖαι αἱ δὲ ἐνθυμηματικαί, καὶ ῥήτορες ὁμοίως οἱ μὲν παραδειγματώδεις οἱ δὲ ἐνθυμηματικοί. And it is also apparent that either form of *oratory* has merit. . . For some *orations* are paradigmatic, some enthymematic; and similarly, some orators are paradigmatic, some enthymematic. (Adapted from Kennedy 1991, 40–41)

(3) Aristotle(?) *Problems* 916b26–27: Διὰ τί τοῖς παραδείγμασι χαίρουσιν ἄνθρωποι ἐν ταῖς ῥητορείαις καὶ τοῖς λόγοις μᾶλλον τῶν ἐνθυμημάτων. Why is it that people enjoy examples in *orations* and arguments more than enthymemes [?] (Adapted from Forster in Barnes 1984, 1427)

(4) Isocrates, *To Philip* (26–27) Καὶ ταῦτ' οὐκ ἀλόγως ἐγνώκασιν· ἐπειδὰν γὰρ ὁ λόγος ἀποστερηθῇ τῆς τε δόξης τῆς τοῦ λέγοντος καὶ τῆς φωνῆς καὶ τῶν μεταβολῶν τῶν ἐν ταῖς ῥητορείαις γιγνομένων, ἔτι δὲ τῶν καιρῶν καὶ τῆς σπουδῆς τῆς περὶ τὴν πρᾶξιν, καὶ μηδὲν ᾖ τὸ συναγωνιζόμενον καὶ συμπεῖθον, ἀλλὰ τῶν μὲν προειρημένων ἁπάντων ἔρημος γένηται καὶ γυμνός, ἀναγιγνώσκῃ δὲ τις αὐτὸν ἀπιθάνως καὶ μηδὲν ἦθος ἐνσημαινόμενος ἀλλ' ὥσπερ ἀπαριθμῶν, εἰκότως, οἶμαι, φαῦλος εἶναι δοκεῖ τοῖς ἀκούουσιν. For when the speech[-text] is separated from the reputation of its speaker and the voice and the variations that in the *orations* are accomplished. (Adapted from Fantham 1992)

(5) Isocrates, *Panathenaicus* (2): ἐπραγματευόμην τοὺς περὶ τῶν συμφερόντων τῇ τε πόλει καὶ τοῖς ἄλλοις Ἕλλησι συμβουλεύοντας, καὶ πολλῶν μὲν ἐνθυμημάτων γέμοντας, οὐκ ὀλίγων δ' ἀντιθέσεων καὶ παρισώσεων καὶ τῶν ἄλλων ἰδεῶν τῶν ἐν ταῖς ῥητορείαις διαλαμπουσῶν καὶ τοὺς ἀκούοντας ἐπισημαίνεσθαι καὶ θορυβεῖν ἀναγκαζουσῶν· I worked at those speeches that give counsel regarding what is useful to the city and to the other Greeks, and that are full of many enthymemes and not a few antitheses and parallelisms and other figures that shine through in the *orations* and compel the approbation and applause of the audience. (Adapted from Too 1995, 20)

Or the abstract noun can refer to a potential or quality of *people*. This is a sense of *rhētoreia* that, arguably, has been underappreciated. Consider the following passage from Isocrates:

(6) Isocrates, *Against the Sophists* (21) Καίτοι τοὺς βουλομένους πειθαρχεῖν τοῖς ὑπὸ τῆς φιλοσοφίας ταύτης προσταττομένοις πολὺ ἂν θᾶττον πρὸς ἐπιείκειαν ἢ πρὸς ῥητορείαν ὠφελήσειεν.

And yet they may help those who are willing to obey the instructions of this philosophy far more quickly toward Equanimity than toward *Oratory*. (Adapted from Norlin 1929, 177)[4]

Two things are noteworthy about this passage. First, it is the earliest surviving use of *rhētoreia*. Though it cannot be proved that *rhētoreia* was first coined by Isocrates, the word cannot be found in earlier documents and the extant texts of the era suggest that it was at least a novelty in 390 B.C.E. Ironically, Isocrates *may* have coined a term designating oratory or rhetoricity not in order to claim it, but to contrast it to the objectives of his pedagogy. Throughout his teaching career Isocrates describes his teaching as "philosophy" and explicitly denies that he is a *Rhētōr* (5.81; 8L.7). In an earlier work (1990a, 465), I speculate that Plato's attack on *rhētorikē* in *Gorgias* may have been intended to identify the art with Isocrates' training: If *Rhētoreia* was a novel term associated with the training offered by Isocrates, then Gorgias' explicit declaration at 449a5 that he teaches the art of oratory would have been a clear signal to fourth-century readers that the target of the passage was Isocrates.

Second, for "Oratory" to be an alternative to the quality of "Equanimity," or the potential to be Fair and Reasonable, as Isocrates proposes in this context, *Rhētoreia* is translated better as "rhetoricity," "rhetorical skill" (Rummel 1979, 35), "facility in Oratory" (Norlin 1928–29), or even "éloquence" (Mathieu and Brémond 1929, 150).[5]

The preceding six examples exhaust the extant usage of *Rhētoreia* in the fourth century B.C.E. They suggest that *Rhētoreia* can denote the general category of Oratory, or an object-class of "things" that are produced by rhetors (as suggested by the word "oratory" or "oration"), or a quality or potential of "oratoricalness" or "rhetoricity." None of these three senses is quite the same as assigning the quality of being "rhetorly" to someone or something as the adjectival use of *rhētorikē* suggests, nor is it the same notion as the distinct "art of the rhetor" denoted by *rhētorikē* when used as an abstract noun.

Rhētoreuein

Like *rhētorikē* and *Rhētoreia, Rhētoreuein* cannot be found in texts prior to the fourth century. Remarkably, only four instances are identifiable

---

4. He continues: "Let no one think I am asserting that justice (*dikaiosynē*) can be taught; for I am absolutely sure that there is no art (*technē*) capable of implanting justice and good behavior (*sōphrosynē*) into those ill-formed by nature for excellence (*aretē*). But I still believe that education in composing political discourse (*tōn logōn tōn politikōn*) would give [students] the most encouragement and practice" (13.21).

5. René Henry's (1959) translation of Photius also often translates *rhētoreia* as "l'éloquence." See, for example, 1:105.86a42; 1:158.101a39; 1:161.105a11.

even in fourth-century texts;[6] all are in treatises written by three educators concerned with the instruction of orators: Isocrates, Plato, and Anaximenes. Liddell and Scott record three of these and translate the infinitive as "to be a public speaker." Given that *Rhētōr* is a quasi-technical term, "to be a rhetor" or "to make public speeches" would be appropriate translations for classical-era texts. The earliest extant use is in Plato's *Gorgias* — a text that is rich with Platonic neologisms including, possibly, *rhetorikē*.

> (7) Plato, *Gorgias* (502d2–3) ἢ οὐ ῥητορεύειν δοκοῦσί σοι οἱ ποιηταὶ ἐν τοῖς θεάτροις. Or don't you think the poets *orate* [or "make speeches"] in the theaters? (Allen 1991, 291)

Plato's choice of words is unusual because, here and in other passages, he is the only classical-era author that stretches the word *Rhētōr* to refer to speakers in settings other than those Aristotle would designate deliberative, forensic, or epideictic (Arthurs 1993). Woodhead's "engage in rhetoric" and Lamb's "use rhetoric" for *Rhētoreuein* make sense in light of current use of "rhetoric" to refer to individual instances of oratory, but are less preferable than R. E. Allen's choice that preserves a distinction between *rhetorikē* and *Rhētoreuein* (see Hamilton and Cairns 1961, 285; and Lamb 1925, 451).

Isocrates employs forms of *Rhētoreuein* twice; the two are dated between 350 and 346 B.C.E. Unlike Plato, Isocrates maintains the more limited and arguably more specialized sense of *Rhētoreuein* as "to be an orator." In both examples the context makes it clear that one orates *orally* and in recognized public settings, such as the assembly.

> (8) Isocrates, *To Philip* (25) Καίτοι μ᾽ οὐ λέληθεν, ὅσον διαφέρουσιν τῶν λόγων εἰς τὸ πείθειν οἱ λεγόμενοι τῶν ἀναγιγνωσκομένων, οὐδ᾽ ὅτι πάντες ὑπειλήφασιν τοὺς μὲν περὶ σπουδαίων πραγμάτων καὶ κατεπειγόντων ῥητο-ρεύεσθαι, τοὺς δὲ πρὸς ἐπίδειξιν καὶ πρὸς ἐργολαβίαν γεγράφθαι. And yet it has not escaped my notice how much spoken arguments are superior in per-suasive power to those read, nor that everyone assumes that arguments about serious and urgent affairs *are orated*, whereas arguments that serve display and are for profit are written down.
>
> (9) Isocrates, *To the Rulers of Mytilene* (7): Ἐγὼ τοῦ μὲν πολιτεύεσθαι καὶ ῥητορεύειν ἀπέστην· οὔτε γὰρ φωνὴν ἔσχον ἱκανὴν οὔτε τόλμαν· I abstained from political activity and from *orating;* for I had neither enough voice nor enough daring. (Adapted from Van Hook 1945, 465)

In these passages Isocrates does not consider himself an orator, for an orator speaks extemporaneously in the assembly while Isocrates writes discourses to

---

6. I set aside, for the moment, two possible uses by Nausiphanes that are reported in Philodemus (see DK 75 B1 and 2).

be read in private. However, in a passage cited earlier from his last work, *Panathenaicus* (#6 above), it is clear that he believes his own works *are* examples of oratory. Thus Isocrates' use of *Rhētoreia* and *Rhētoreuein* include oral and written speech.

The late fourth-century B.C.E. *Rhetoric to Alexander* never uses the words *Rhētōr, Rhētoreia,* or *rhētorikē,* and uses *Rhētoreuein* only once (1444a34 = 36.39.6). The author suggests that one can defend oneself from charges of preparing a forensic speech by contrasting such behavior with the litigiousness of one's opponent; surely it is more beneficial to the polity "to learn to be an orator (*manthanein Rhētoreuein*) than to be a sycophant" (*sykophantēs*).

> (10) Anaximenes(?), *Rhetoric to Alexander* (1444a33–34= 36.39.5–6): ὥστε λυσιτελὲς φανεῖται τοῖς πολίταις κἀκεῖνον μανθάνειν ῥητορεύειν· So that it would apparently be advantageous for the citizens if he also learned *orating*. (Adapted from Forster in Barnes 1984, 2310)

Discussion

The question that gave rise to this study is whether, and in what ways, the development of additional disciplinary terms such as *Rhētoreia* and *Rhētoreuein* altered the ways in which discourse was conceptualized and taught. The extremely limited number of surviving usages of these terms, especially in contrast to other technical terms used to categorize and describe the teaching of discourse (such as *rhētorikē* or *dialektikē*), suggest that the conceptual work to which *Rhētoreia* and *Rhētoreuein* were put was extremely limited. In the classical era, neither term is used to mark off discrete phenomena in the consistent manner that "kind terms" can. To be most useful in theorizing, same-order kind-terms should not overlap. So, according to Aristotle, a particular oration is deliberative *or* forensic *or* epideictic. Identify an oration as one kind and you know that it has certain qualities and lacks others. Because there were ample constructions of *Rhētōr, legō,* and *logos* available to describe speakers, speaking, and speeches, the more convoluted constructions of *Rhētoreia* and *Rhētoreuein* were typically unnecessary. At least in the fourth century, these words were not used often or consistently enough to catch on as useful classifiers; oratory could be written or oral, public or private, political or nonpolitical.

Nevertheless, the preceding analysis suggests that translations of *Rhētoreia* and *Rhētoreuein* in certain classical texts of the fourth century are in need of correction. The general tendency, corrected in the examples quoted in this presentation, is to translate *Rhētoreia* and *Rhētoreuein* taking "rhetoric" as the semantic kernel to be harvested. Because "rhetoric" was and is a rather highly charged and equivocal term, the relevant texts will be understood better if it is recognized that *Rhētōr* by the end of the fifth century had a consistent, limited quasi-technical use and is both morphologically and conceptually the root of such fourth-century neologisms as *Rhētoreia, rhētorikē,* and *Rhētoreuein.* The sociopolitical role of the orator is what gives most of the preceding fourth-century passages their bite. Only well after the fourth century, when the term *Rhētōr* became a more generic label for *any* speaker, do such terms as *Rhētoreia, rhētorikē,* and *Rhētoreuein* become increasingly aestheticized or depoliticized and thus more akin to the contemporary uses of the words *oratory, rhetoric,* and *orate.*[7]

7. I am grateful to John T. Kirby, André Lardinois, Terry L. Papillon, and Michael Tiffany for the helpful comments on earlier drafts of this chapter.

10

Isocrates' Philosophia

The study of the Sophists, rhetorical theory, and American Pragmatism has enjoyed a renaissance in the twentieth century, especially in the past few decades. That all three areas of inquiry have become the cutting edge of various disciplines is no mere coincidence. A profound dissatisfaction with both the transcendental metaphysics of Plato and the brute empiricism of Positivism has rekindled interest in alternative perspectives. As a recent collection by Steven Mailloux illustrates (1995), the ideas and interests associated with the Sophists, rhetorical theory, and American Pragmatism combine and interact in provocative ways.

My objective in this chapter is to provide a reading of Isocrates that attempts to locate him as one of the first philosophers in Western history to address the central concerns that we now identify with Pragmatism. The chapter is divided into four parts: in the first, I argue that Isocrates ought to be viewed as a part of the history of philosophy as much as he has been viewed a part of the history of rhetoric. Part two describes Isocrates' vision of philosophy based on his extant texts, and part three contrasts this vision with how Isocrates saw rival approaches to higher education. Part four locates Isocrates vis-à-vis the concerns and interests of contemporary Pragmatism.

Isocrates and the History of Philosophy

The disciplines of Philosophy and Rhetoric have treated each other throughout much of Western history as hostile neighboring countries. Temporary visas have been permitted to allow crossover efforts to engage in the "philosophy of rhetoric" and for rhetorical theorists to engage in philosophy, but permanent residency is purchased at the price of renouncing one's past and declaring allegiance to the powers-that-be. With respect to the famous Sophists of ancient Greece, the habit for more than two thousand years has been to follow Plato's suggestion that Sophistry and Rhetoric are inextricably "mixed together" (*Gorgias* 465c4–5). When the Sophists engaged in intellectual pursuits that we might be tempted to call philosophical, it was only with an eye toward captivating their audiences and hence capturing more students. In short, it was not "real" Philosophy at all but either a cheap knock-off designed to fool the unsuspecting or, occasionally, simply an accidental by-product of rhetorical pursuits (Classen 1976, 246–47; Gomperz [1912] 1985, 35–49).

Over the past century or so, relations have begun to warm. It is too soon to call for live television coverage of the demolition of the divide between Philosophy and Rhetoric; indeed, one can still sniff out ample evidence of marking behavior.[1] A growing number of historians of philosophy have begun slowly, sometimes grudgingly, to include chapters or volumes on the Sophists. Like the past actions of the resident alien with suspect past political affiliations, however, the rhetorical activities of the Sophists are downplayed or treated with a certain amount of embarrassment (Kerferd 1981b, 82). Demolishing the wall between Philosophy and Rhetoric remains unfinished business both in general and, in particular, with respect to the Sophists. The categories of Philosophy and Rhetoric still exert a strong influence over how the Sophists are understood by friend and foe alike.

The received opinion concerning Isocrates is a useful case in point. Isocrates traditionally is described as a fourth-century B.C.E. representative of "sophistic rhetoric" (Kennedy 1980, 31–36). Beginning as a logographer, or speechwriter, he repudiated his first vocation and in around 392 opened a school for young men interested in participating in civic life. His teaching practices are described by Kennedy as more respectable than those of previous Sophists: he did not travel around, he took a personal interest in his students, and his school featured a "stable" and "consistent" curriculum (1980, 32).

Throughout his long teaching career Isocrates consistently describes his

---

1. See, e.g., Peter Munz (1990).

teaching as Philosophy and explicitly denies that he is a *rhētōr* (5.81; 8L.7).[2] There are two common reactions to this self-report. The first is simply to ignore it. You will not find him discussed in that discipline's histories because historians of philosophy believe that Isocrates was not "really" doing philosophy. The *Encyclopedia of Philosophy,* which purports to "cover the whole of philosophy" and that "made it a special point to rescue from obscurity unjustly neglected figures," does not include an entry for Isocrates (Edwards 1967, 1:ix–x). Later commentators, including the Loeb edition's translators George Norlin and LaRue Van Hook, tend to discount the philosophical content of Isocrates' teachings — to the point of selectively translating the Greek word for philosophy (*philosophia*) as "rhetoric" (Norlin 1928, 1:124; Van Hook 1945, 3:438). Even as sympathetic a reader of the Sophists as John Poulakos asserts that Isocrates "often uses *philosophy* to mean rhetoric" (1995, 116). Similarly, in his otherwise excellent book on Isocrates, Yun Lee Too parenthetically remarks that when Isocrates uses the term *philosophy* "he means 'rhetoric'" (1995, 190). Werner Jaeger typifies the modern opinion when he describes the conflict between Plato and Isocrates as "the first battle in the centuries of war between philosophy and rhetoric" (1943, 46). So, the thinking goes, regardless of what Isocrates claimed he was doing, he was really teaching and engaging in Rhetoric and not Philosophy.

The alternative reaction to Isocrates' self-portrayal as a teacher of philosophy is to consider him half-blooded; an intellectual mutt. Plato describes Isocrates (without mentioning him by name) in the *Euthydemus* as dwelling on the "boundary between philosopher and politico" and denigrates Isocrates' halfheartedness as evading all risk and struggle: "The fact is that these people, participating in both sides, are inferior to both with respect to each reason for which Politics and Philosophy are important; and so they are in truth in third place though they wish to be thought in first" (305c7, 306c2–5). In his dissertation on Isocrates, Allan Bloom notes that Isocrates appears "to be holding a precarious balance between rhetoric and philosophy, fulfilling the true function of neither. . . . So we find Isocrates in a no man's land between rhetoric and philosophy — too philosophic for the politician, and too aware of the immediate and the changing for the philosopher" (1955, 3). According to Bloom,

2. The Greek text of Isocrates' compositions is available in Blass (1913–1937); Georges Mathieu and Emile Brémond (1929–1962); Norlin (1928–1929) and Van Hook (1945). Each text has a traditional number assigned to it, followed by a section number. Accordingly, 5.81 = Oration 5 (*To Philip*), section 81. The following is a key to the orations and letters cited: 1. *To Demonicus*; 2. *To Nicocles*; 3. *Nicocles*; 4. *Panegyricus*; 5. *To Philip*; 6. *Archidamus*; 7. *Areopagiticus*; 8. *On the Peace*; 9. *Evagoras*; 10. *Helen*; 11. *Busiris*; 12. *Panathenaicus*; 13. *Against the Sophists*; 15. *Antidosis*; 8L. Eighth Letter.

Isocrates' mixed pedigree results in a twofold negative verdict: "Isocrates' anomalous position is the consequence of the fact that when he is looked upon as an advocate of the same pursuits as Demosthenes, he is found wanting; and when he is measured up against Plato, he appears trivial. Because he has eluded pigeonholing, his thought is almost never taken seriously anymore" (1955, 3–4).

A variation of the half-blooded "mutt" theme is the contention that Isocrates was essentially a rhetorician, but that he tried to give his teaching of rhetoric a philosophical grounding. Kennedy's account is typical: "Since he had apparently come under some influence from Socrates, he presents his teaching as 'philosophy.' In his own way, Isocrates sought to answer the kind of criticism of rhetoric found in the *Gorgias*" (1991, 11). Such an account supposes that *philosophia* had a fairly fixed meaning and a self-sufficient credibility, while *rhētorikē* had an unclear or controversial status. Isocrates' use of the term *philosophia* to describe his teaching, therefore, is interpreted as proof that he wanted to legitimize his rhetorical training by aligning it with the better known and respected discipline of philosophy (Heilbrunn 1967, 188). Michael Cahn even suggests that Isocrates' self-description may have been deliberately deceptive. According to Cahn, Isocrates established "his own school of rhetoric which he advertises under the name of another institution: Philosophy" (1989, 134).

Two recent developments, one in classical philology and one in philosophy, encourage us to reconsider the texts of Isocrates with a somewhat different set of conceptual lenses. The first development has been described in earlier chapters as the origins-of-*rhētorikē* thesis. *Logos* was the significant theoretical term most often discussed by the Sophists of the fifth century B.C.E. Prior to the coining of *rhētorikē,* the verbal arts were understood as less differentiated and more holistic in scope than they were in the fourth century B.C.E., and the teaching associated with *logos* shows considerably less tension between the goals of seeking success and seeking truth than is the case once Rhetoric and Philosophy were defined as distinct disciplines. Even in the fourth century, the use of the term *rhētorikē* to designate a specialized skill or art is exceedingly rare outside of the writings of Plato and Aristotle (Cole 1991a, 115–58). Most important for the purposes of this chapter is the fact that the word *rhetoric* is not found in the writings of Isocrates—even in the various texts in which Isocrates explicitly describes and defends his teachings (noted also by Cole 1991a, 2). The absence of *rhētorikē* in Isocrates' texts gives us cause to reconsider precisely how he described his own teaching (Poulakos 1997, 69–72).

The second development can be described as the "end of philosophy" movement occurring among certain contemporary academic philosophers. Fueled by critiques of philosophy as a privileged way of knowing, certain Pragmatist and continental philosophers seek not to end philosophy, per se, but to reformulate what it means to philosophize in such a way as to break from the vision of philosophy as found in Plato; that is, as producing a "God's eye view" of reality (Magnus 1985, 2–10). There is, according to a recent account of American Pragmatism, "a widespread disenchantment with the traditional image of philosophy as a transcendental mode of inquiry, a tribunal of reason which grounds claims about Truth, Goodness, and Beauty" (West 1989, 3).

These developments open up a conceptual space from which to question the appropriateness of casting Isocrates into the role of "Rhetoric" in the hackneyed play of "Rhetoric versus Philosophy." If we reject the notions that Rhetoric and Philosophy represent timeless Forms, invariant categories, or labels for natural kinds, then a more productive exploration of the struggle to give meaning to these terms at different points in history is possible. There are two obvious starting points from which to define a canon for the history of philosophy commonly referred to as the *real* and *nominal* approaches to definition. The traditional preference is to posit a "real" definition or description of philosophy that sets out criteria for people or ideas to be dubbed "philosophical," then utilizes the criteria to canonize those previous authors and speakers who appear to fit the bill. An alternative would be to take a nominalist approach: Those people or ideas that are self-identified as philosophical or are considered such by their peers are, presumptively, part of the history of Philosophy. Such an approach avoids claims about who is "really" a philosopher and who is not, and instead asks the questions: Who are the people and what are the ideas that have tried explicitly to join the conversation known as Philosophy? Apart from what Philosophy may mean to us today, what has it meant to thinkers in other places and times?

The choice between a real and nominal approach to canon formation is certainly not either-or. There are current needs and interests that are served by contemporary philosophers selecting some figures to study to the neglect of others, regardless of how those "Others" see themselves. Nonetheless, I want to press the idea that a productive and provocative history of philosophy ought to take seriously the self-proclaimed philosophical claims put forward by certain historical figures that have been marginalized or ignored by the traditional canon (Grimshaw 1986; Waithe 1987). As Susan Jarratt (1991) points out, the strategies for marginalizing people that we see as radically Other (that is, people very different from our "selves") is similar to those who used to marginalize certain thinkers from the history of Philosophy. If X does not match our current conception of what is *really* or *normally* Y, then X is, by definition, other than Y. The question facing the historian of Philosophy is, then, how does one respond to the claims of someone traditionally understood as "philosophically" Other?

Earlier I argued that there are important differences between historical reconstructions and contemporary appropriations of the Sophists (1991, 64–81). A historical interpretation attempts to empathize with a historical figure in order to understand the "proposed world" found in historical texts as best we can (Ricoeur 1981, 143). Interpretation without presupposition is impossible, of course, but the point of historical interpretation is to try to understand what is alien (or Other) about the text—what is not already articulated in our current thinking. By contrast, I describe contemporary theorizing and criticism as laudable but different tasks where one freely borrows and purposefully transforms an ancient text in order to contribute to some contemporary conversation (Rorty 1984, 49–75).

There is an analogy between the most productive way to engage a historical text and the most ethical way to engage an Other. My argument is that understanding a person very different from oneself (for me, a white male, this could be a Black female) is an ethically prior goal to valuing (or "using") that person for one's own immediate ends. If I remain "self-centered" and habitually define myself as "normal," then I will simply translate the Other's features accordingly: I value the person only in terms of what I define as salient similarities and differences. But I have both mistreated that Other and I have failed to learn anything new. If, on the other hand, my goal is empathy—that is, if I try to understand who that person is from the "inside out"—then not only will I treat her more ethically, as a full human being and not just by mere difference, I will also learn and grow as a person myself (Rogers 1980, 137–61). My understanding of what it is to be human has been expanded. True, I can never empathize to the point of achieving complete identification. But the more I empathize, the closer I come to engaging her on her own terms, and the more I learn.

Having treated the person ethically and broadened my understanding, I may very well gain insights that are "useful" to me in my life. The more alien a text or Other, the more likely it is that I will learn something new by empathizing. In fact, I am more likely to enrich myself by empathizing than by remaining persistently self-centered. The connection between historical interpretation and interpersonal relations was noted by Hans-Georg Gadamer in his description of the requisite openness of the *historically effected consciousness:* "It too has a real analogue in the I's experience of the Thou. In human relations the important thing is, as we have seen, to experience the Thou truly as a Thou—i.e., not to overlook his [or her] claim but to let him [or her] really say something to us. Here is where openness belongs" (1989, 361). Gadamer insists that "without such openness to one another there is no genuine human bond" and he suggests that there is a direct "parallel to the hermeneutical experience" of historical texts (1989, 361). Similarly, Paul Ricoeur describes the interpretive process as an ongoing dialectic of *distanciation* and *appropriation* — as a "struggle between the otherness that transforms all spatial and temporal distance into cultural estrangement and the ownness by which all understanding aims at the extension of self-understanding" (1976, 43). Ricoeur describes appropriation not as a kind of possession of the Other but as a "moment of dispossession of the narcissistic ego" (1981, 192). That is, only by empathizing with the other "self" found in the text can one transcend the limits of one's self in order to broaden one's understanding of the world.

> [E]ven when we read a philosophical work, it is always a question of entering into an alien work, of divesting oneself of the earlier "me" in order to receive, as in play, the self conferred by the work itself. . . . Only the interpretation which satisfies the injunction of the text, which follows the "arrow" of meaning and endeavors to "think in accordance with" it, engenders a new *self*-understanding. By the expression "*self*-understanding," I should like to contrast the *self* which emerges from the understanding of the text to the *ego* which claims to precede this understanding. It is the text . . . which gives a *self* to the *ego*. (1981, 190, 192–93)

In sum, the historical understanding of past philosophical texts is both an ethically and logically prior task to that of "using" the text to warrant contemporary projects. Furthermore, there is no prima facie reason for rejecting Isocrates' own words when trying to come to a historical understanding of his texts. The initial question is not how is Isocrates' work "different" from "real" philosophy, but what does Isocrates say about *philosophia*? What is his understanding and practice of Philosophy? To answer these questions, part two of this chapter revisits his texts to try to understand what he had to say about philosophy, discourse, and education.

Isocrates' Philosophia

Philosophia is Isocrates' term of choice to denote higher learning. It is the most frequent "disciplinary" word he uses and it appears in the pivotal passages in which he describes his own teaching (Timmerman 1998). A characteristic passage appears in a discourse written for a young Cyprian monarch named Demonicus: "I see that fortune is on our side and that the present circumstances are in league with us; for you are eager for education and I profess to educate; you are ripe for philosophy, and I lead students of philosophy" (1.3).[3] Isocrates announces in his first publication as an educator that the pursuit he advocates is philosophy (13.1). Near the conclusion of the extant text of *Against the Sophists,* Isocrates describes the promises of his *philosophia* as follows:

> [T]hose who are willing to obey the instructions of this philosophy would be aided far more quickly toward Equanimity (*epieikeia*) than toward Oratory (*rhētoreia*). Let no one think I am asserting that justice (*dikaiosynē*) can be taught; for I am absolutely sure that there is no art (*technē*) capable of implanting justice and good behavior (*sōphrosynē*) into those ill-formed by nature for excellence (*aretē*). But I still believe that education in composing political discourse (*tōn logōn tōn politikōn*) would give [students] the most encouragement and practice. (13.21)

As noted in the previous chapter, the use of *rhētoreia* in this passage is the earliest surviving use of the Greek word that normally would be translated as Oratory. Here I must revisit the point about this passage made earlier: For "Oratory" to be an alternative to the end-state of "Equanimity," *rhētoreia* is explained better in this context as "rhetoricity," "rhetorical skill," "facility in Oratory," "eloquence," or "rhetorical fluency."[4] The word *rhētōr* was used in Isocrates' time to designate a very specific group of people; namely, the more or less professional politicians who spoke often in the courts or in the assembly. The neologism *rhētor-eia* creates an abstract noun that denotes some "thing" that has the enduring character of the *rhētōr* where the "thing" could be a product of the rhetor (as suggested by the word "oratory") or a state-of-being ("oratoricalness" or "rhetoricity"). This is not the same as assigning the (potentially temporary) quality of being "rhetorly" or "rhetorical" to someone or something as the adjective *rhētorikē* suggests, nor is it the same notion as the distinct "art of the rhetor" denoted by *rhētorikē* when used as an abstract noun. Instead, *rhētoreia* refers to a possible end-state that, at least in this passage, functions as an *alternative* to Equanimity. Though it cannot be proved that *rhētoreia* was first coined by Isocrates, the word cannot be found in earlier documents and the extant texts of the era suggest that it was at least a novelty in 390 B.C.E. In other words, Isocrates may have coined a term designating oratory or rhetoricity not in order to claim it, but to contrast it to the objectives of his pedagogy.

---

3. Unless otherwise indicated, all translations of Isocrates are adapted from the translations in the Loeb editions (Norlin 1928–29; Van Hook 1945) or from unpublished translations by Elaine Fantham (1992).

4. Cf. the translation above with that of Erika Rummel (1979, 35); and Mathieu and Brémond (1929, 150).

Second, philosophy and the "study of political discourse" are treated as equivalent; both are means toward a just character, but not necessarily toward oratorical proficiency. Isocrates' text makes clear that he can differentiate between moral and technical excellence in political discourse. While Isocrates does not deny that his educational program assists in the production of discourse appropriate to the *rhētōr,* he chooses instead to emphasize the goal of *epieikeia*—which also can be translated as fairness, reasonableness, or virtuousness. Indeed, on more than one occasion Isocrates specifically ranks the goal of producing students of good character higher than that of producing clever speakers (1.4, 12.87). The sentiments found in such passages, which, as I will show, are repeated throughout the texts of Isocrates, clearly call into question interpretations of his teaching that portray it as purely "rhetorical" (see also Wagner 1922, 328–37).

Isocrates also calls his philosophical training *logōn paideia* (15.180). While *paideia* readily translates as "education," *logos* is one of the most equivocal terms of the period.[5] Norlin translates the phrase *logōn paideia* in a variety of ways, including "teaching of rhetoric," "teaching of eloquence," and "education of an orator." Since Norlin interprets Isocrates' *philosophia* as "rhetoric," such translations of *logōn paideia* would appear to follow naturally. But Isocrates could have said "teaching of rhetoric" (*rhētorikē* or *rhētoreia*), "teaching of eloquence" (*kalliphōnia*), or "education of an orator" (*rhētōr*) had he wanted to do so. That he did not do so suggests that *logōn paideia* is a more "dense" phrase than Norlin's translation suggests. Though "education in discourse" is less precise, it may be a more accurate way to represent the breadth of learning that Isocrates denotes with the phrase *logōn paideia.* Consider the following passage from the section in *Antidosis* in which Isocrates explicitly sets out to give an account, "like a genealogist," of *logōn paideia:*

> For it is agreed that our nature is composed of *psychē* and body (*sōma*): of these two no one would deny that the *psychē* is more fit to lead and more important. Its function is to deliberate (*bouleuesthai*) about public and private matters, whereas the body's function is to serve the decisions of the *psychē*. Hence certain of our ancestors, seeing that arts (*technai*) had been created for many other things, but that nothing of the kind had been devised for the body and for the *psychē,* invented and bequeathed to us two disciplines, that of the trainer, of which gymnastics is a part, for the body, and for the *psychē,* philosophy. . . . For when they take on pupils, the physical trainers teach their students the stances and postures devised for combat, and the teachers of philosophy go through with their students all the forms of thought encountered in the use of discourse (*logos*). (15.180–183)

5. For an alternative account of Isocrates and *logos* that reads Isocrates through a Heideggerian lens, see Samuel Ijsseling (1976, 18–25).

Psychē is a notoriously polysemic word in ancient Greek. The oldest meaning of *psychē* is "life" or "breath." As ancient writers began to theorize about the *psychē,* the term sometimes was used to refer to a hypothesized "life-force" or "soul-breath." Barnes suggests that early Greek philosophers understood the *psychē* as "that part or feature of an animate being which endows it with life; and since the primary signs of life are cognition and mobility, the *psychē* is the source of knowledge and the source of locomotion" (1979, 2:170). The "nature" of the *psychē* became a widely disputed philosophical issue: the available descriptions disagree whether the *psychē* is corporeal or not, immortal or not, and whether it can exist apart from human bodies (Rohde 1925, 362–89; Barnes 1979, 2:170–205; Bremmer 1983). By Isocrates' time it is fair to say that the term covered a range of cognitive, emotional, and even "spiritual" phenomena. Translators of Isocrates tend to supply "mind" in contexts that emphasize cognitive skills (such as deliberation), and "soul" in contexts that emphasize matters of character. In what follows I leave *psychē* untranslated to underscore my belief that for Isocrates, as for other humanist philosophers, *psychē* "is a collective expression for all the [human] powers of thought, desire, and will" (Rohde 1925, 365).

The analogy between philosophy as training for the *psychē* and gymnastics as training for the body is developed at length by Isocrates. Beginning in his earliest works as an educator, Isocrates describes philosophical education as *tēs psychēs epimeleian:* the cultivation, the giving of attention to, or the concern for developing the *Psychē* (13.8). He repeats this theme both in his deliberative orations (1.6, 9.41, 9.80) and in his texts that explicitly concern his educational program (13.17; 15.181, 250, 290, 304). The relationship *"philosophia* is to *psychē* as gymnastics is to body" is articulated in texts from throughout Isocrates' career (1.40; 2.11; 15.210), usually as part of a defense of higher learning in general. For example, Isocrates complains that "it is most irrational to rank the *psychē* as superior to the body but, despite this belief, show more good will to athletes than to students of philosophy" (15.250).

The importance of cultivating the *psychē* to match the training of the body was not wholly original with Isocrates. One finds the germ of the idea in the Homeric passage where Phoenix reminds Achilles that he has taught him to be a "teller of tales and a doer of deeds" (*Iliad* 9.443). Democritus, in the mid-fifth century B.C.E., is said to have claimed, "It is fitting for people to set more store by their psyches than by their bodies; for perfection of *psychē* corrects wickedness of body, but strength of body without reasoning (*logismos*) makes the *psychē* no better at all" (Barnes [1951] 1989, 2:183 §187). But the more specific claim that it is the province of *philosophia* to train the *psychē* as it is the province of gymnastics to train the body may well have originated with Isocrates.

It did not take long for a rival teacher, Plato, to question Isocrates' self-description. It is worth keeping in mind Ostwald's observation that "the Athenian public made no attempt to differentiate Sophists from philosophers" (1986, 259n). The distinctions familiar to us between "sophistry" and "philosophy" from Plato's and Aristotle's writings were by no means commonly known — let alone accepted — by most people during most of the fifth and fourth centuries B.C.E. In fact, Isocrates' vocabulary generally is much closer to common Greek than either Plato's or Aristotle's. *Philosophia* — literally, the love of wisdom — in this period denotes "higher learning" in general (Wilcox 1943, 115n). As Athens' first permanent school, Isocrates' training would have been regarded by most Greeks as every bit as "philosophical" as that of his later rivals Plato and Aristotle.

I have argued previously that Plato's *Gorgias* probably was intended largely as a critique of Isocrates' training and a programmatic defense of Plato's own new school (1991, 40–49). Plato suggests that there are two sets of arts for the *psychē* and *sōma*, one set that aims at true health and improvement, the other aims merely at the appearance of health and improvement (*Gorgias* 463e–466a). Gymnastics and the medical arts are the "true" arts for the care of the body, just as law-giving (*nomothetikē*) and justice (*dikaiosynē*) are the true arts for the *psychē*. Cosmetics and pastry-cooking are "false" arts that bring pleasure but not real health to the body, just as sophistic (*sophistikē*) and rhetoric (*rhētorikē*) — which are "mixed together" and difficult to separate — are the false arts of the *psychē*. Elsewhere in the dialogue these sets of arts are aligned with two ways of life: the life of true philosophy and the life of active involvement in civic affairs. There can be no doubt that the former is promoted in Plato's educational program, while the latter is portrayed by Plato as advocated by Isocrates' approach to schooling. Plato's *Gorgias* champions a separation of philosophy from direct involvement in civic affairs that was anathema to Isocrates.

The point of Plato's *Gorgias* is summed up by Socrates in his argument with Callicles: "Our argument now concerns . . . the way one ought to live: whether it is the life to which you summon me, doing such manly things as speaking in public, practicing rhetoric, engaging in politics as you do now; or whether it is this life of mine in philosophy; and how this life differs from that" (*Gorgias* 500c1–8, trans. Allen 1984, 289). Isocrates' philosophy shows no evidence of such a dichotomy. In a passage in *Busiris*, Isocrates undertakes to describe the contributions of the Egyptians. He notes that "for the *psychē* they laid down a course of philosophy able to legislate laws and investigate the nature of things" (11.22). Here, and elsewhere in the speech, Isocrates makes clear that philosophy is coterminous with civic life (11.17). In *Panegyricus* Isocrates claims that Philosophy "has helped to discover and establish all [civic] institutions, and has educated us for public affairs and made us gentle toward each other" (4.47). As Norlin notes, the conclusion of *On the Peace* demonstrates that the state of politics and philosophy are intertwined; for Isocrates, philosophy "is the salvation of the state" (1929, 97).

It is easy for us now to separate many of the concepts that were intimately fused and connected in Isocrates' thought. For example, we readily acknowledge the possibility that someone could have a sound intellectual training, yet think and act perversely. We actively distinguish between politics and non-politics, between education and civic life. Isocrates' tendency to see education as moral may have been encouraged by the polysemy of the word *psychē*, which in Isocrates' texts seem to fuse ideas we would identify with such words as "mind," "character," "personality," and "soul." Some of the passages discussed above where Isocrates likens philosophy to training of the *psychē* have been translated by Norlin as training of the "soul." The result of a good philosophical education was, for Isocrates, what we would now call a good mind and a good soul: "As it is the nature of the body to be developed by appropriate exercises, it is the nature of the *psychē* to be developed by serious-minded argument (*tois spoudaiois logois*)" (1.12). In Plato's and Aristotle's writings, the *psychē* becomes the composite of distinct specialized functions — such as in Plato's myth of the charioteer in *Phaedrus* (246a). One result of Plato's distinctions was that it became easy to associate rhetoric with able minds but corrupt souls. Isocrates is certainly capable of distinguishing between political success and moral worth, but the unity of philosophy and civic virtue, mind and soul, and speech and thought in his writing suggests that Isocrates would attribute unsound discourse to unsound intellect: "For the power to speak well is taken as the surest sign of a sound understanding, and discourse that is true and lawful and just is the outward image of a good and faithful *psychē*" (3.7). Refusing to separate thought from expression, Isocrates suggests that learning "to speak and to think well will come together for those who feel a love of wisdom and love of honor" (15.277). In other words, Isocrates believes that moral and intellectual development are closely linked; training his students to think and speak nobly encourages them to *be* noble. A similar sentiment can be found in Aristotle's *Nicomachean Ethics* where he argues that there are two kinds of excellence (*aretē*): intellectual (*dianoētikē*) and moral (*ēthikē*), both of which can be improved through training and teaching (1103a14–18). Isocrates' prescription for the best discourse is compatible with the vision of moral discourse described by Plato in the *Phaedrus*. In the *Panathenaicus*, Isocrates concludes by enjoining his readers to consider discourse that is composed for "instruction and with skill, to prefer them over others written for display or for contests," and to prefer discourses "that aim at truth over those that mislead the opinions of the hearers; discourses that rebuke our faults and admonish us to those that are spoken for our pleasure and gratification" (12.271).

Isocrates' vision of *philosophia* can be summarized as follows: philosophy provides training for the *psychē* just as gymnastics provides training for the body. The goal of Isocrates' schooling, *logōn paideia,* is to produce leaders of high moral worth to provide counsel and advice on matters of civic importance. Philosophy is not above or apart from civic affairs: the two are consubstantial. Philosophy is understood by Isocrates as cultivating the *Psychē* of individual students, and by extension, the *psychē* of the *polis* (7.14; 12.138; see Poulakos 1997). His advice to Demonicus, typical of Isocrates' stated values, can withstand comparison to the advice found in the mouth of Socrates:

> Give careful heed to all that concerns your life, but above all train your own practical wisdom (*phronēsis*); for the greatest thing in the small compass is a good mind (*nous*) in a human body. Strive with your body to be a lover of toil, and with your *psychē* to be a lover of wisdom (*philosophos*), so that with the one you may have the strength to carry out your resolves, and with the other the knowledge to foresee what is for your good. (1.40)

Is what Isocrates teaches philosophy? Must we, following Russell H. Wagner and others, leave "philosophy" in quotation, noting that Isocrates did not use the term "as we understand it today" (1922, 328)? Nehamas observes that one cannot "neutrally" distinguish between philosophy and non-philosophy in classical Greece; that is, you cannot exclude someone like Isocrates from philosophy without taking the partisan position that someone else's (typically Plato's) definition of philosophy is true (1990, 13). The textual evidence that Isocrates portrays his own teaching as philosophy in a consistent and coherent manner, combined with the high esteem in which antiquity held him, suggests that failing to take him seriously as a philosopher amounts to special pleading by his detractors. Even if it is granted that Isocrates taught philosophy, the portrait provided here is far from complete. We can further our understanding of Isocrates' notion of philosophy by examining how he contrasts his *philosophia* to that of his competitors. That is, in addition to what Isocrates claims *is* philosophy, what does he say is *not*?

Isocrates and His Rivals

Isocrates consistently distinguishes his teaching from two competing approaches. We need not assume that Isocrates' educational accomplishments always matched his lofty goals in order to understand and appreciate the distinctions he made among different pedagogical practices. The first rival practice he refers to is *erides,* which is best understood as "disputation." We cannot be sure to whom Isocrates is referring, but at the time of the publication of *Against the Sophists* (390 B.C.E.), it cannot be Plato or Aristotle. Norlin suggests that Isocrates is referring to Socratics such as Antisthenes and Eucleides, and "such quibblers as are later shown up in Plato's *Euthydemus*" (1929, 162). Given that *Euthydemus* may be one of Plato's early dialogues (ca. 380), it seems safe to assume that the sort of "wrangling" one finds in *Euthydemus* typifies the kind of early fourth-century disputation Isocrates opposes. He specifies that those claiming to know the future are promising the impossible, as are those trying to persuade their students "that if they associate with them [the Sophists] they will know how to act and achieve success through this knowledge" (13.3). He rounds out his critique of this group of teachers by noting that they charge so little that their wares cannot be worthwhile, and that they are so insecure as to charge their payment in advance.

Isocrates notes that the teachers of Eristics, the *eristikoi,* are criticized by others for wasting their students' time since none of what they teach "is applicable either to private or public affairs, and their studies do not persist in the memory of students for any length of time because they do not serve life or assist in business, but are entirely apart from essential needs" (15.262). Isocrates agrees with such criticism, but acknowledges that students develop helpful learning skills from eristical exercises: "By studying the subtleties of astronomy and geometry and paying attention to difficult material, even by acquiring the habit of persevering and toiling over what is said and demonstrated and not letting their attention wander, so as to exercise and sharpen their wits, students become able to take in and learn more easily and quickly matters that are more worthwhile and important" (15.265). The critical references to disputation and geometry in Isocrates' later texts suggest that Plato's school is not an exception to his critique. It is clear from passages in *Antidosis* and in *Helen* that Isocrates does not approve of the sorts of Eleatic metaphysical speculation with which Plato's academy would have been associated (10.3–5, 15.268). The problem, from Isocrates' perspective, is that eristical disputation becomes an end in itself, rather than contributing to civic virtue.

Isocrates often describes the activities of a well-trained student as including *bouleuesthai,* which generally means "deliberation" or "taking good counsel." The term is from *euboulia,* which means good or wise counsel. Prior to Isocrates, Protagoras may have linked *euboulia* to the notion of "right discourse," *orthos logos* (Schiappa 1991, 184–85). And subsequent to Isocrates, in Aristotle's *Rhetoric,* the relationship between speech (*logos*) and judgment (*krisis*) is made explicit (1391b7). It is clear from texts spanning Isocrates' career that he saw deliberation concerning actions of the *polis* to be an important philosophical task. As Takis Poulakos notes in his recent book on Isocrates, "By bringing *phronein* in contact with *legein,* he made the affairs of the polis the object of reflection and gave wisdom a practical orientation" (1997, 69). Isocrates suggests that all teachers of philosophy agree that the well-educated person must acquire "the ability to deliberate" (2.51; see also 4.5). Isocrates equates *bouleuesthai* with rational policy-making, and he often gives advice on how to deliberate well. "The greatest incentive you can have to deliberation," he notes, "is to observe the misfortune from the lack of it" (1.35). In his eulogy for Evagoras, Isocrates attributes his success to the fact that "he spent most of his time in inquiring (*zētein*) and in pondering (*phrontizein*) and in taking counsel (*bouleuesthai*), for he believed that if he should prepare his intellect (*phronēsis*) well, all would be well with his kingdom also" (9.41). Similarly, he argued that rulers "reign well or ill according to the manner in which they equip their own minds (*gnōmas*); therefore, no athlete is so called upon to train his body as is a ruler to train his *psychē*" (2.10).

In contrast to his use of *bouleuesthai* and related terms, Isocrates rarely uses the word *dialegesthai,* which was a term commonly associated with philosophers and denotes "holding discussion." *Dialegesthai* becomes a "professionalized" verbal art in Plato's texts where it is formalized as *dialektikē,* or Dialectic (Timmerman 1993, 116–23). Both *dialegesthai* and *bouleuesthai* denote a process of deliberation and thought, but *dialegesthai* and later, dialectic, took on a sense of a private and often agonistic process, while *bouleuesthai* suggests a more public and evaluative activity — one that has the goal of arriving at "advice" concerning public policy. In a typical passage from *Antidosis,* Isocrates notes that "when danger threatens the city, they seek counsel from those who can speak best on the question at issue and act upon their advice" (15.248). Accordingly, from Isocrates' perspective, dialectic as practiced in Plato's academy, and later in Aristotle's Lyceum, amounts to eristical disputation and not *bouleuesthai.*

Isocrates even argues that he has doubts about whether the sort of teaching provided by Plato ought to be called "philosophy": "I do not think we should give the name *philosophia* to a study that has no immediate benefit for speaking (*legein*) or action (*prattein*); instead I call it mental exercise and preparation for philosophy" (15.266). When Isocrates notes, "I hold that what some people call 'philosophy' is not entitled to that name" (15.270), it scarcely can be doubted that he includes Plato in this group (Nehamas 1990, 4–5). How does Isocrates define "philosophy"? "My opinion is quite simple. Since it is not in human nature to acquire knowledge (*epistēmē*) that would make us certain what to do or say, I consider one wise who has the ability through conjecture (*doxai*) to attain the best choice: I call *philosophers* those that engage themselves with that from which this sort of practical wisdom (*phronēsis*) is speedily grasped" (15.271). In short, since complete certainty is unattainable, Isocrates suggests that only education aimed at developing practical wisdom warrants the title of philosophy. He elaborates on the description just quoted by describing the sorts of discourses appropriate for students to compose. As one might expect, Isocrates commends discourse that offers advice and counsel on civic affairs. In the process, he condemns a second set of his competitors.

The second rival practice he criticizes is that of some of "those who profess to teach political discourse" (*politikos logos*). These teachers are "indifferent to truth" (*alētheia*), but make extravagant promises about the power they can convey. They offer poorly written speeches to their students to memorize, they fail to consider the necessity of natural ability and practical experience, and they neglect the need for speeches to utilize "the right responses and achieve appropriate and novel form" (13.9–13). These teachers "encouraged their pupils to study political discourse, and then, disregarding the good qualities of this practice, took it on themselves to be instructors in troublemaking and greed" (13.20). The distinctions Isocrates makes between his teaching of "political discourse" and those of his rivals are significant, for they further delimit his vision of philosophy and distinguish it from what later will be canonized as the "Art of Rhetoric" by Aristotle (Too 1995).

Isocrates distances his students' and his own efforts to compose political discourse from those of his competitors using three criteria for evaluating discourse: style, content, and purpose (Rummel 1979). Isocrates considers style important because such elements as rhythm, melodious phrasing, and a compelling organizational pattern can have a positive psychological impact on the audience. Furthermore, "the Greeks were inclined to regard the beautiful form of a speech as guaranteeing the truth of its contents, just as they were apt to regard corporeal beauty as a sign of mental superiority" (Verdenius 1981, 122). Accordingly, it is reasonable to assume that Isocrates believed the more aesthetically pleasing the text is, the better the argument it constituted. As Rummel points out, however, style is the least important of the three criteria one can identify in Isocrates' writings (1979, 30). To the extent that form and content are separable, form is subservient to the content and moral purpose of political discourse.

Isocrates urged students of his *philosophia* to limit the "content" of their speeches to important and ethical matters (Too 1995, Poulakos 1997). For the most part, this means that he prefers deliberative oratory above all. He generally disparages forensic oratory as unimportant and self-serving, involving "petty matters" and "private contracts" (12.11). Isocrates criticizes display speeches praising "bumblebees or salt" as trifling and insignificant. But he does not reject all display oratory; in fact, several of Isocrates' own more famous essays are of this kind. To be honorable, such discourse must avoid overly eristical arguments and be aimed at ethical ends. Isocrates concludes *Busiris* with a peroration on arguing justly, suggesting that Polycrates' defense of Busiris is too paradoxical to be a good example for student-philosophers. His statement is not unlike some of the words with which Plato provides Socrates in the *Apology:* "I think it has now been made clear to you, even if you were previously in ignorance, that an accused person would sooner gain acquittal by not uttering a word than by pleading his case in this way. And, furthermore, this too is evident, that philosophy, which is already in mortal jeopardy and is hated, will be detested even more because of such discourses" (11.48–49). As Rummel notes, Isocrates' own epideictic speeches consistently address their subject matter with a careful eye toward the ethical lessons that can be drawn, regardless of the putative subject matter (1979, 30–31).

Isocrates' chief preference, however, is to write about "the affairs of Greece and of kings and of states" (12.11). In order "to speak or to write discourses (*logoi*) worthy of praise and honor," students must choose to write about matters that are "great and honorable and philanthropic and of the common interest" (15.276). The selection of such topics will compel students to draw upon examples that are equally noble. Familiarity with such material will, in modern terminology, condition or socialize students to handle their own affairs in a noble way, "so that speaking and thinking well will bring together the love of wisdom (*philosophōs*) and love of honor (*philotimōs*) to those well-disposed toward discourse" (15.277).

In practice, Isocrates' preference for deliberative discourse calls for his students to address contemporary practical problems facing the polity. He is not particularly interested in what we would call political theory; in fact, a passage in *Antidosis* appears to be a rebuke to Plato's *Laws* (de Vries 1953, 41): "You should acknowledge that thousands of Greeks and even barbarians can draft laws but very few can speak about the interest of the city in a manner worthy of Athens and of Greece. For this reason you should value those who make it their task to devise this kind of discourse more highly than those who propose and write down laws, since such discourse is rarer and more difficult and requires a wiser intellect, especially nowadays" (15.80–81). People prefer the oldest laws but the newest discourse (15.82), so Isocrates defends his choice of deliberative discourse because it is more difficult to formulate, thus benefiting the students, and because it does more to contribute to the public good (15.83–85). In what is perhaps a direct comment on Plato, Isocrates decries obscure writings suggesting that "the life of beggars and exiles is enviable." He declares that it is "absurd to try to persuade us of their political knowledge (*epistēmē*) through this kind of discourse, when they could give a demonstration in the area in which they advertise" (10.8–9). There is no honor in such discourse, Isocrates suggests, in part because there is no competition: "Those who lay a claim to wisdom and call themselves teachers should excel not in fields neglected by others but in matters where everyone is competing against them; this is where they should surpass amateurs" (10.9). Once again, Isocrates implies that studies that do not contribute to the common good are not worthy of the label of philosophy. Accordingly, only the study of political discourse that is aimed at addressing the great contingencies of public life will help students develop into good speakers and thinkers (cf. Too 1995, 10–35).

The purpose of discourse, according to Isocrates, is to contribute to civic virtue: both that of the speaker and of the *polis* the speaker addresses. The close connection between civic virtue and philosophy finds expression both in Isocrates' educational theory and in his discursive practice. In his address *To Demonicus,* Isocrates claims to have written a moral treatise: "I am going to counsel you on the objects to which young men should aspire and from what actions they should abstain" (1.5). Virtue (*aretē*), claims Isocrates, "is the one possession which abides with us in old age; it is better than riches and more serviceable than high birth; it makes possible what is for others impossible; it supports with fortitude that which is fearful to the multitude; and it considers sloth a disgrace and toil an honor" (1.7).

Indeed, the vast majority of Isocrates' texts are explicitly moral and political. He wrote *Panegyricus* when Athens' fortunes were at their worst. To end the battles among the various Greek states and to escape from "intolerable" circumstances of poverty, civil strife, and piracy, Isocrates advocated panhellenic unity to wage war against the incursions of Persia. He claimed that "I have singled out as the most excellent sort of discourse that which deals with the greatest affairs and, while best displaying the ability of those who speak, brings most advantage to those who hear; this discourse is of that sort" (4.4).

Isocrates' texts typically are assumed to have been composed for the sole purpose of providing his students with appropriate models to emulate. Such a view is mistaken, for many of his compositions addressed actual, not hypothetical audiences and were intended to move them toward specific actions. His essays were political and moral not only in content but also in their objectives. Isocrates urged young leaders such as Nicocles, Demonicus, and Alexander the Great to study philosophy and live just lives. Following the ill-conceived "Social War" he tried to persuade his fellow Athenians to reverse the policy of aggression. After the Thebans destroyed Plataea, Isocrates encouraged Athenians to help their long-time ally to rebuild. A long-standing opponent of the anti-Macedonian war party, he hailed the peace between Philip and Athens in 346 B.C.E. He wrote to encourage Timotheus to continue to pursue a milder and more democratic course of leadership than Timotheus' father had shown. His several discourses on behalf of panhellenic unity, urging that Greek city-states should cease warring against each other, became famous in his own time, and this theme remains his best known.

Though Isocrates was not as influential as active orators such as Demosthenes, Mathieu has argued that Isocrates, in fact, did influence Greek politics far more than did other philosophers and many orators of his own time (1925, 222–23). Mathieu rejects the belief that Isocrates' orations were merely the idealist dreams of an armchair critic. Instead, he contends that Isocrates directly influenced certain policy choices by the Athenian *polis* and played an important role in shaping public opinion for later reorganization of the Greek world (Mathieu 1925, 189–99, 208–24). De Romilly points out that the second Athenian Confederation was created in 377 B.C.E., "two years after Isocrates had written his *Panegyricus,* and it follows several of the suggestions he had made in that treatise" (1992b, 11). Some years later, Philip created the League of Corinth in which "Isocrates' influence is even more conspicuous":

> It shows in even more insistent precautions against the role of the leader. The freedom and autonomy of all members are firmly asserted. Philip is to be the leader, but as a purely personal charge: his country was not even a member of the league. And the League meant a common peace for all Greeks, but was expected to fight against the Persians: this twin purpose was in agreement with Isocrates' obstinate plea. It didn't work, for Philip died almost immediately afterwards. Isocrates himself was already dead. But the 4th century offers a convergence of ideas, which was largely due to his influence, and which almost took shape at the time of his death. (de Romilly 1992b, 11)

In short, there was parsimony between Isocrates' theory and practice: He advocated an active role in the *polis* through which wisdom is put to the service of the common good, and that is what he and his students did their best to do. The *philosophia* he preached was the *philosophia* he practiced.

Isocrates and Contemporary Pragmatism

My remaining task is to consider the implications that Isocrates' self-description and self-understanding might have for reformulating our conception of philosophy and the relevance of such a reformulation to the current turn to Pragmatism. I begin by noting that a more empathetic reading of Isocrates than has been practiced traditionally suggests that the battle between him and Plato (later, between him and Aristotle) is less accurately portrayed as

"Rhetoric versus Philosophy" than it is as between two competing views of higher education in general, and between two rival definitions of *philosophia* in particular (cf. Poulakos 1997, 69–73). It is important to recognize that the sort of professional vocabulary we take for granted today was far from stable during the sixth, fifth, and most of the fourth century B.C.E. in ancient Greece. Prior to Plato, those figures we typically call philosophers (from Thales to Socrates) were more likely to be called "sophists" than "philosophers" (Kerferd 1950, 8–10). Most of these figures led lives that defy the sort of easy categorization historians prefer. They moved from politics to religious mysticism to natural philosophy to anthropocentric studies without a blink. The fifth-century follower of Parmenides, Melissus of Samos, both wrote arguments extending Eleatic philosophy and defeated Pericles in a battle at sea. The point is that it was not unusual for people we now label "philosophers" to have been active in areas we now consider far afield from philosophy. But such estrangement is our problem, not theirs.

It is not until the fourth century B.C.E. that philosophy begins to be treated as a distinct profession (Charlton 1985; Havelock 1983, 7–82; Nehamas 1990; Robb 1994; Striker 1996, 5). Both Plato and Isocrates sought to "professionalize" and "disciplinize" the term *philosophia,* but in decidedly different ways. Interestingly enough, it was Isocrates "who educated fourth-century Greece," and it was Isocrates who exercised the more profound influence on how higher education was modeled throughout much of western history (Marrou 1956, 79–80; Finley 1975, 198–99). Yet it is Plato's vocabulary that we embrace today and that creates what Kenneth Burke calls a "terministic screen" (1966, 44–62) through which we tend to see Plato and Isocrates. It is ironic, indeed, that Isocrates consistently is viewed as a central figure in the early history of *Rhetoric*—a word he conspicuously avoided—while being largely ignored as a contributor to the history of *Philosophy*—a term he conspicuously embraced and promoted.

In the process of constructing a history of philosophy, contemporary historians have the option of whom to pick as their forebears (Rorty 1979, see esp. 131–39). If adding certain authors to the philosophical canon is to endorse the intellectual lineage with which such authors are associated, then Isocrates' day has arrived. Isocrates' vision of philosophy resonates nicely with a number of the beliefs and practices associated with contemporary Pragmatism. Three interrelated themes in Isocrates' writings that have obvious contemporary Pragmatist parallels are his regard for the importance of informed opinion (*doxa*) and doubts about certainty (*epistēmē*); his belief that pedagogy ought to be moral and aimed at preparing students for participation in civic affairs; and his general preference for practical over speculative philosophy.

To begin with, the quest for certainty promoted by early Positivists and some contemporary Realists is addressed by a variety of Pragmatist texts. There is a strong "Isocratean" flavor to Stephen Toulmin's rejection of the Platonic goal of certainty resulting from "geometrical" reasoning and his contention that philosophers need to return to the study of persuasive argumentation (Toulmin 1958). No doubt Isocrates would agree with John Dewey's claim that "there is no knowledge self-guaranteed to be infallible, since all knowledge is the product of special acts of inquiry" (1929, 193). And Isocrates would applaud efforts to describe science — the contemporary practice that most claims *epistēmē* — in terms of persuasively induced "solidarity" rather than in terms of "objective truth" (Rorty 1991, 35–45).

The parallels between Isocrates and recent efforts to reinvigorate the sociopolitical dimension of contemporary composition pedagogy have been noted explicitly in recent works by Jarratt (1991, 80–117), Jasper Neel (1988), and Kathleen Welch (1990, esp. 123–28). All three authors support the Isocratean notion that education ought to be "a study of how to make choices and a study of how choices form character and make good citizens" (Neel 1988, 211). In a similar vein, Frank Lentricchia (1983), Robert Scholes (1985), and Omar Swartz (1997) argue that viewing academic life as apolitical and somehow above and apart from the "real world" is intellectually indefensible and politically disabling. It is not surprising that two fine recent books on Isocrates both emphasize the relevance of Isocrates' doctrines for contemporary educational practices (Too 1995, 221–32; Poulakos 1997, 93–104).

Toulmin has proffered an eloquent argument for a return to "practical philosophy," the sort of philosophy that engages contemporary social concerns. Specifically, he suggests that the line between politics and philosophy (hence Rhetoric and Philosophy) is no longer helpful in an age when "matters of practice" are literally "matters of life and death" (1988, 343). Toulmin notes that contemporary "philosophers are increasingly drawn into public debates about environmental policy, medical ethics, judicial practice, or nuclear politics. . . . These practical debates are no longer 'applied philosophy': they are philosophy itself" (1988, 345). It is difficult not to hear the echo of Isocrates when Toulmin concludes by declaring that "it is time for philosophers to come out of their self-imposed isolation and reenter the collective world of practical life and shared human problems" (1988, 352). Similarly, Cornel West's call for an activist "neopragmatism" shares an Isocratean distaste for excessively obscure speculation and philosophy that eschews political involvement:

The goal of a sophisticated neopragmatism is to think genealogically about specific practices in light of the best available social theories, cultural critiques and historiographical insights and to act politically to achieve certain moral consequences in light of effective strategies and tactics. This form of neo-pragmatism explodes the preoccupation with transient vocabularies and discourses. . . . This focus indeed takes seriously the power-laden character of language — the ideological weight of certain rhetorics and the political gravity of various discourses. (1989, 209)

The previous paragraphs are intended to suggest, in a preliminary fashion, how the substantive arguments fueling the current "rhetorical turn" (Simons 1990) and the resurgence of Pragmatism help us to understand and appreciate Isocrates' conception of philosophy better, and vice versa. Furthermore, there is an important symbolic value in being able to point to an alternative to Plato's conception of philosophy that was alive and well in Athens at the same time. There are clear rhetorical advantages to being in a position to argue that today's call for a practical, politically engaged philosophy has ancient and venerable roots. In short, our understanding of the history and practice of philosophy will suffer as long as Isocrates' vision of *philosophia* is not considered as a live alternative to the Platonic-Aristotelian tradition.

As West notes, to historicize philosophy is to politicize it: "To tell a tale about the historical character of philosophy while eschewing the political content, role, and function of philosophies in various historical periods is to promote an ahistorical approach in the name of history" (1989, 208). Accordingly, as pragmatists revisit Isocrates' texts, it is important to acknowledge the ideological baggage that we do not want to carry (Too 1995, 234). As far as we know, women were not allowed in Isocrates' school. In a provocative rereading of Isocrates, Jane Sutton argues that his treatment of *logos* and the myth of the Amazon constructs a repressive image of women and femininity (1992, 100–101). Isocrates' school did not escape the sexism of his time. An Isocratean pedagogy oriented toward the production of public discourse should not be allowed to obscure the fact that important matters often have been marginalized by relegating them to a feminized, private sphere of discourse (Schiappa 1989). Furthermore, Isocrates' school was available only to the small class of wealthy patrons who could afford it. Only those properly endowed by nature (*physis*) were considered educable, and in practice this meant only members of the leisure class (Finley 1975, 195–99). Isocrates' orations often show a disdain for the general populace. He is equivocal about the Athenian form of democracy, and when the Athenian public fails to be swayed by his discourses, he appeals to monarchs such as Philip and Alexander to pursue his panhellenic dream. His panhellenic ambitions have been particularly controversial, for the price of unity for Greece in Isocrates' vision is an imperialist war against Persia. As Mathieu observed in 1925 (perhaps somewhat nervously), Isocrates found the most favor with certain German classicists who noted, with approval, the parallels between Isocrates' vision of panhellenism and advocates of German unity (1925, 220–21).

Nevertheless, Isocrates' texts remain an interesting and important chapter in the history of ideas: all the more so if we make the effort to understand Isocrates on his own terms rather than translate him into a Platonically defined tradition. His texts remind us that the process of definition and canon-formation are thoroughly contingent and rhetorical. *Philosophy* and *Rhetoric* are not "givens" but are "takens" (Dewey 1929, 178). That is, they are not naked data, but are important entitlements we use to indicate that an activity is to be taken *as* philosophy or *as* rhetoric. Naming a practice facilitates it becoming a site of power and knowledge. Especially when the terms are used as opposites and one is treated as superior to the other, the choice of what is taken as which is far from trivial. An important historical lesson afforded by Isocrates' texts is that what constitutes Philosophy or Rhetoric was not "given" in fourth-century B.C.E. Greece any more than it is today. For historians, this means we need to correct our accounts of ancient Greek thought that reify such categories and anachronistically impose them on the texts of the period. In particular, we should refuse to continue to repeat the Rhetoric versus Philosophy turf battle when interpreting the contributions of the ancient Greek Sophists. That particular map of ideas is no longer believable, nor is it helpful. The task for historians as well as contemporary theorists is not simply to switch our pledges of allegiance from Philosophy to Rhetoric or from Plato to the Sophists, but to call into question the assumption that the choice must be either one or the other.

Philosophically, pedagogically, and politically, the tasks Isocrates gave himself were unprecedented in the society in which he was born. His was the first permanent school of higher learning in ancient Greece. His was the first explicit effort in western history to influence the events around him strictly through the moral education of others and through written discourse. That he found new ways to contribute to the political life of the community in which he found himself suggests, for contemporary Pragmatists, that the last message provided by Isocrates' texts is that our own roles in society are limited only by our ingenuity.[6]

6. My thanks to David Dunlap, Mary Keehner, Steven Mailloux, Ramsey Eric Ramsey, William K. Rawlins, Kathleen E. Welch, and especially John T. Kirby for their helpful comments on earlier versions of this chapter.

Aristotle's Disciplining of Epideictic

WRITTEN WITH DAVID M. TIMMERMAN

Aristotle's formulation of three genres of rhetoric — deliberative, judicial, and epideictic — is assumed to represent, or at least to make sense of, fourth-century B.C.E. Greek rhetorical practice. Most historians take Greek rhetorical practice as a set of "givens" that Aristotle is merely describing, albeit in a more systematic manner than his predecessors, rather than as a prescription for future rhetorical practices. The argument in this chapter is that Aristotle's description of epideictic rhetoric is highly original and, in fact, redescribes and reconfigures a set of previously disparate rhetorical practices — the speech of praise (*enkōmion*), the festival oration (*panēgyrikos logos*), and the Athenian funeral oration (*epitaphios logos*) — into one large category of "epideictic" that was largely untheorized prior to Aristotle's *Rhetoric*. In particular, I examine how Aristotle's formulation of epideictic subsumes and subverts these ideologically significant genres of speech-making.

The chapter is divided into three parts. The first part briefly situates the study with respect to recent scholarship reexamining the history of early Greek rhetorical theory. The second part describes three rhetorical practices of the late fifth and fourth century B.C.E. as they were understood prior to Aristotle's *Rhetoric*. The third part of the chapter analyzes how Aristotle's *Rhetoric* redescribes these practices into subsets of the genre of epideictic rhetoric and identifies some of the social and political implications of such a redescription.

Once *named,* intellectual practices can become what we can loosely call a discipline; a common set of issues can be identified as its focus. Almost immediately, further categorization and specialization occur. Foucault refers to disciplines or institutions of knowledge as developing "authorities of delimitation" that, in effect, define the scope of permissible objects and objectives (1972, 40–49). Accordingly, in works such as Aristotle's *Rhetoric,* the scope and function of the discipline of Rhetoric are of central concern. Such works provide what Foucault calls "grids of specification"; systems according to which the objects and objectives of a discipline are "divided, contrasted, related, regrouped, classified," and so on (1972, 41–42). As a discipline matures, parameters exclude some concerns to focus efforts on others. Disciplinary vocabularies create "terministic screens" that select and direct attention in certain directions and deflect it from others (Burke 1966, 44–62). Accordingly, because it reconfigures the previous theoretical vocabulary that describes and categorizes the rhetorical practices of his time, Aristotle's formulation of epideictic in *Rhetoric* is important to understand both for a thorough history of early Greek rhetorical theory and as an interesting case study in the ideological work of theoretical treatises. Through his redescription, Aristotle combines three rhetorical practices under the rubric of epideictic and, I would contend, his text acts to blur the distinct social and political functions of these practices.

Enkōmion, Panegyric, Epitaphios Logos

The conceptual clarity of dividing discourse into the three categories of deliberative, judicial, and epideictic has proven to be compelling for students of Rhetoric over the ages. In the sense that this act of description and category-construction by Aristotle facilitated his discussion of the characteristics of each genre and its relevant subject matter, there is no question that his categories have proven useful. However, Aristotle was not merely repeating commonly understood ways of describing the rhetorical practices of his time. As Eugene Garver notes, "Aristotle finds the existence of the three kinds of rhetoric as unproblematic as he finds most of his conclusions," yet his formulation of these categories is "a large achievement" in the conceptualization of rhetoric (1994, 52). In particular, his description of epideictic rhetoric is original in important respects. First, his treatment was the first effort that we know of to define and describe a discrete genre of rhetorical practice called "epideictic." Second, the manner in which he combines three different practices (*enkōmion, panegyric,* and *epitaphios*) was an original synthesis that offered a somewhat different understanding of the social and political functions of such discourse than what can be detected from the available historical evidence. I turn now to a brief discussion of each type as a means of viewing the rhetorical landscape prior to Aristotle's *Rhetoric*.

ENKŌMION

The verb *enkōmiazein* means to praise, extol, or laud. The noun *enkōmion* originally was a term used to describe a poem celebrating a victory in competition. In fact, there are no extant examples of a prose composition being called an *enkōmion* prior to Gorgias' *Helen* in the late fifth century B.C.E. (Blass 1887, 72; Duncan 1938, 405). As Dover notes, "*enkōmion* and *enkōmiazein* are freely used in the fourth century of formal praise in prose or verse, but in fifth-century usage *enkōmion* is especially a poem celebrating someone's victory" (1968a, 237). Such use is found in Pindar and Aristophanes, but not in any extant prose writer (see Harvey 1955, 163–64). Though it is possible that "*enkōmion*" was added to the formal title at some later date, Gorgias explicitly calls his discourse "an *enkōmion* of Helen" in the final sentence of the speech—a self-reference that implies a relationship between his speech and the poetic tradition. Given that subsequent to Gorgias' *Helen* more and more prose writers began to refer to compositions as *enkōmia*, the most probable inference is that Gorgias—intentionally or otherwise—helped to inaugurate a tradition of prose *enkōmia* (see chapter 7).

Though Gorgias calls his speech an *enkōmion*, his *Helen* has little in common with poetic *enkōmia* celebrating victories. Only about one-tenth of the speech (3–5) is devoted to praise of Helen. Most of the speech is a fairly rationalistic effort to exonerate Helen from the charge of starting the Trojan War by running away with Paris. Gorgias describes his purpose in his introduction as "I wish to offer reasoning by means of argument to free the accused of blame and to show that her critics are lying and to demonstrate the truth and to put an end to ignorance" (adapted from Kennedy 1991, 284). He argues that Helen was not responsible for her actions because she was the victim of fate or the wishes of the Gods, or else she was taken by force, or compelled by force of speech (*logos*), or maddened by love. Most historians of rhetoric have found the most interesting part of the speech to be the section on *logos* where the speech engages in relatively systematic, secular, physical explanation and description. The speech is not particularly notable for its praise of Helen but as one of the first serious accounts of the workings of *logos* on the psyche.

Even though Gorgias' *Helen* only partially resembles the poetic tradition of *enkōmia*, the rhetorical tradition after Gorgias expanded the use of the term *enkōmion* to include prose speeches of praise. It is important to recognize that, during the classical era, Greece was experiencing a rapid rise in literacy, and composition habits of prose were evolving quickly during the fifth and fourth centuries B.C.E. (Enos 1993). Gorgias' texts, in particular, suggest that the sort of compositional and stylistic expectations that would later be firmly associated with specific genres of prose discourse were far from fixed in the late fifth and early fourth centuries. Indeed, poetic and prose styles, mythical and logical appeals freely mixed in the texts of the Old Sophists in a way that would be considered odd a few decades later (Jarratt 1991, 31–61).

Gorgias' *Helen* was composed sometime between 415 and 393 B.C.E. (Blass 1887, 72–75).[1] Around 370 B.C.E., Isocrates composed his *Helen,* traditionally categorized as an *enkōmion* (Van Hook 1945, 59). What is significant about both speeches is that each author refers to his speech as an *enkōmion.* Isocrates praises Gorgias, but claims that Gorgias committed a small mistake: "Although he asserts that he has written an *enkōmion* of Helen, it turns out that he has actually spoken a defense (*apologia*) of her conduct . . . for a plea in defense (*apologeisthai*) is appropriate only when the defendant is charged with a crime, whereas we praise those who excel in some good quality" (adapted from Van Hook 1945, 67).

Here we have a remarkably clear example of what I mean by the disciplining of discourse. A poetic tradition of celebration and praise is adapted into prose by Gorgias. Interestingly enough, Gorgias does so primarily by referring to his speech as an *enkōmion* in his conclusion. Gorgias' speech becomes "paradigmatic" in Kuhn's sense; namely, that it becomes a shared example that later writers imitate and further develop. Indeed, late fifth-century and early fourth-century speakers must have followed suit because, as we learn from both Plato's *Symposium* (177a–c) and Isocrates' *Helen* (12), speeches of praise were composed on such topics as bumble bees, salt, and mythical figures like Heracles. The genre of prose *enkōmia* must have still been evolving in the late 360s B.C.E. as Isocrates claims that an effort "to eulogize in prose" (*dia logōn enkōmiazein*) the virtues of a mortal man has not been attempted previously (*Evagoras* 8). Isocrates is very much aware of the relationship of prose *enkōmia* to the poetic tradition (Race 1987), as he argues that his task is far more difficult than it would be for a poet. Not only can poets make use of exotic words, figures of speech, and mythical figures, they also can charm their listeners with meter and rhythm; while Isocrates cannot share in any of these advantages (*Evagoras* 9–10).

Plato is also aware of the close connection of the poetic and prose traditions

---

1. Aristotle reports in the *Rhetoric* that Gorgias also wrote an *enkōmion* to the Greek city of Elis, though nothing more than the opening phrase of the speech survives (1416a1).

of *enkōmia*. Though we do not know precisely when Plato's *Symposium* was composed, it was probably sometime after 385 B.C.E. (Allen 1991, 4–5; Guthrie 1975, 365; cf. Nails 1995). When Eryximachus proposes the theme of love for speeches in *Symposium,* songs of praise composed by the poets are described as analogous to the written prose speeches of praise by the Sophists, such as Prodicus's lesson about Heracles (177a–b). Indeed, the speeches given in *Symposium* are offered as *enkōmia* of the god of Love (177a–e). Thus by the first half of the fourth century the practice of prose *enkōmia* is sufficiently well established that educators such as Isocrates and Plato can cite common examples and refer to the genre's poetic antecedents. Both Plato's and Isocrates' texts indicate an awareness of expectations associated with different genres of discourse. Nonetheless, it is not until the later half of the fourth century that one finds texts such as Aristotle's *Rhetoric* or the *Rhetoric to Alexander* offering what can be described as explicit "rules for the genre" of *enkōmia* (Dover 1980, 12).

With hindsight, Isocrates' *Helen* and Plato's *Symposium* can be placed in a period of time after the genre of prose *enkōmia* was named and recognized but prior to any systematic or in-depth theoretical treatment of prose genres. Thus, Isocrates and Plato provide good exemplars of *enkōmia* that are useful for the purpose of understanding the context in which Aristotle encountered and studied contemporary rhetorical practices. How Aristotle redescribed the genre is addressed below. For the moment it is sufficient to note that the speeches by such writers as Gorgias, Prodicus, Plato, and Isocrates dubbed by themselves or others as examples of *enkōmia* were both morally and educationally oriented. Though we know nothing of the content of the reported *enkōmia* of salt and bees, we do know that the *enkōmia* that survived had a strong moral message. The most salient examples of prose *enkōmia* for Aristotle's generation were openly didactic in their praise of personal qualities of such mythical figures such as Heracles and Helen in addition to those of real historical figures such as Evagoras and Socrates. Even speeches that are not strictly speeches of praise, such as Gorgias' *Helen* and Prodicus's *Choice of Heracles,* offer their listeners instruction on their respective topics — in Gorgias' case, the workings of *logos;* in Prodicus's case, the value of a life of virtue. Implicitly in the other surviving examples of *enkōmia,* and explicitly in the writings of Isocrates, the importance of the genre is to praise actions and qualities that the audience should emulate. Takis Poulakos argues that Isocrates' *Evagoras,* for example, functions deliberatively because it uses the opportunity to praise Evagoras as a means "to persuade Nicocles to pursue actively the study of philosophy" (1987, 325). As Erika Rummel notes, Isocrates' *enkōmia* consistently address their subject in order to draw out ethical lessons, regardless of the putative topic (1979, 30).

PANĒGYRIKOS LOGOS

The word *panēgyris* refers to a gathering of the whole people in a single location. The dominant types of such gatherings were festivals held to commemorate particular events or institutions and athletic games such as those held at Olympia, Pythia, Nemea, and Isthmia. Though speeches probably were a common event at such gatherings, the specific name of *panēgyrikos logos* is not recorded prior to the fourth century B.C.E. Gorgias' speech at the Olympic festival in 408 is referred to by Aristotle as an *Olympikos logos* (*Rhet.* 1414b31) and Lysias's speech in 388 is traditionally titled *Olympiakos* (Lamb 1930, 684), even though later commentators refer to both speeches as panegyrics. According to Liddell and Scott (1940, 1297) and data gathered from the *Thesaurus Linguae Graecae* database (cf. Berkowitz and Squitier 1990), Isocrates may have been the first to give a specific name to speeches given at such gatherings by naming his famous appeal for Hellenic unity *Panēgyrikos* in 380 B.C.E. This was Isocrates' most famous composition and may well have popularized the use of the term to describe a particular type of speech. Isocrates uses the term *generically* to refer to festival speeches in his *Antidosis* (46), probably written about 354 B.C.E., and again in his *Panathenaicus* (263) finished about 339 B.C.E. Subsequently, speeches given at such events commonly came to be referred to as panegyrics (*panēgyrikoi logoi*) by Aristotle and other rhetorical writers.

Kennedy lists what became the traditional elements in such speeches: "A panegyric, the technical name for a festival speech, consists normally of praise of the god associated with the festival, praise of the city in which the festival is held, praise of the contest itself and of the crown awarded, and finally, praise of the king or officials in charge" (1963, 167). However, an examination of panegyric speeches prior to Aristotle's *Rhetoric* reveals an additional characteristic: early panegyrics contained an unmistakable deliberative dimension. That is, they were openly political in orientation and aimed at encouraging the audience to follow a course of action.

The earliest example about which we have any information is Gorgias' Olympic speech, believed to have been given in 408 B.C.E. Plutarch refers to the speech as being about "concord among the Greeks" (Sprague 1972, 49), which would be a fitting topic for a panhellenic gathering such as the Olympic games. In 408, six years after Athens' disastrous expedition to Sicily (Gorgias' home) and just three years after the anti-democratic revolution of 411 B.C.E. in Athens, the Peloponnesian War was still in progress as fighting continued sporadically throughout Greece (Sealey 1976, 348–384). Concerning the details of Gorgias' address we can only conjecture, though speeches on the same topic by Lysias and Isocrates may be instructive.

Lysias's *Olympiakos* of 388 B.C.E. is chronicled by two sources, Dionysius of Halicarnassus (*Lysias* 29) and Diodorus Siculus (14.109). Both make the political purposes of the speech very clear. Lysias was originally a native of Syracuse, but his family settled as resident aliens in the Peiraeus—the most important of the harbors of Athens located a few miles from the city. Lysander's successful blockade and defeat of Athens in 404 B.C.E. brought famine, humilation, and tyranny to Athens. The rule of the so-called "Thirty" affected Lysias directly—his brother was executed and Lysias was forced to escape to Megara after being arrested. Less than ten years later, the peace that was supposed to accompany the end of the Peloponnesian War was shattered by the start of the Corinthian War in 395 B.C.E.—a war that was still in progress when Lysias gave his address. His Olympic oration therefore presented him with an opportunity to offer a speech that his status as a resident alien denied him at home: "Debarred at Athens, as a resident alien, from public speech, he seizes the opportunity allowed him at Olympia of arousing hostility against the unscrupulous master of his native city, Syracuse, and of his Sicilian compatriots" (Lamb 1930, 682). His particular focus was on Dionysius the powerful ruler at Syracuse and Artaxerxes of Persia. After paying tribute to Heracles, the founder of the Olympic contests, Lysias shifts his focus and explains his reason for doing so: "But I think it behooves a man of principle and civic worth to be giving his counsel on the weightiest questions, when I see Greece in this shameful plight, with many parts of her held subject by the foreigner, and many of her cities ravaged by despots" (*Olympic Oration* 3, in Lamb 1930).

Lysias did more than address and praise the general theme of Greek unity, he advocated the cessation of the Corinthian War, the removal of Dionysius as "tyrant" of Sicily, and a return to the example of their ancestors when Athens led the effort to drive the Persians out of Greece. Though the complete text of Lysias's speech no longer survives, Dionysius of Halicarnassus reports that he urged the crowd to tear down the fine tents that housed the delegates Dionysius had dispatched as his representatives to the festival (*Lysias* 29). In a similar yet less violent vein, Diodorus Siculus reports that Lysias "urged the multitude not to admit to the sacred festival the representatives from a most impious tyranny" (14.109).

The most famous panegyric is, of course, that by Isocrates. Ironically, Isocrates almost certainly did not present his *Panēgyrikos* in person, as tradition holds that he did not deliver his speeches in public. It is possible that someone presented the speech for him. Additionally, written copies were widely distributed among the reading public (Norlin 1928, 119). Not unlike Gorgias and Lysias before him, Isocrates forcefully argues for Greek unity and an end to war. Specifically, he advocates a policy for Athens and Sparta to unite in opposition to the great power of Persia. As George Norlin puts it, "The *Panegyricus* was published at a time when the power and influence of Athens were at a low ebb and when the Hellenic world generally was in a sorry state" (1928, 116). A few years earlier, the Greeks had formally submitted themselves to the rule of Persia in order to end war and avoid famine, yet bloodshed among the Greek city-states continued. Though the speech spends considerable time retelling the history of Athens and recounting the glory days of Greece when Hellenic unity defeated Persia, Isocrates turns to the specifics of current events, first offering examples of ill-founded conflicts to illustrate the dangers of current policies, then offering examples of recent Greek military victories against the Persians to prove success is possible (134 ff.). There is no question about the deliberative orientation of the address. He discusses a number of specific contemporary events and policies, and it is clear that his call for Greek unity and war against Persia is a policy urged *now* (380 B.C.E.): "So it seems to me that the motives which summon us to enter upon a war against them are many indeed; but chief among them is the present opportunity, which we must not throw away.... Indeed what further advantage could we desire to have on our side when contemplating a war against the King beyond those which are now at hand?" (160).

Some historians argue that Isocrates' *Panēgyrikos* was indeed successful *as* deliberative discourse. Mathieu contends that Isocrates directly influenced Greek politics through his writings, and played an important part in shaping public opinion for later policies that reorganized the Greek world (1925, 189–99, 208–24). M. L. W. Laistner also credits Isocrates for contributing to the "practical politics" of Athens both through his public writings — most notably his *Panegyricus, De Pace,* and *Panathenaicus* — and his tutelage of such important leaders as Timotheus (1930, 129–30).

In short, the term *panēgyrikos* is used only rarely prior to Aristotle's *Rhetoric*. It appears it may have originated with Isocrates naming his treatise *Panēgyrikos* in 380 B.C.E., though the term caught on as a category for all speeches given at festivals. The best-known examples of panegyrics prior to Aristotle's *Rhetoric* include the Olympic addresses of Gorgias and Lysias, along with Isocrates' *Panēgyrikos,* all of which explicitly addressed important political topics and at least two of which advocated a specific course of action to be followed by the audience.

EPITAPHIOS LOGOS

The *epitaphios logos* was a funeral oration given periodically during wartime by leading Athenian figures. Though many cultures produce eulogies for the dead, the *epitaphios* was a distinctly Athenian rhetorical practice (Loraux 1986). Thucydides' description of Pericles' Funeral Oration includes details concerning how Athens handled the death of her soldiers: "When the remains have been laid away in the earth, a man chosen by the state, who is regarded as best endowed with wisdom and is foremost in public esteem, delivers over them an appropriate eulogy (*epainos*). After this the people depart. In this manner they bury; and throughout the war, whenever occasion arose, they observed this custom" (2.34.6).[2] The *epitaphioi* probably began in the 460s and remained an important Athenian institution at least until 322 B.C.E. (Ziolkowski 1981, 13–21; Loraux 1986). Nicole Loraux (1986) argues in her highly influential work on the *epitaphios* that Athen's military and political demise after its surrender to Antipater in 322 B.C.E. led to the decline of the importance of the *epitaphios* as anything more than a literary genre. While the Athenian democracy was intact, however, the *epitaphios* was an important political institution.

Surviving examples of *epitaphioi* are few in number and somewhat problematic as historical sources (Loraux 1986, 8–14). Thucydides (2.35) provides a reconstructed version of Pericles' Funeral Oration given in 431 B.C.E. that, despite being a reconstruction, remains as the most famous example of the *epitaphios*. There remains only a small fragment of an *epitaphios* composed by Gorgias late in the fifth century B.C.E., though as a non-Athenian he would not have been able to perform it except as a demonstration of his skills.[3] Lysias wrote an *epitaphios* during the Corinthian War, probably in 392 B.C.E. Some historians suggest that, as a resident alien, he would probably not have been selected to present an offical *epitaphios;* other historians suggest that he may have written the speech for someone else to give, while still others say that Lysias wrote it purely as a rhetorical exercise (Lamb 1930, 28–29). Plato

2. All translations of Thucydides are based on the Loeb translations by Smith (1919–23).

3. For an interesting reading of Gorgias' *epitaphios* that positions it as simultaneously affirming and subverting the sort of Athenian jingoism typical of the genre of *epitaphios,* see Takis Poulakos: "Gorgias' *Epitaphios* is governed by the simultaneous glorification of two co-existing but contradictory political formations, the politics of city-state imperialism and the politics of Hellenic imperialism. Marking a rift within the political subject produced by these two political formations, the discourse of glorification challenges the sovereignty of both" (1989b, 96).

wrote a sample *epitaphios* in his *Menexenus* sometime after 387 B.C.E., but it is clear from the introduction and his position on flattery in the *Gorgias* that Plato was mocking the institution of the *epitaphios* (Allen 1984, 319–27). Demosthenes gave an *epitaphios* in 338 B.C.E. after the battle of Chaeronea, though a few historians dispute the authenticity of the surviving manuscript (DeWitt 1949, 3–5). We also have parts of an *epitaphios* given by Hyperides in 322 B.C.E. early in Athens' effort to rebel against Macedonia after the death of Alexander the Great.

Despite the problems facing the historical reconstruction of the *epitaphios,* the commonalities among the extant texts and other historical evidence about the speeches allow us to identify some of the social and political functions the *epitaphioi* played in Athenian culture. Kennedy contends that a particular set of topics (*topoi*) and a particular arrangement of those *topoi* appears to have developed within the *epitaphioi* over time: "Pericles' opening words clearly indicate that a traditional pattern was expected, beginning with a commendation of the custom of such speeches and continuing on to the deeds of ancestors and then of the present generation. From the accounts in later rhetoricians it appears that the usual structure was threefold: praise, lament (sometimes a denial of the propriety of lamentation), consolation" (1963, 155). Loraux likewise notes the stability of these *topoi* across the extant funeral orations and contends that "the unity of the genre is constructed out of these 'commonplaces'" (1986, 223). The repetition of these *topoi* in a setting that brought together all Athenians on a fairly regular basis performed important sociopolitical functions of defining Athenian identity, justifying the loss of life caused by war, and consoling the bereaved. Loraux argues that "the funeral oration must be regarded as an integral part of Athenian political practice: no doubt the epitaphioi tend to autonomize *hē polis;* but if the Athenians conceived of themselves as a city through the mediation of this entity, it is certainly a political act that they are performing in listening to the oration" (1986, 336).

In the case of Pericles' Funeral Oration, the political aspects of the speech are hard to miss: Athens is a state worthy of the ultimate sacrifice and those who have given it should be honored. Pericles praises Athenian democracy and the manner in which that democracy leads to better relations between its citizens (Thucydides 2.37). He praises Athens for its superiority in terms of leisure activities and the training of its soldiers for battle. He praises Athens for the character of its citizens, in particular the character they demonstrate through involvement in public affairs: "for we alone regard the man who takes no part in public affairs, not as one who minds his own business, but as good for nothing" (Thucydides 2.40). All of these bring Pericles to praise Athens for its greater grandeur and power in comparison to its neighbors. Pericles concludes this section by explaining his purpose in giving such an extended praise of the Athenian state: "It is for this reason that I have dwelt upon the greatness of our city; for I have desired to show you that we are contending for a higher prize than those who do not enjoy such privileges in like degree" (Thucydides 2.42).

After establishing the worth of Athens, Pericles moves on to the individuals who have died on her behalf. These individuals and their sacrifice are described, honored, and praised. Pericles states that these men "bore themselves after a manner that befits our city" and that they acted with "manly courage." And Pericles declares that those who have died have more than made up for any "harm they have done by their private lives" (Thucydides 2.42). This section concludes with what Kennedy has praised as "one of the most emotional, and perhaps finest, sentences in Greek prose" (1963, 156): "And then when the moment of combat came, thinking it better to defend themselves and suffer death rather than to yield and save their lives, they fled, indeed, from the shameful word of dishonor, but with life and limb stood stoutly to their task, and in the brief instant ordained by fate, at the crowning moment not of fear but of glory, they passed away" (Thucydides 2.42).

Pericles then addresses himself directly to those who have survived. He challenges his audience to make those who have fallen their examples, to be lovers of Athens and to likewise meet her enemies with great courage. He encourages parents who have lost sons to view their loss as an honor: "It is to be accounted good fortune when men win, even as these now, a most glorious death" (Thucydides 2.44). He comforts the widows and brothers and sisters of the fallen in similar fashion. Finally, he declares that the state will "maintain their children at the public expense until they grow to manhood" (Thucydides 2.46).

The *epitaphioi* thus served several purposes: To valorize and make heroes out of those who had fallen in battle, to validate the ongoing sacrifices of the Athenians for their country, and to praise Athens and Athenian values as worthy of the sacrifices of her people. Particularly in a democracy where persuasion must replace force, the *epitaphios* played an important persuasive function to maintain the will of the citizenry to meet the ongoing institutional needs of Athens (e.g., finances, soldiers, unity), reinforce commitment to Athenian-style democracy, support the current military policies (whether imperialistic or defensive) and, in short, to assure the continued existence of Athens as a political institution (Loraux 1986; T. Poulakos 1989, 1990).

Such purposes are supported by reference to the *epitaphios* attributed to Lysias. The speech was composed early in the Corinthian War (395–386 B.C.E.), and most of the oration is devoted to a recounting of the battles between Athens and her allies and Sparta. Statements within the oration indicate that the practice of funeral orations had become institutionalized by this point. The speaker notes at the beginning that his oration will be placed in comparison to the orations that have preceded it (2). A similar statement is found at the outset of the funeral oration of Demosthenes (60.2). Lysias begins the oration by presenting a clear rationale for the address: "For they also are events which all men ought to remember, glorifying them in their songs, and describing them in the sage sayings of worthy minds; honouring them on such occasions as this, and finding in the achievements of the dead so many lessons for the living" (*Funeral Oration* 3, in Lamb 1930). In modern terms, we can say that the *epitaphios* became an important cultural institution that played an important role in socializing citizens as to what it meant to be Athenian.

Lysias' oration, like that of Pericles, includes an explicit charge to the living that evidences its political character. The speaker describes those who have fallen as the most happy of men, and the honor they have received as a result of "every man's envy" (*Funeral Oration* 79, in Lamb 1930). "We have but one way, as it seems to me, of showing our gratitude to those who lie here: it is to hold their parents in the same high regard as they did, to be as affectionate to their children as though we were ourselves their fathers, and to give such support to their wives as they did while they lived" (*Funeral Oration* 75, in Lamb 1930). Thus, the actions of the soldiers are glorified, and the living are charged to honor them, to regard their efforts as the most noble efforts possible for Athenians, and to duplicate the fallen's love for Athens in their own lives.

Plato was the first theorist we know of to draw critical attention to the political function of the *epitaphios logos*. Prior to presenting his own funeral oration, Plato portrays Socrates as making the following (arguably cynical) comments to Menexenus:

> Actually, Menexenus, in many ways it's a fine thing to die in battle. A man gets a magnificent funeral even if he dies poor, and people praise him even if he was worthless. Wise men lavish praise on him, and not at random but in speeches prepared long in advance, and the praise is so beautiful that although they speak things both true and untrue of each man, the extreme beauty and diversity of their words bewitches our souls. For in every way, they eulogize the city and those who died in battle and all our forebears, and even us who are still alive. (*Menexenus* 234c–235a, translation by Allen 1984)

Plato has Socrates claim that Pericles' consort, Aspasia, actually taught him the *epitaphios* he is about to present. Most commentators believe that such a claim is a jest intended to further lampoon the genre of the *epitaphios*, though recent work by feminist scholars takes the claim more seriously, particularly in light of other historical evidence of Aspasia's significance and influence (Glenn 1994; Henry 1995).

Socrates' oration follows the standard pattern of praising the fallen for their birth, their education, and finally their deeds. Included is praise for the Athenian political structure as nurturing such qualities and actions. The oration recounts past Athenian military campaigns, given in some detail, but often containing significant anachronisms. The fallen are praised for their courage and wealth, beauty, and strength (246e). The children of the fallen possess a "noble and splendid treasure" that exceeds any monetary inheritance or other distinctions (247b). The final sections include a charge to the state and to the survivors. Only by bearing the loss of their loved ones with joy will the survivors live up to the honor of the dead (247c). "Socrates" exhorts the state to care for the children and parents of the dead, children to imitate their fathers, and parents to "have no fear for themselves" but to trust the state for their well being (248d–e). The relationship of the state to the fallen is described: "And thus, in simple fact, she stands towards the fallen in the position of son and heir, towards the sons in that of father, and towards the parents of the dead in that of guardian, thus exercising towards all all manner of care throughout all time" (249c).

Despite the critical preface to the *epitaphios* found in Plato's *Menexenus,* the speech was treated with respect by Dionysius of Halicarnassus and by Hermogenes centuries later. Cicero reports that the speech was so popular that it was read publicly every year in Athens (*Orator* 44.151), rather as Lincoln's Gettysburg Address is often recited in local settings on the Fourth of July in the United States. R. E. Allen argues that our understanding of the *Menexenus* should be shaped by juxtaposing the text with Plato's *Gorgias.* From such a perspective, the *epitaphios* is "base rhetoric" because it engages in mere flattery and does not tell the truth. Despite Plato's condemnation of the genre of *epitaphioi,* Allen points out Plato still produced a fine example of its kind (1984, 320–21).

It is not necessary to describe the *epitaphioi* of Demosthenes and Hyperides other than to note that they also address a common set of *topoi* and, particularly given the wartorn era in which they were presented, played an important role in reinforcing Athenian values and identity during a time of political stress. Other than emphasizing the political importance of the *epitaphios,* it remains only to observe that the genre was remarkably successful in molding subsequent Greek opinions about the glory of Athens. Loraux argues that the *topoi* of the *epitaphios* became well known and influential for centuries after

Athens lost all significant military and political power; she traces how the *epitaphios* evolved after 322 B.C.E. into a declamation topic yet continued to influence Greek attitudes about the reputation of Athens (1986, 252–62).

Aristotle's Reconfiguration: From Politics to Aesthetics

Aristotle's *Rhetoric* is the first theoretical explication of a genre called epideictic. I contend that Aristotle's use of the term *epideiktikē* in *Rhetoric* redescribes and reconfigures a set of rhetorical practices and turns epideictic discourse into what Foucault calls an "object of discourse" (1972). Naming is never neutral, and the choice to describe the *enkōmion, panēgyrikos logos,* and *epitaphios logos* under the rubric of "epideictic" has significant consequences.

A key to understanding Aristotle's disciplining of epideictic is recognizing how the term *epideiktikē* is used and transformed by him. The earliest extant use of the word is in Plato's *Sophist* (224b5), where it is used to describe "the art of display" that helps to define the profession of the Sophists. The *Sophist* was one of Plato's later dialogues, however, and the absence of the word in earlier texts that survive suggests that it *may* have been prompted by fourth-century Sophists and has been applied only with hindsight to those of the previous century. *Epideiktikē* might have been yet another example of Plato's original and prolific construction of *-ikē* words to designate specific arts or skills (Ammann 1953; Chantraine 1956, 97–151).

Cole contends that the word "epideictic" is part of a later developed standard terminology that has its roots in the "preanalytic stage" of the history of rhetoric. He suggests that what marks a speech as an *epideixis* is that it is *written to be presented* rather than the quality of "showing off" (1991a, 89). The verb *epideiknunai* is typically translated as "to display" or "to show," and *epideixis* denotes a particular exhibition or demonstration. Most commentators on the history of epideictic emphasize the performance aspect of the classical conception of epideictic (Beale 1978; Burgess 1902). As Cole points out, prior to Aristotle the word *epideixis* was used to designate a quality or characteristic of discourse rather than a genre of discourse. There is no evidence that anyone ever described a genre of rhetorical practice with the term "epideictic" prior to Aristotle.

The semantic field associated with *epideiktikē* therefore was primarily aesthetic and emphasized the performance aspect of the genre rather than the content of the speeches. As a typical example, the adjective *epideiktikōs* was used by Isocrates in reference to oratory that is "elaborated with extreme care" and that evidenced style in contrast to oratory that was plain (*Panegyricus* 11).

Isocrates employed the term as he contrasted his discourse with that of "the sophists." While their discourse evidenced mere display his was of the highest quality because it addressed the most significant topics while maintaining a high degree of style, "I have singled out as the highest kind of oratory that which deals with the greatest affairs and, while best displaying (*epideiknumi*) the ability of those who speak, brings most profit to those who hear" (*Panegyricus* 4).

Two passages in *Rhetoric* discuss the genre of epideictic in some detail: Book 1, chapter 3 describes the three kinds of rhetoric Aristotle discusses — deliberative, judicial, and epideictic. Book 1, chapter 9 is devoted wholly to discussing epideictic. By contrast, Aristotle devotes five chapters to discussing deliberative rhetoric (1359a30–1366a22) and six chapters to judicial rhetoric (1368b1–1377b12).

Students of Aristotle's *Rhetoric* know well book 1, chapter 3. In it this chapter lays out a description of the aims of discourse that have been described as coming close to representing "universals in the analysis of discourse" (Kennedy 1995, 730). A speech situation consists of a speaker, a discourse, and an audience. Each type of rhetoric can be distinguished by its distinctive temporal orientation, subject, and the type of audience action called for:

Type of Rhetoric	Temporal Orientation	Means	End	Audience
Deliberative	Future	Exhort/Dissuade	Expediency	Judge (*kritēs*)
Judicial	Past	Accuse/Defend	Justice	Judge
Epideictic	Present	Praise/Blame	Honorable	Spectator

Most commentators agree that Aristotle's description of deliberative and judicial rhetoric more or less correctly corresponds to Athenian rhetorical practices in the assembly (*ekklēsia*), the council (*boulē*), and such judicial settings as the popular people's courts (*dikastēria*) (Ober 1989, 127–48). Discussion in judicial and deliberative settings typically was followed by a nearly immediate vote on an accusation, motion, or decree, so that the audience served as judges (*kritai*) and were empowered to take action on the matter at hand. Since direct and immediate action was not normally associated with *enkōmia*, panegyrics, or *epitaphioi*, Aristotle describes the audience member for such speeches as a "spectator" (*theōros*) — not unlike an audience for a poetry performance or the theater. The similiarity is no accident, for Aristotle's description of epideictic rhetoric as *prose* speeches of praise and blame reproduces the longstanding tradition of *poetry* of praise and blame, called *ainos* or *epainos* and *psogos*, respectively (Nagy 1979, 222–42).

Aristotle's description of epideictic in 1.3 is not unqualified.[4] Regarding the audience's spectator status, Aristotle acknowledges that sometimes the audience must make decisions about the speaker's performance (though it should be noted that this is an aesthetic rather than a political judgment). Regarding the temporal orientation of each type of rhetoric, Aristotle says, "speakers praise or blame in regard to existing qualities" but notes that speakers remind audiences of the past and project future actions when it is appropriate to do so (1358b18). Nonetheless, Aristotle's notion of epideictic rhetoric is generally understood as describing the audience as *mere* spectators to discourse that has little or no consequence: "Those who go to be amused or interested by the show-speeches, or *epideixeis,* the Panegyrics (in two senses), funeral orations, burlesques, or whatever other form may be taken by speeches composed merely to display skill in composition without practical interest" (Cope 1877, 52; see also Cope 1867, 121).

Aristotle's description of epideictic in 1.3 arguably does not do justice to the range of rhetorical objectives and activities previously described by *enkōmion, panēgyrikos logos,* and *epitaphios logos* (Kennedy 1994, 62; see also Carter 1991, Duffy 1983, and Poulakos 1988). As Garver observes, "pure induction observing Athenian rhetorical practice would never come up with precisely these three kinds" of rhetoric — deliberative, judicial, and epideictic (1994, 93).[5] In an important sense, it is misleading to treat *enkōmion,* panegyric, *epitaphios,* and epideictic as interchangable categories, as Aristotle and some of his commentators did (Cope 1867, 121–22). The two most significant characteristics to emphasize are how the audience members are conceptualized as passive spectators and how the relationship of the speaker to the "ends" of epideictic are described in terms that minimize the social and political importance of *enkōmia,* panegyrics, and *epitaphioi.* Despite the explicit social and political dimensions of these three rhetorical practices, audience members in Aristotle's scheme are considered either as passive witnesses of a mostly aesthetic performance (not a civic action) or, if seen as active agents, they are merely judging the artistry of the rhetorical performance. The specific policy actions advocated in such speeches as Isocrates' *Panēgyrikos* or Lysias' *Olympiakos* are ignored by Aristotle, perhaps because he supposed that the

---

4. Translations from Aristotle's *Rhetoric* are taken from Kennedy (1991).

5. For an argument concerning Aristotle's somewhat misleading categorizations and descriptions of literary traditions in his *Poetics,* see Nagy (1979, 252–56).

attending audience could not immediately vote and act on those policies (though recall that one account of Lysias' speech claims he advocated an immediate action against the tents of Dionysius). The important political agendas enacted through the *epitaphios* — so obvious to his teacher Plato — are not acknowledged or discussed by Aristotle. The moral issues sometimes discussed in *enkōmia* are turned into topics to be considered under the rubric of epideictic, but the didactic function of such speeches receives no mention.

The lone chapter Aristotle devotes to epideictic is traditionally described as having three parts: the first identifies the general *topoi* useful in epideictic rhetoric and describes the virtues and "the honorable" as sources of praise (1366a23–1367a33), the second offers prescriptive advice for how to employ topics of praise and blame (1367a33–1368a9), and the third explains why amplification is characteristic of epideictic rhetoric (1368a10–1368a37). Aristotle provides a definition and description of *to kalon*, "the honorable," which is the "end" or *telos* of the epideictic genre. The relationship between *to kalon* and *aretē* ("excellence" or "virtue") is described. Aristotle then provides a list of qualities useful for the hypothetical epideictic speaker. The list of praiseworthy qualities described by Aristotle would be appropriate primarily for *enkōmia* — "justice, manly courage [*andreia*], self-control, magnificence, magnanimity, liberality, gentleness, prudence, and wisdom" (1.9.5). Aristotle continues by describing different sorts of things and deeds people find honorable and praiseworthy, most of which are appropriate for an *enkōmion* but a few of which could be used in an *epitaphios*. Aristotle sometimes shifts from describing to prescribing advice for the would-be epideictic speaker. The section bothers many commentators because Aristotle's advice is purely strategic and implies that speakers should stretch the truth where necessary. For example, Aristotle suggests that one should call "an irascible and excitable person 'straightforward' and an arrogant person 'high-minded' and 'imposing' and (speak of) those given to excess as actually in states of virtue, for example the rash one as 'courageous,' the spendthrift as 'liberal'; for this will seem true to most people and at the same time is a fallacious argument" (1367a33–1367b4). The key relativizing move made by Aristotle is the notion of audience adaptation: "Consider also the audience before whom the praise (is spoken); for, as Socrates used to say, it is not difficult to praise Athenians in Athens" (1367b7–9). Furthermore, Aristotle is not above advocating the use of claims that he knows to be false but are persuasive: "One should take coincidences and chance happenings as due to deliberate purpose; for if many similar examples are cited, they will seem to be a sign of virtue and purpose" (1367b25–27).

An interesting passage draws a distinction between speeches in praise of a person's qualities (*epainos*) and an *enkōmion,* which praises particular deeds (1367b28–34). It would be difficult to identify distinct traditions of *epainos* and *enkōmia* since most examples of *enkōmia,* panegyrics, and *epitaphioi* contain praise of both qualities and deeds; thus it may be with good reason that some commentators doubt the authenticity of this and following passages, or it may be that Aristotle wished to describe a conceptual difference not previously acknowledged (see Grimaldi 1980, 213–14).

An important passage makes it clear that Aristotle recognized that deliberative and epideictic rhetoric are not easily disentangled: "Praise and deliberations are part of a common species (*eidos*) in that what one might propose in deliberation becomes encomia when the form of expression is changed" (1367b37–1368a1; cf. 1418a21–33). However, Aristotle reinforces the analytic framework that separates the different kinds of rhetoric by urging the speaker to "change the form of expression" and to use "praise" or "propositions" depending on which kind of rhetoric one is producing (1368a1–8). To put the matter in Aristotelian terms (but not the ones he uses here), though Aristotle seems to recognize the *potential* deliberative functions of certain forms of "epideictic" rhetoric, those functions are recognized as being *actual* only in the traditional decision-making settings of the assembly, council, or court.

Aristotle concludes the chapter by noting that the rhetorical technique of amplification (*auxēsis*) is most appropriate for epideictic rhetoric. By contrast he notes that argument from example (*paradeigma*) is most appropriate in deliberative discourse and enthymematic argument most appropriate to judicial rhetoric. It is interesting to note that the other two kinds of rhetoric are defined, in part, by reference to the *logic* most appropriate to them, while epideictic is defined, in part, by its dependence on a technique (cf. Grimaldi 1980, 221–22).

Aristotle's classificatory scheme was important for its role in influencing subsequent rhetorical theorists' discussions of epideictic rhetoric (Timmerman 1996). Kennedy suggests that Aristotle's *Rhetoric* was not particularly influential throughout much of the history of rhetorical theory (1991, 305–9). Though many of the specifics of Aristotle's treatise may have been superseded by other writings, the tripartite scheme of deliberative, judicial, and epideictic has proved to be his "most distinctive contribution" (1994, 58). As Kennedy notes, "most later Greek and Latin rhetoricians accept Aristotle's definition of epideictic" (1994, 61). By focusing on the aesthetic and performance aspects of certain rhetorical practices (*enkōmia,* panegyrics, *epitaphioi*), the social and political dimensions were neglected, and the degree of overlap with other rhetorical practices minimized. In antiquity, for example, Cicero and Quintilian would later expand the epideictic category to include poetry and history. And "modern rhetoricians prefer to think of epideictic rhetoric as a discourse in any literary genre" that does not urge specific action (Kennedy 1994, 61–62).[6] Similarly, Aristotle's characterization of epideictic's dependence on technique and style functions to link the genre to the aesthetics of performance: "Amplification is especially characteristic of epideictic and contributes to its role as the species of rhetoric in which the speaker's skill or cleverness is demonstrated" (Kennedy 1991, 85n). Many commentators share Cope's belief that "the real object" of the epideictic speaker is "the display of his own powers" made "for ostentations's sake and to gain applause" (1867, 120). Though some twentieth-century scholars, most notably Perelman and Olbrechts-Tyteca (1969), have theorized about the social and political importance of epideictic rhetoric, most of the history of rhetorical theory has been dominated by Aristotle's aesthetic-performance orientation. Loraux claims that "Aristotle's classificatory and normative thought, triumphant in antiquity still dominates all modern analyses of the history and function of Greek prose" (1986, 224).

Conclusion

I conclude this chapter by offering speculations concerning why Aristotle's treatment of epideictic deemphasized the social and political importance of epideictic. I offer three possible hypotheses: one philosophical, one ideological, and one epistemological. The hypotheses are not meant to be exclusive or exhaustive. They are simply educated guesses as to why Aristotle's treatment of epideictic turned out the way it did.

The philosophical hypothesis is that Aristotle's attitude toward epideictic is influenced significantly by Plato's critique of flattery and "base rhetoric" in the *Gorgias*. As Whitney Oates notes, one finds "frequent evidence of amoralism or even on occasion immoralism" in Aristotle's text (1974, 112). Though such evidence can be found throughout the text, the examples in Aristotle's treatment of epideictic are conspicuous (see 1367a33–1367b27). Such practices fulfill Plato's dire warnings about base rhetoric in *Gorgias*. In particular, Plato's sample *epitaphios*, the *Menexenus* — a clear example of epideictic rhetoric in Aristotle's framework — illustrates many of the concerns about base rhetoric articulated in *Gorgias*:

> As Socrates himself suggests, it is witchcraft or enchantment which is eminently gratifying but which produces false beliefs (235a–c); it is flattery, prais-

6. For a contemporary treatment of Aristotle's *Rhetoric* that accepts the description of epideictic rhetoric as accurate and unproblematic, see Garver (1994, 69–73, 93–96).

ing the Athenians to their faces (235d, 236a); it does not aim at truth, but consciously says both what is true and what is false (234e, cf. 249d–e); it is organized randomly, "glued together" with leftovers from Pericles's Funeral Oration, some of it composed before, and some made up on the spot (236b). (Allen 1984, 320–21)

Allen concludes that "The speech is no doubt good of its kind, but its kind is not good: it is base rhetoric" (1984, 321). And its kind, in Aristotelian terms, is epideictic. One might conjecture, therefore, that Aristotle's conceptualization of epideictic is somewhat trivializing because, for him, the practices of *enkōmia,* panegyrics, and *epitaphioi* are far less important and less ethically defensible than deliberative or judicial rhetoric. Over the years many have joined Cope's opinion that deliberative is "first and noblest" of the genres, and that epideictic "is inferior" to the deliberative and judicial genres "in extent, importance and interest" (1867, 119, 121). It is even possible that Aristotle simply recognized no connection between epideictic discourse and the art of politics (Garver 1996).

The ideological hypothesis is that Aristotle's status as a non-Athenian may have led him to minimize the political significance of certain Athenian practices, or at least led him when teaching and writing about such practices to downplay characteristics of particular significance to Athenians. As Kennedy notes, the outside dates "for the development of the *Rhetoric* are from about 360 to about 334" B.C.E. (1991, 301). Given Kennedy's (1991, 299–305) and Rist's (1989, 85–86, 136–44) analysis of the composition of Aristotle's *Rhetoric,* it is likely that the treatment of epideictic in 1.3 and 1.9 was part of an "early core" of his lectures on rhetoric composed around 350 B.C.E. If so, not only would Plato's influence on Aristotle's thinking be more pronounced (which supports the philosophical hypothesis) but political tensions between Aristotle's homeland of Macedonia and Athens throughout the 350s also would have been significant — indeed, such tensions often erupted into warfare (Sealey 1976, 441–53). Aristotle had ties to Philip and then Alexander during the period during which it is supposed *Rhetoric* was composed and revised. Probably not long after composing the "early core," Aristotle was asked by Philip to return to Macedon to serve as a tutor for Alexander, and it is probable that during this time (343–340 B.C.E.) the instruction included rhetoric (Kennedy 1991, 6). Years later, faced with significant anti-Macedonian sentiments, Aristotle left Athens upon the death of Alexander. In short, throughout the period of time Aristotle taught and wrote about rhetoric, he would have been interacting with students and audience members with conflicting political allegiances — even if, as Cope and Kennedy claim, *Rhetoric* is written "primarily" for an Athenian audience (Cope 1877, 173; Kennedy 1991, 301).

Aristotle could not have described such ideologically charged practices as panegyrics and *epitaphioi* in a politically neutral manner in a time when Athenian patriotism would have had, by definition, a strong anti-Macedonian flavor (and vice versa). To take the politically important genre of *epitaphios*, for example, and "reduce" it to a subset of the apparently politically benign genre of *epideictic* is to rob the *epitaphios* of its ideological significance — a particularly important act taken by a non-Athenian toward a uniquely Athenian institution. Nonetheless, a treatment that reconceptualizes such practices as part of a genre characterized by its aesthetic-performative qualities may have been the least provocative direction to go.

Finally, the epistemological hypothesis is that Aristotle often failed to appreciate the more poetic styles of certain composition traditions; such a habit may have led him to underestimate the significance of certain forms of epideictic address. As noted previously, prose *enkōmia* evolved from a poetic tradition.[7] And for Aristotle, the panegyrics of Isocrates and Gorgias, and the preserved *epitaphioi* of Pericles (in Thucydides) and Plato (in the *Menexenus*) represented a form of literature in contrast to the urgent and fierce political and judicial debates taking place in the assembly and in the courts (Trevett, 1996). Two attitudes demonstrated by Aristotle and other early literary critics toward the performance of prose literature are relevant here. First, the assessment of literature qua literature typically emphasized stylistic evaluation above all — social and political dimensions were secondary at best (see Trevett 1996).[8] Second, the critical assessment of the more "poetic" literary styles often found in epideictic addresses reflects a class bias that underestimates (or perhaps fears) the social and political significance of such speeches. These two attitudes cumulatively point to an epistemological divide between the masses and the more literate elites (cf. Ober 1989).

Though a sort of basic literacy was fairly widespread among male Athenian citizens, what we might call "book-oriented" literacy was rare and usually the sign of being part of the intellectual elite (Schiappa 1991, 25–26). Even by the middle of the fourth century B.C.E., the literacy rate for Attica was not likely to

---

7. On the close relationship between the epideictic genre and poetry in general, see Burgess (1902, 166–80).

8. For example, though Aristotle may acknowledge the healthy role that tragic catharsis may provide, tragedy as a genre simply does not have the philosophical, social, or political importance that other forms of discourse have: "To Aristotle, it was possible to acclaim tragedy as a pleasant medicine, because he had banished tragedy from the sphere of religion, ethics and pedagogy, in short, from cosmology" (Oudemans and Lardinois 1987, 214). For Aristotle, the social consequences of tragedy, like epideictic, are more aesthetic than practical.

have been "much above 10–15%" (Harris 1989, 328). Most audiences for what Aristotle calls epideictic rhetoric probably were made up of people at best only partially literate compared to the sort of reading fluency attained by the literati (Swearingen 1986, 150–52). Once it is recognized that such speeches were composed for oral performance for audiences with aural pre-dilections, it is possible to reconcile their popularity with the relatively unflattering treatment such works later often received at the hands of critics.

The literati of ancient Greece represent a privileged economic and social class (Ostwald 1986, 213). As written manuscripts were scarce and expensive, the only group with the interest and ability to own and, in turn, to write about them would have been the leisure class. Accordingly, their reactions should not be taken as typical of the large live audiences to which panegyrics and *epitaphioi,* in particular, would have been addressed. The experience of performing a text to oneself is very different from hearing a text performed by its creator in person. The public performance gives the control of the auditory experience more to the speaker, adds a visual dimension to the performance, and creates greater excitement with the presence of an expectant audience (Dufrenne 1973, 37–41). The "same" text that is aesthetically pleasurable and highly persuasive in one context (for a live mass audience, say) may not be pleasurable or persuasive in another context, such as being read alone by Aristotle or by a later literary critic. Aristotle's derisive comment about Gorgias' "poetic" style in *Rhetoric* is telling: "Even now, the majority of the uneducated think such speakers speak most beautifully" (1404a26–28).

When one considers Plato's philosophical attack on base rhetoric in *Gorgias,* the ideological pressures on a Macedonian philosopher living in a sometimes hostile city, and the epistemological differences between the average Athenian audience and a highly literate and rationalistic philosopher, Aristotle's treatment of *enkōmia,* panegyrics, and *epitaphioi* under the rubric of epideictic rhetoric makes more sense. Of course, even if such hypotheses are wholly wrong, the theoretical and ideological work performed by Aristotle's text remains an important historical legacy. Aristotle's treatment of epideictic rhetoric will continue to be useful as a case study of the "disciplining" of rhetoric.

References

Allen, R. E., trans. 1984–91. *The Dialogues of Plato.* 2 vols. New Haven: Yale University Press.

Ammann, A. N. 1953. *IKOS bei Platon.* Freiburg: Paulusdruckerei.

Arieti, James A., and John M. Crossett. 1985. *Longinus: On the Sublime.* New York: Edwin Mellen Press.

Arthurs, Jeffrey. 1994. The Term *Rhetor* in Fifth- and Fourth-Century Greek Texts. *Rhetoric Society Quarterly* 23: 1–10.

Atkins, J. W. H. 1949. Rhetoric, Greek. *Oxford Classical Dictionary.* Oxford: Clarendon.

Austin, Scott. 1986. *Parmenides: Being, Bounds, and Logic.* New Haven: Yale University Press.

Baldwin, Charles Sears. 1924. *Ancient Rhetoric and Poetic.* New York: Macmillan.

Barilli, Renato. 1989. *Rhetoric.* Trans. Giuliana Menozzi. Minneapolis: University of Minnesota Press.

Barnes, Jonathan. 1982. *The Presocratic Philosophers.* London: Routledge and Kegan Paul.

———. 1983. Aphorism and Argument. In *Language and Thought in Early Greek Philosophy,* ed. Kevin Robb, 91–109. La Salle, Ill.: Hegeler Institute.

———, ed. 1984. *The Complete Works of Aristotle.* Princeton: Princeton University Press.

———. 1987. *Early Greek Philosophy.* London: Penguin Books.

Barrett, Harold. 1987. *The Sophists.* Novato, Calif.: Chandler and Sharp.

Beale, Walter H. 1978. Rhetorical Performative Discourse: A New Theory of Epideictic. *Philosophy and Rhetoric* 11: 221–46.

Bekker, I. 1831. *Aristotelis opera*. Vol. 2. Berlin: Reimer.

Berkowitz, Luci, and Karl A. Squitier. 1990. *Thesaurus Linguae Graecae: Canon of Greek Authors and Works*. 3d ed. New York: Oxford University Press.

Berlin, James A. 1990. Polylog: Professing the New Rhetorics. *Rhetoric Review* 9: 5–35.

Biesecker, Susan. 1990. Feminist Criticism of Classical Rhetorical Texts: A Case Study of Gorgias' *Helen*. In *Realms of Rhetoric: Phonic, Graphic, Electronic*, ed. Victor J. Vitanza and Michelle Ballif, 67–82. Arlington, Tex.: Rhetoric Society of America.

Blass, Friedrich. 1887. *Die attische Beredsamkeit*. 2d ed. Vol. 1. Leipzig: Teubner.

Blass, Friedrich. 1913–37. *Isocratis Orationes*. 2 vols. Leipzig: Teubner.

Blank, David L. 1985. Socratics vs. Sophists on Payment for Teaching. *Classical Antiquity* 16: 1–49.

Bloch, Maurice, ed. 1975. *Political Language and Oratory in Traditional Society*. London: Academic Press.

Bloom, A. D. 1955. The Political Philosophy of Isocrates. Ph.D. diss., University of Chicago.

Bremmer, Jan N. 1983. *The Early Greek Concept of the Soul*. Princeton: Princeton University Press.

Brown, Roger W. 1956. Language and Categories. In *A Study in Thinking*, ed. J. S. Bruner, J. J. Goodnow, and G. A. Austin, 247–310. New York: John Wiley and Sons.

Brown, Roger W., and E. H. Lenneberg. 1954. A Study in Language and Cognition. *Journal of Abnormal Psychology* 59: 452–62.

Bryant, Donald C. 1968. *Ancient Greek and Roman Rhetoricians*. Columbia, Mo.: Artcraft Press.

Buchheim, Thomas 1989. *Gorgias von Leontini: Reden, Fragmente und Testimonien*. Hamburg: Meiner.

Buchler, Justus. 1955. *Philosophical Writings of Peirce*. New York: Dover.

Burke, Kenneth. 1966. *Language as Symbolic Action*. Berkeley: University of California Press.

———. 1973. *Philosophy of Literary Form*. 3d ed. Berkeley: University of California Press.

Burger, Ronna. 1980. *Plato's* Phaedrus: *A Defense of a Philosophical Art of Writing*. University, Ala.: University of Alabama Press.

Burgess, Theodore C. 1902. Epideictic Literature. *University of Chicago Studies in Classical Philology* 3:89–254.

Burnet, John. 1930. *Early Greek Philosophy*. 4th ed. London: Adam and Charles Black.

Burnet, John. 1959. *Platonis Opera*. Vol. 2. Oxford: Clarendon.

Bury, R. G. 1935. *Sextus Empiricus II*. Cambridge, Mass.: Harvard University Press.

Buxton, R. G. A. 1982. *Persuasion in Greek Tragedy: A Study of Peithō*. Cambridge: Cambridge University Press.

Cahn, Michael. 1989. Reading Rhetoric Rhetorically: Isocrates and the Marketing of Insight. *Rhetorica* 7: 121–44.

Calogero, Guido. 1932. *Studi sull'Eleatismo*. Rome: Tipografia del Senato.

Cantarella, Eva. 1987. *Pandora's Daughters: The Role and Status of Women in Greek and Roman Antiquity*. Baltimore: John Hopkins University Press.

Carter, Michael F. 1991. The Ritual Functions of Epideictic Rhetoric: The Case of Socrates' Funeral Oration. *Rhetorica* 9: 209–32.

Casertano, G. 1986. L'Amour entre *Logos* et *Pathos:* Quelques Considérations sur L'*Hélène* de Gorgias. In *Positions de la sophistique,* ed. Barbara Cassin, 211–20. Paris: Vrin.

Cassin, Barbara. 1980. *Si Parménide.* Lille: Presses Universitaires de Lille.

——, ed. 1986. *Positions de la sophistique.* Paris: Vrin.

——. 1995. *L'effet sophistique.* Paris: Editions Gallimard.

Chantraine, Pierre. 1956. Le suffixe grec -IKOS. *Etudes sur le vocabulaire grec.* Paris: Klincksieck. 97–171.

Charlton, William. 1985. Greek Philosophy and the Concept of an Academic Discipline. *History of Political Thought* 6: 47–61.

Chase, Richard. 1961. The Classical Conception of Epideictic. *Quarterly Journal of Speech* 47: 293–300.

Cherniss, Harold. 1935. *Aristotle's Criticism of Presocratic Philosophy.* New York: Octagon Books.

Chiesi, H. L., G. J. Spilich, and J. F. Voss. 1979. Acquisition of Domain-Related Information in Relation to High and Low Domain Knowledge. *Journal of Verbal Learning and Verbal Behavior* 18: 257–73.

Clark, D. L. 1957. *Rhetoric in Greco-Roman Education.* New York: Columbia University Press.

Classen, Carl Joachim. 1959. The Study of Language Amongst Socrates' Contemporaries. *Proceedings of the African Classical Association.* 2: 33–49.

——, ed. 1976. *Sophistik.* Wege der Forschung 187. Darmstadt: Wissenschaftliche Buchgesellschaft.

——. 1981. Aristotle's Picture of the Sophists. In *The Sophists and Their Legacy,* ed. G. B. Kerferd, 7–24. Wiesbaden: Franz Steiner.

Cole, Thomas. 1972. The Relativism of Protagoras. *Yale Classical Studies* 22: 19–45.

——. 1991a. *The Origins of Rhetoric in Ancient Greece.* Baltimore: Johns Hopkins University Press.

——. 1991b. Who Was Corax? *Illinois Classical Studies* 16: 65–84.

Conley, Thomas M. 1985. Dating the So-called *Dissoi Logoi:* A Cautionary Note. *Ancient Philosophy* 5: 59–65.

Connors, Robert J. 1986. Greek Rhetoric and the Transition from Orality. *Philosophy and Rhetoric* 19: 38–65.

——. 1988. [Review of] *The Muse Learns to Write* By Eric A. Havelock. *Quarterly Journal of Speech* 74: 379–81.

Consigny, Scott. 1992. Gorgias's Use of the Epideictic. *Philosophy and Rhetoric* 25: 281–97.

——. 1994. Nietzsche's Reading of the Sophists. *Rhetoric Review* 13: 5–26.

——. 1995. Review of *Protagoras and Logos: A Study in Greek Philosophy and Rhetoric* by E. Schiappa. *Rhetoric Society Quarterly* 25: 217–20.

——. 1996. Edward Schiappa's Reading of the Sophists. *Rhetoric Review* 14: 253–69.

Cooper, Lane. 1932. *The Rhetoric of Aristotle.* Englewood Cliffs, N.J.: Prentice-Hall.

Cope, Edward M. 1855. On the Sophistical Rhetoric. *Journal of Classical and Sacred Philology* 2:129–69.

———. 1856. On the Sophistical Rhetoric. *Journal of Classical and Sacred Philology* 3: 34–80, 252–88.

———. 1867. *An Introduction to Aristotle's Rhetoric.* London: Macmillan.

———. 1877. *The Rhetoric of Aristotle with a Commentary.* 3 vols. Cambridge: Cambridge University Press.

Corrigan, Roberta. 1989. Introduction. *Linguistic Categorization.* Roberta Corrigan, Fred Eckman, Michael Noonan, eds. Philadelphia: John Benjamin.

Coxon, A. H. 1986. *The Fragments of Parmenides.* Assen: Van Gorcum.

Crowley, Sharon. 1988. Octalog: The Politics of Historiography. *Rhetoric Review* 7: 5–49.

———. 1989. A Plea for the Revival of Sophistry. *Rhetoric Review* 7: 318–34.

Culler, Jonathan. 1977. *Ferdinand de Saussure.* New York: Penguin.

Curd, Patricia. 1998. *The Legacy of Parmenides : Eleatic Monism and Later Presocratic Thought.* Princeton: Princeton University Press.

Daly, Mary. 1985. *Beyond God the Father.* 2d ed. Boston: Beacon Press.

de Groot, A. W. 1918. *A Handbook of Antique Prose-Rhythm.* Groningen: J. B. Wolters.

Denniston, J. D. 1927. Technical Terms in Aristophanes. *Classical Quarterly* 21: 113–21.

Denniston, J. D. 1952. *Greek Prose Style.* Oxford: Clarendon Press.

———. 1954. *The Greek Particles.* 2d ed. Oxford: Clarendon Press.

de Romilly, Jacqueline. 1975. *Magic and Rhetoric in Ancient Greece.* Cambridge, Mass.: Harvard University Press.

———. 1988. *Les Grands Sophistes dans l'Athènes de Pèriclés.* Paris: Fallois.

———. 1992a. *The Great Sophists in Periclean Athens,* trans. Janet Lloyd. Oxford: Clarendon Press, 1992.

———. 1992b. Isocrates and Europe. *Greece and Rome* 39: 2–13.

Derrida, Jacques. 1981. *Dissemination.* Trans. Barbara Johnson. Chicago: University of Chicago Press.

———. 1988. *Limited Inc.* Evanston: Northwestern University Press.

de Saussure, Ferdinand. 1973. *Cours de linguistique générale.* Ed. Tullio de Mauro. Paris: Payot.

De Witt, Norman W., and Norman J. De Witt, trans. 1949. *Demosthenes. Funeral speech, LX. Erotic essay, LXI. Exordia and Letters.* Cambridge, Mass.: Harvard University Press.

de Vries, G. J. 1953. Isocrates' Reaction to the *Phaedrus. Mnemosyne* 6: 41–49.

———. 1969. *A Commentary on the Phaedrus of Plato.* Amsterdam: Adolf M. Hakkert.

Dewey, John. 1929. *The Quest for Certainty: A Study of the Relation of Knowledge and Action.* New York: Minton, Balch and Co.

Diels, Hermann, and Walther Kranz. 1951–52. *Die Fragmente der Vorsokratiker.* 6th ed. Dublin and Zurich: Weidmann.

Dik, Helma. 1995. *Word Order in Ancient Greek.* Amsterdam: J. C. Gieben.

Dodds, E. R. 1959. *Plato's GORGIAS:* Oxford: Clarendon Press.

Douglas, A. E. 1955. The Aristotelian *Synagōgē Technōn* after Cicero *Brutus* 46–48. *Latomus* 14:536–9.

Dover, Kenneth J. 1960. *Greek Word Order*. Cambridge: Cambridge University Press.

———. 1968a. *Aristophanes CLOUDS*. Oxford: Clarendon Press.

———. 1968b. *Lysias and the corpus Lysiacum*. Sather Classical Lectures 39. Berkeley: University of California Press.

———. 1972. *Aristophanic Comedy*. Berkeley: University of California Press.

———. 1976. The Freedom of the Intellectual in Greek Society. *Talanta* 7: 24–54.

———. 1980. *Plato: SYMPOSIUM*. Cambridge: Cambridge University Press.

Drerup, Engelbert. 1902. Die Anfänge der rhetorischen Kunstprosa. *Jahrbücher für klassische Philologie*, Supplementband 27.2: 219–351.

Duffy, Bernard K. 1983. The Platonic Functions of Epideictic Rhetoric. *Philosophy and Rhetoric* 16: 79–93.

Dufrenne, Mikel. 1973. *The Phenomenology of Aesthetic Experience*. Evanston: Northwestern University Press.

Duncan, Thomas Shearer. 1938. Gorgias' Theory of Art. *Classical Journal* 33: 402–15.

Dupréel, Eugène. 1948. *Les Sophistes*. Neuchâtel: Editions du Griffon.

Eagleton, Terry. 1981. *Walter Benjamin, or, Towards a revolutionary criticism*. New York: Verso.

Edwards, M. W. 1991. *The Iliad: A Commentary. Vol. 5, books 17–20*. Cambridge: Cambridge University Press.

Edwards, Paul, ed. 1967. *The Encyclopedia of Philosophy*. Vol. 1. New York: Macmillan.

Engnell, Richard A. 1973. Implications for Communication of the Rhetorical Epistemology of Gorgias of Leontini. *Western Journal of Speech Communication* 37: 175–84.

Enos, Richard Leo. 1976. The Epistemology of Gorgias's Rhetoric: A Re-examination. *Southern Speech Communication Journal* 42: 35–51.

———. 1988. *The Literate Mode of Cicero's Legal Rhetoric*. Carbondale: Southern Illinois University Press.

———. 1993. *Greek Rhetoric Before Aristotle*. Prospect Heights, Ill.: Waveland Press.

Enos, Theresa. 1989. The Course in Classical Rhetoric: Definition, Development, Direction. *Rhetoric Society Quarterly* 19: 45–48.

Erickson, Keith V., ed. 1974. *Aristotle: The Classical Heritage of Rhetoric*. Metuchen, N.J.: Scarecrow Press.

———. 1979. *Plato: True and Sophistic Rhetoric*. Amsterdam: Rodopi.

Evelyn-White, Hugh G., trans. 1936. *Hesiod*. Cambridge, Mass.: Harvard University Press.

Fantham, Elaine. 1992. Unpublished translations of selected texts of Isocrates.

Farenga, Vincent. 1979. Periphrasis on the Origin of Rhetoric. *Modern Language Notes* 94: 1033–55.

Finley, M. I. 1968. *A History of Sicily*. London: Chatto and Windus.

———. 1975. *The Use and Abuse of History*. New York: Viking.

Foss, Sonja K., Karen A. Foss, and Robert Trapp. 1991. *Contemporary Perspectives on Rhetoric*, 2d ed. Prospect Heights, Ill.: Waveland Press.

Foucault, Michel. 1972. *The Archaeology of Knowledge*. Trans. A. M. Sheridan Smith. New York: Pantheon.

———. 1979. *Discipline and Punish*. Trans. Alan Sheridan. New York: Vintage.

———. 1980. *Power/Knowledge*. Ed. Colin Gordon. New York: Pantheon.

Fowler, H. N. 1914. *Plato: Euthuphro, Apology, Crito, Phaedo, Phaedrus*. Cambridge, Mass.: Harvard University Press.

———. 1925. *Plato: Statesman, Philebus, Ion*. Cambridge, Mass.: Harvard University Press.

Freeman, K. 1946. *The Murder of Herodes and Other Trials from the Athenian Law Courts*. London: MacDonald.

Fuller, Benjamin. 1945. *A History of Philosophy*, rev. ed. New York: Henry Holt.

Furley, David J., and Alexander Nehamas, eds. 1994. *Aristotle's Rhetoric*: Philosophical Essays. Princeton: Princeton University Press.

Furth, Montgomery. 1968. Elements of Eleatic Ontology. *Journal of the History of Philosophy* 7: 111–32.

Gadamer, Hans-Georg. 1989. *Truth and Method*. 2d rev. ed. Trans. Joel Weinsheimer and Donald G. Marshall. New York: Crossroad.

von Gaertringen, F. Hiller, ed. 1924. *Inscriptiones Graecae*. Vol. 1 ed. minor. Berlin: De Gruyter.

Gagarin, Michael. 1968. Plato and Protagoras. Ph.D. diss., Yale University.

———. 1990. The Nature of Proofs in Antiphon. *Classical Philology* 85: 22–32.

———. 1994. Probability and Persuasion: Plato and Early Greek Rhetoric. In *Persuasion: Greek Rhetoric in Action*, ed. Ian Worthington, 46–68. London: Routledge.

Gallop, David. 1984. *Parmenides of Elea*. Toronto: University of Toronto Press.

Garner, Richard. 1987. *Law and Society in Classical Athens*. New York: St. Martin's Press.

Garver, Eugene. 1994. *Aristotle's Rhetoric*: An Art of Character. Chicago: University of Chicago Press.

———. 1996. The Political Irrelevance of Aristotle's *Rhetoric*. *Philosophy and Rhetoric* 29: 179–99.

Gercke, A. 1897. Die alte *Technē Rhētorikē* und ihre Gegner. *Hermes* 33: 348–59.

Gigon, Olaf. 1936. Gorgias über das Nichtsein. *Hermes* 71: 186–213.

Glenn, Cheryl. 1994. sex, lies, and manuscript: Refiguring Aspasia in the History of Rhetoric. *College Composition and Communication* 45: 180–99.

Goebel, George H. 1989. Probability in the Earliest Rhetorical Theory. *Mnemosyne* 42: 41–53.

Golden, James L., Goodwin F. Berquist, and William E. Coleman. 1993. *The Rhetoric of Western Thought*, 5th ed. Dubuque, Iowa: Kendall/Hunt.

Gomperz, Heinrich. [1912] 1985. *Sophistik und Rhetorik*. Reprint. Aalen: Scientia.

Green, Mark, and Gail MacColl. 1983. *There He Goes Again: Ronald Reagan's Reign of Error*. New York: Pantheon.

Gregg, Richard B. 1984. *Symbolic Inducement and Knowing*. Columbia: University of South Carolina Press.

Grimaldi, William M. A. 1980. *Aristotle, Rhetoric* I: A Commentary. New York: Fordham University Press.

———.1996. How do We Get from Corax-Tisias to Plato-Aristotle in Greek Rhetorical Theory? In *Theory, Text, Context: Issues in Greek Rhetoric and Oratory*, ed. Christopher Lyle Johnstone, 19–43. Albany: State University of New York Press.

Grimshaw, Jean. 1986. *Philosophy and Feminist Thinking*. Minneapolis: University of Minnesota Press.

Gronbeck, Bruce E. 1972. Gorgias on Rhetoric and Poetic: A Rehabilitation. *Southern Speech Communication Journal* 38: 27–38.

Grote, George. 1851. *A History of Greece*. 2d ed. Vol. 8. London: Murray.

Groten, F. J., Jr. 1955. The Tradition of the Helen Legend in Greek Literature. Ph.D. diss., Princeton University.

Guthrie, W. K. C. 1957. Aristotle as Historian. *Journal of Hellenic Studies* 77: 35–41.

———. 1962. *The Earlier Presocratics and the Pythagoreans*. Cambridge: Cambridge University Press.

———. 1965. *The Presocratic Tradition from Parmenides to Democritus*. Cambridge: Cambridge University Press.

———. 1971. *The Sophists*. Cambridge: Cambridge University Press.

———. 1975. *Plato: The Man and His Dialogues, Earlier Period*. Cambridge: Cambridge University Press.

———. 1981. *Aristotle: An Encounter*. Cambridge: Cambridge University Press.

Halliwell, Stephen. 1994. Philosophy and Rhetoric. In *Persuasion: Greek Rhetoric in Action*, ed. Ian Worthington, 222–43. London: Routledge.

Halporn, James W., Martin Ostwald, and Thomas G. Rosenmeyer. 1980. *The Meters of Greek and Latin Poetry*. Rev. ed. Norman: University of Oklahoma Press.

Hamilton, Edith, and Huntington Cairns. 1961. *The Collected Dialogues of Plato*. Princeton: Princeton University Press.

Hansen, M. H. 1981. Initiative and Decision: The Separation of Powers in Fourth-Century Athens. *Greek, Roman, and Byzantine Studies* 22: 345–70.

———. 1983a. The Athenian "Politicians," 403–322 B.C. *Greek, Roman, and Byzantine Studies* 24: 33–55.

———. 1983b. *Rhetores* and *Strategoi* in Fourth-Century Athens. *Greek, Roman, and Byzantine Studies* 24: 151–80.

Harnad, Stevan. 1987. Category Induction and Representation. In *Categorical Perception*, ed. Stevan Harnad, 535–65. Cambridge: Cambridge University Press.

Harris, William V. 1989. *Ancient Literacy*. Cambridge, Mass.: Harvard University Press.

Harvey, A. E. 1955. The Classification of Greek Lyric Poetry. *Classical Quarterly* 5: 152–74.

Haslett, Michael. 1995. Sophisticated Burke: Kenneth Burke as a Neosophistic Rhetorician. *Rhetoric Review* 13: 271–90.

Havelock, Eric A. 1957. *The Liberal Temper in Greek Politics*. New Haven: Yale University Press.

———. 1963. *Preface to Plato*. Cambridge, Mass.: Harvard University Press.

———. 1978. *The Greek Concept of Justice*. Cambridge, Mass.: Harvard University Press.

———. 1982. *The Literate Revolution in Greece and Its Cultural Consequences*. Princeton: Princeton University Press.

———. 1983. The Linguistic Task of the Presocratics. In *Language and Thought in Early Greek Philosophy*, ed. Kevin Robb, 7–82. La Salle, Ill.: Hegeler Institute.

Hegel, G. W. F. 1914. *Lectures on the Philosophy of History*, trans. J. Sibree. London: G. Bell and Sons.

Henry, Madeline M. 1995. *Prisoner of History: Aspasia of Miletus and Her Biographical Tradition*. Oxford: Oxford University Press.

Henry, René. 1959. *Photius: Bibliothèque*. Vol. 1. Paris: Les Belles Lettres.

Hett, W. S. 1936. *Aristotle: Minor Works*. Cambridge, Mass.: Harvard University Press.

Heilbrunn, Gunther. 1967. An Examination of Isocrates' Rhetoric. Ph.D. diss., University of Texas.

Hinks, D. A. G. 1936. Tria Genera Causarum. *Classical Quarterly* 30: 170–76.

———. 1940. Tisias and Corax and the Invention of Rhetoric. *Classical Quarterly* 34: 61–69.

Holtsmark, Erling B. 1968. *Ancient Greek and Roman Rhetoricians*. Columbia, Mo.: Artcraft Press.

Hommel H. [and Konrat Ziegler]. 1972. Rhetorik. *Der Kleine Pauly*. Vol. 4 Munich: Druckenmüller.

Howland, R. L. 1937. The Attack on Isocrates in the *Phaedrus*. *Classical Quarterly* 31: 151–59.

Hubbell, H. M. 1949. *Cicero II*. Cambridge, Mass.: Harvard University Press.

Hunt, Everett Lee. 1925. Plato and Aristotle on Rhetoric and Rhetoricians. In *Studies in Rhetoric and Public Speaking in Honor of James Albert Winans*, ed. A. M. Drummond, 3–60. New York: Century.

Ijsseling, Samuel. 1976. *Rhetoric and Philosophy in Conflict: An Historical Survey*. The Hague: Nijhoff.

Jacob, Bernard. 1996. What If Aristotle Took Sophists Seriously? New Readings in Aristotle's *Rhetoric*. *Rhetoric Review* 14: 237–52.

Jacoby, F. 1947. The First Athenian Prose Writer. *Mnemosyne* 13: 13–64.

Jaeger, Werner. 1943. *Paideia: The Ideas of Greek Culture*. Vol. 2. Trans. Gilbert Highet. New York: Oxford University Press.

Jamieson, Kathleen Hall. 1988. *Eloquence in an Electronic Age*. New York: Oxford University Press.

Jarratt, Susan C. 1991. *Rereading the Sophists: Classical Rhetoric Refigured*. Carbondale: Southern Illinois University Press.

Jebb, R. C. [1893] 1962. *The Attic Orators from Antiphon to Isaeos*. 2d ed. 2 vols. New York: Russell and Russell.

Johnstone, Jr., Henry W. 1996. On Schiappa versus Poulakos. *Rhetoric Review* 14: 438–40.

Jones, H. S. and J. E. Powell. 1942. *Thucydidis historiae*. 2nd ed. Oxford: Clarendon Press.

Jones, W. H. S. 1923. Breaths. *Hippocrates*. Vol. II. Cambridge, Mass.: Harvard University Press.

Kahn, Charles H. 1960. *Anaximander and the Origins of Greek Cosmology*. New York: Columbia University Press.

Kahn, Charles H. 1966. The Greek Verb "to be" and the Concept of Being. *Foundations of Language* 2: 245–65.

———. 1973. *The Verb "Be" in Ancient Greek*. Dordrecht, Holland: D. Reidel.

———. 1979. *The Art and Thought of Heraclitus*. Cambridge: Cambridge University Press.

Karp, Andrew J. 1977. Homeric Origins of Ancient Rhetoric. *Arethusa* 10: 237–58.

Kastely, James L. 1997. *The Clouds:* Aristophanic Comedy and Democratic Education. *Rhetoric Society Quarterly* 27: 25–46.

Keil, Frank C. 1989. *Concepts, Kinds, and Cognitive Development.* Cambridge, Mass.: MIT Press.

Kennedy, George A. 1959. The Earliest Rhetorical Handbooks. *American Journal of Philology* 80:169–78.

———. 1963. *The Art of Persuasion in Ancient Greece.* Princeton: Princeton University Press.

———. 1972a. *The Art of Rhetoric in the Roman World.* Princeton: Princeton University Press.

———. 1972b. Gorgias. In *The Older Sophists,* ed. Rosamond Kent Sprague, 30–67. Columbia: University of South Carolina Press.

———. 1980. *Classical Rhetoric and Its Christian and Secular Tradition from Ancient to Modern Times.* Chapel Hill: University of North Carolina Press.

———, ed. 1989. *The Cambridge History of Literary Criticism.* Vol. 1. Cambridge: Cambridge University Press.

———. 1991. *Aristotle ON RHETORIC: A Theory of Civic Discourse.* New York: Oxford University Press.

———. 1994. *A New History of Classical Rhetoric.* Princeton: Princeton University Press.

———. 1995. Rhetorical Questions. *The Review of Politics* 57: 729–32.

Kerferd, G. B. 1950. The First Greek Sophists. *Classical Review* 64: 8–10.

———. 1955. Gorgias on Nature or That Which is Not. *Phronesis* 1: 3–25.

———. 1967. Protagoras. *The Encyclopedia of Philosophy.* Vol. 6. New York: Macmillan.

———, ed. 1981a. *The Sophists and Their Legacy.* Wiesbaden: Franz Steiner.

———. 1981b. *The Sophistic Movement.* Cambridge: Cambridge University Press.

———. 1984. Meaning and Reference: Gorgias and the Relation between Language and Reality. In *The Sophistic Movement,* 215–22. Papers Read at the First International Symposium on the Sophistic Movement Organised by the Greek Philosophical Society 27–29 Sept. 1982. Athens: Athenian Library of Philosophy.

Keuls, Eva C. 1985. *The Reign of the Phallus: Sexual Politics in Ancient Athens.* New York: Harper.

Kimball, B. A. 1986. *Orators and Philosophers: A History of the Ideal Liberal Education.* New York: Columbia University Teachers College Press.

Kirby, John T. 1990. The "Great Triangle" in Early Greek Rhetoric and Poetics. *Rhetorica* 8: 213–28.

———. 1992. Rhetoric and Poetic in Hesiod. *Ramus* 21: 34–60.

Kirk, G. S., J. E. Raven, and Malcolm Schofield. 1983. *The Presocratic Philosophers: A Critical History with a Selection of Texts,* 2d ed. Cambridge: Cambridge University Press.

Kopff, E. Christian. 1990. The Date of Aristophanes, *Nubes* II. *American Journal of Philology* 113: 18–29.

Kroll, Wilhelm. 1940. Rhetorik. *Paulys Real-Encyclopädie der classischen Altertumswissenschaft.* Supp. 7: 1039–1138.

Kuhn, Thomas S. 1970. *The Structure of Scientific Revolutions*. 2d ed. Chicago: University of Chicago Press.

——. 1977. *The Essential Tension*. Chicago: University of Chicago Press.

——. 1987. What Are Scientific Revolutions? In *The Probabilistic Revolution,* ed. Lorenz Krüger, Lorraine J. Daston, and Michael Heidelberger, 7–22. *The Probabilistic Revolution,* vol. 1. Cambridge, Mass.: MIT Press.

——. 1989. Possible Worlds in History of Science. In *Possible Worlds in Humanities, Arts, and Sciences,* ed. Sture Allén, 9–32. Berlin: De Gruyter.

——. 1990. Dubbing and Redubbing: The Vulnerability of Rigid Designation. *Minnesota Studies in the Philosophy of Science* 14: 298–318.

Laistner, M. L. W. 1930. The Influence of Isocrates's Political Doctrines on Some Fourth Century Men of Affairs. *The Classical Weekly* 23: 129–31.

Lamb, W. R. M., trans. 1925. *Plato: Lysis, Symposium, Gorgias*. Cambridge, Mass.: Harvard University Press.

——. 1930. *Lysias*. Cambridge, Mass.: Harvard University Press.

Lanham, Richard A. 1968. *A Handlist of Rhetorical Terms*. Berkeley: University of California Press.

Lardinois, André. 1997. Modern Paroemiology and the Use of Gnomai in Homer's *Iliad*. *Classical Philology* 92: 213–34.

Latour, Bruno, and Steve Woolgar. 1979. *Laboratory Life: The Social Construction of Scientific Facts*. Beverly Hills, Calif.: Sage.

Leff, Michael C. 1987. Modern Sophistic and the Unity of Rhetoric. In *The Rhetoric of the Human Sciences,* ed. J. S. Nelson, A. Megill, D. N. McCloskey, 19–37. Madison: University of Wisconsin Press.

Lentricchia, Frank. 1983. *Criticism and Social Change*. Chicago: University of Chicago Press.

Lentz, Tony M. 1989. *Orality and Literacy in Hellenic Greece*. Carbondale: Southern Illinois University Press.

Levin, S. 1983. The Origin of Grammar in Sophistry. *General Linguistics* 23: 41–47.

Liddell, H. G., and R. Scott. 1940. *A Greek-English Lexicon*. 9th ed. Revised and augmented by H. S. Jones. Oxford: Clarendon Press.

Lindblom, Kenneth J. 1996. Toward a Neosophistic Writing Pedagogy. *Rhetoric Review* 15: 93–107.

Lloyd, G. E. R. 1987. *The Revolutions of Wisdom*. Berkeley: University of California Press.

Lloyd, M. 1992. *The Agon in Euripides*. Oxford: Clarendon Press.

Loraux, Nicole. 1986. *The Invention of Athens: The Funeral Oration in the Classical City*. Trans. Alan Sheridan. Cambridge, Mass.: Harvard University Press.

Lu, Xing. 1998. *Rhetoric in Ancient China, Fifth to Third Century BCE: A Comparison with Classical Greek Rhetoric*. Columbia: University of South Carolina Press.

Lucy, John A., and James V. Wertsch. 1987. Vygotsky and Whorf: A Comparative Analysis. In *Social and Functional Approaches to Language and Thought,* ed. Maya Hickman, 67–86. Orlando, Fla.: Academic Press.

Maas, Peter. 1962. *Greek Metre*. Oxford: Clarendon.

MacDowell, D. M. 1982. *Gorgias: Encomium of Helen, Translation and Commentary.* Bristol: Bristol Classical Press.

MacIntyre, Alasdair. 1988. *Whose Justice? Which Rationality?* Notre Dame, Ind.: Notre Dame University Press.

Magnus, Bernd. 1985. The End of "The End of Philosophy." In *Hermeneutics and Deconstruction,* ed. Hugh J. Silverman and Don Ihde, 2–10. Albany: State University of New York Press.

Maidment, K. J. 1953. *Minor Attic Orators: Antiphon, Andocides.* Cambridge, Mass.: Harvard University Press.

Mailloux, Steven. 1989. *Rhetorical Power.* Ithaca: Cornell University Press.

Mailloux, Steven, ed. 1995. *Rhetoric, Sophistry, Pragmatism.* Cambridge: Cambridge University Press.

Major, Wilfred E. 1996. Aristophanes: Enemy of Rhetoric. Ph.D. diss., Indiana University, Bloomington.

Major, Wilfred E., and Edward Schiappa. 1997. Gorgias's "Undeclared" Theory of Arrangement. *Southern Communication Journal* 62: 149–52.

Makin, Stephen. 1988. How Can We Find Out What Ancient Philosophers Said? *Phronesis* 33: 121–32.

Mansfeld, Jaap. 1985. Historical and Philosophical Aspects of Gorgias' "On What is Not." *Siculorum Gymnasium* 38: 243–71.

———. 1988. De Melisso Xenophone Gorgias: Pyrrhonizing Aristotelianism. *Rheinisches Museum* 131: 239–76.

Marchant, E. C., trans. 1923. *Xenophon: Memorabilia, Oeconomicus, Symposium, Apology.* Cambridge, Mass.: Harvard University Press.

Marrou, H. I. 1956. *A History of Education in Antiquity.* Trans. George Lamb. New York: Sheed and Ward.

Martin, Josef. 1974. *Antike Rhetorik: Technik und Methode.* Munich: Beck.

Mathieu, Georges. 1925. *Les Idées Politiques d'Isocrate.* 2d ed. Paris: Les Belles Lettres.

Mathieu, Georges, and Emile Brémond. 1929–62. *Isocrate. Discours.* Paris: Les Belles Lettres.

Matsen, Patricia P., Philip Rollinson, and Marion Sousa. 1990. *Readings from Classical Rhetoric.* Carbondale: Southern Illinois University Press.

Mazzara, Giuseppe, 1982. *Gorgia: Ontologo e metafisico.* Palermo: ili palma.

McComiskey, Bruce. 1993. Postmodern Sophistics: Appearance and Deception in Rhetoric and Composition. In *Rhetoric in the Vortex of Cultural Studies,* ed. Arthur Walzer, 83–91. Minneapolis: Rhetoric Society of America/Burgess.

———. 1994. Neo-Sophistic Rhetorical Theory: Sophistic Precedents for Contemporary Epistemic Rhetoric. *Rhetoric Society Quarterly* 24: 16–24.

McDiarmid, J. B. 1953. Theophrastus on the Presocratic Causes. *Harvard Studies in Classical Philology* 6: 85–156.

Meiggs, Russell, and David Lewis. 1969. *A Selection of Greek Historical Inscriptions to the End of the Fifth Century B.C.* Oxford: Oxford University Press.

Menzel, Adolf. 1910. Protagoras, der älteste Theoretiker der Demokratie. *Zeitschrift für Politik* 3: 205–38.

Minar, E. L. 1949. Parmenides and the World of Seeming. *American Journal of Philology* 70: 41–53.

Morrison, J. S. 1941. The Place of Protagoras in Athenian Public Life. *Classical Quarterly* 35: 1–16.

Moss, Roger. 1982. The Case for Sophistry. In *Rhetoric Revalued*, ed. Brian Vickers, 207–24. Binghamton, N.Y.: Center for Medieval and Early Renaissance Studies.

Mourelatos, Alexander P. D. 1970. *The Route of Parmenides*. New Haven: Yale University Press.

———. 1985. Gorgias on the Function of Language. *Siculorum Gymnasium* 38: 607–38.

Müller, Reimer. 1986. Sophistique et démocratie. In *Positions de la sophistique*, ed. Barbara Cassin, 179–93. Paris: Vrin.

Munz, Peter. 1990. The Rhetoric of Rhetoric. *Journal of the History of Ideas* 51: 121–42.

Murphy, C. T. 1938. Aristophanes and the Art of Rhetoric. *Harvard Studies in Classical Philology* 49: 69–113.

Murphy, James J. 1972. *A Synoptic History of Classical Rhetoric*. New York: Random House.

———. 1997. Review of *Writing Histories of Rhetoric* (Edited by Victor Vitanza). *Quarterly Journal of Speech* 83: 267–68.

Mutschmann, Hermann. 1918. Die Älteste Definition der Rhetorik. *Hermes* 53: 440–43.

Mutschmann, H., and J. Mau. 1961. *Sexti Empirici opera*, 2d ed., vol. 2. Leipzig: Teubner.

Nagy, Gregory. 1979. *The Best of the Achaeans: Concepts of the Hero in Archaic Greek Poetry*. Baltimore: Johns Hopkins University Press.

———. 1989. Early Greek Views of Poets and Poetry. In *The Cambridge History of Literary Criticism, vol. 1*, ed. George A. Kennedy, 1–77. Cambridge: Cambridge University Press.

Nails, Debra. 1995. *Agora, Academy, and the Conduct of Philosophy*. Dordrecht: Kluwer Academic Publishers.

Neel, Jasper. 1988. *Plato, Derrida, and Writing*. Carbondale: Southern Illinois University Press.

Nehamas, Alexander. 1985. *Nietzsche: Life as Literature*. Cambridge, Mass.: Harvard University Press.

———. 1990. Eristic, Antilogic, Sophistic, Dialectic: Plato's Demarcation of Philosophy from Sophistry. *History of Philosophy Quarterly* 7:3–16.

Nestle, Wilhelm. 1966. *Vom Mythos zum Logos*. 2d ed. Aalen: Scientia Verlag.

Newiger, Hans-Joachim. 1973. *Untersuchungen zu Gorgias' Schrift uber das Nichtseiende*. Berlin: de Gruyter.

Norden, Eduard. 1958 [1900–1902]. *Die Antike Kunstprosa*. 2 vols. Stuttgart: Teubner.

Norlin, George, trans. 1928–29. *Isocrates*. 2 vols. Cambridge, Mass.: Harvard University Press.

Novick, Peter. 1988. *That Noble Dream: The Objectivity Question and the American Historical Profession*. Cambridge: Cambridge University Press.

Oates, Whitney J. 1974. Aristotle and the Problem of Value. In *Aristotle: The Classical Heritage of Rhetoric*, ed. Keith V. Erickson, 102–16. Metuchen, N.J.: Scarecrow Press.

Ober, Josiah. 1989. *Mass and Elite in Democratic Athens: Rhetoric, Ideology, and the Power of the People*. Princeton: Princeton University Press.

Oldfather, C. H., trans. 1954. *Diodorus of Sicily*. Vol. 6. Cambridge, Mass.: Harvard University Press.

Ong, Walter J. 1982. *Orality and Literacy: The Technologizing of the Word*. London: Methuen.

Oravec, Christine. 1976. "Observation" in Aristotle's Theory of Epideictic. *Philosophy and Rhetoric* 9: 162–74.

Ostwald, Martin. 1986. *From Popular Sovereignty to the Sovereignty of Law: Law, Society, and Politics in Fifth-Century Athens*. Berkeley: University of California Press.

O'Sullivan, Neil. 1992. *Alcidamas, Aristophanes, and the Beginnings of Greek Stylistic Theory*. Stuttgart: Steiner, 1992.

———. 1993. Plato and *hē kaloumenē rhētorikē. Mnemosyne* 46: 87–89.

———. 1996. Written and Spoken in the First Sophistic. In *Voice into Text: Orality and Literacy in Ancient Greece,* ed. Ian Worthington, 115–27. Leiden: Brill.

Otterlo, W. A. A. van. 1944. *Untersuchungen über Begriff, Anwendung, und Entstehung der griechischen Ringkompositionen*. Amsterdam: Mededeelingen der Nederlandsche Akademie van Wetenschappen, Afdeeling Letterkunde. N.S. pt. 7 no. 3.

Oudemans, T. C. W., and A. P. M. H. Lardinois. 1987. *Tragic Ambiguity: Anthropology, Philosophy and Sophocles' Antigone*. Leiden: E. J. Brill.

Papillon, Terry L. 1995. Isocrates' *Techne* and Rhetorical Pedagogy. *Rhetoric Society Quarterly* 25: 149–63.

———. 1996. Isocrates on Gorgias and Helen: The Unity of the *Helen. Classical Journal* 91: 377–91.

Perelman, Chaïm, and Lucie Olbrechts-Tyteca. 1969. *The New Rhetoric: A Treatise on Argumentation*. Trans. J. Wilkinson and P. Weaver. Notre Dame, Ind.: Notre Dame University Press.

Pilz, Werner. 1934. *Der Rhetor im attischen Staat*. Weida: Thomas and Hubert.

Pirsig, Robert M. 1974. *Zen and the Art of Motorcycle Maintenance*. New York: Morrow.

Poulakos, John. 1983a. Aristotle's Indebtedness to the Sophists. In *Argument in Transition: Proceedings of the Third Summer Conference on Argumentation,* ed. David Zarefsky, Malcolm O. Sillars, and Jack Rhodes, 27–42. Annandale, Va.: Speech Communication Association.

———. 1983b. Gorgias' *Encomium to Helen* and the Defense of Rhetoric. *Rhetorica* 1: 1–16.

———. 1983c. Toward a Sophistic Definition of Rhetoric. *Philosophy and Rhetoric* 16: 35–48.

———. 1984. Rhetoric, the Sophists, and the Possible. *Communication Monographs* 51: 215–26.

———. 1986. Gorgias's and Isocrates' Use of the Encomium. *Southern Speech Communication Journal* 51: 300–307.

———. 1987. Sophistical Rhetoric as a Critique of Culture. In *Argument and Critical Practice,* ed. Joseph W. Wenzel, 97–101. Annandale, Va.: Speech Communication Association.

——. 1990. Interpreting Sophistical Rhetoric: A Response to Schiappa. *Philosophy and Rhetoric* 23: 218–28.

——. 1995. *Sophistical Rhetoric in Classical Greece*. Columbia: South Carolina University Press.

Poulakos, Takis. 1987. Isocrates's Use of Narrative in the *Evagoras:* Epideictic Rhetoric and Moral Action. *Quarterly Journal of Speech* 73: 317–28.

——. 1988. Towards a Cultural Understanding of Classical Epideictic Oratory. *Pre/Text* 9: 147–65.

——. 1989a. Intellectuals and the Public Sphere: The Case of the Older Sophists. In *Spheres of Argument*, ed. Bruce E. Gronbeck, 9–15. Annandale, Va.: Speech Communication Association.

——. 1989b. The Historical Intervention of Gorgias' Epitaphios: The Genre of Funeral Oration and the Athenian Institution of Public Burials. *Pre/Text* 10: 90–99.

——. 1990. Historiographies of the Tradition of Rhetoric: A Brief History of Classical Funeral Orations. *Western Journal of Speech Communication* 54: 172–88.

——. 1997. *Speaking for the Polis: Isocrates' Rhetorical Education*. Columbia: South Carolina University Press.

Powell, J. Enoch. 1977. *A Lexicon to Herodotus*. 2d ed. Hildesheim: Georg Olms.

Quandahl, Ellen. 1989. What Is Plato? Inference and Allusion in Plato's *Sophist. Rhetoric Review* 7: 338–48.

Rabe, Hugo. 1931. *Prolegomenon Sylloge, Rhetores Graeci*. XIV. Leipzig: Teubner.

Race, William H. 1981. The Word *kairos* in Greek Drama. *Transactions of the American Philological Association* 111: 197–213.

——. 1987. Pindaric Encomium and Isokrates' *Evagoras. Transactions of the American Philological Association* 117: 131–55.

Rackham, H. 1937. *Rhetorica ad Alexandrum*. Cambridge, Mass.: Harvard University Press.

Radermacher, Ludwig. 1951. Artium scriptores: Reste der voraristotelischen Rhetorik. *Osterreichische Akademie der Wissenschaften: Philosophisch-historische Klasse,* Sitzungsberichte, 227. Band 3 (1951) B XXII 15 (135–41).

Reckford, Kenneth J. 1987. *Aristophanes' Old-and-New Comedy*. Vol. 1. Chapel Hill: University of North Carolina Press.

Reid, Robert S. 1997. "Neither Oratory nor Dialogue": Dionysius of Halicarnassus and the Genre of Plato's *Apology. Rhetoric Society Quarterly* 27: 63–90.

Rhode, Erwin. 1925. *Psyche: The Cult of Souls and Belief in Immortality among the Greeks*. Trans. W. B. Hillis. London: Routledge and Kegan Paul.

Ricoeur, Paul. 1981. *Hermeneutics and the Human Sciences*. Ed. and trans. John B. Thompson. Cambridge: Cambridge University Press.

Ricoeur, Paul. 1976. *Interpretation Theory: Discourse and the Surplus of Meaning*. Fort Worth: Texas Christian University Press.

Rist, John M. 1989. *The Mind of Aristotle: A Study in Philosophical Growth*. Toronto: University of Toronto Press.

Robb, Kevin. 1994. *Literacy and Paideia in Ancient Greece*. New York: Oxford University Press.

Roberts, W. Rhys. 1932. Demetrius. In *Aristotle: The Poetics, "Longinus": On the Sublime, Demestrius: On Style*. Cambridge, Mass.: Harvard University Press.

Roberts, Jennifer Tolbert. 1994. *Athens on Trial: The Anti-Democratic Tradition in Western Thought*. Princeton: Princeton University Press.

Robin, Léon. 1985 [1933]. Introduction. In *Phedre/Platon*, i–ccxxxiii. Paris: Les Belles Lettres.

Robinson, John M. 1973. On Gorgias. In *Exegesis and Argument*, ed. E. N. Lee, A. P. D. Mourelatos, R. M. Rorty, 49–60. Assen: Van Gorcum.

Robinson, Richard. 1953. *Plato's Earlier Dialectic*. 2d ed. Oxford: Clarendon.

———. 1977. A Sophist on Omniscience, Polymathy, and Omnicompetence: D. L. 8.1–13. *Illinois Classical Studies* 7: 125–35.

Robinson, Thomas M. 1979. *Contrasting Arguments: An Edition of the DISSOI LOGOI*. Salem, N.H.: Ayer.

Rogers, B. B. 1924. *Aristophanes*. 3 vols. Cambridge, Mass.: Harvard University Press.

Rogers, Carl R. 1980. *A Way of Being*. Boston: Houghton Mifflin.

Rorty, Amélie Oksenberg, ed. 1996. *Essays on Aristotle's Rhetoric*. Berkeley: University of California Press.

Rorty, Richard. 1979. *Philosophy and the Mirror of Nature*. Princeton: Princeton University Press.

———. 1984. The Historiography of Philosophy: Four Genres. In *Philosophy in History: Essays on the Historiography of Philosophy*, ed. Richard Rorty, J. B. Schneewind, Quentin Skinner, 49–75. Cambridge: Cambridge University Press.

———. 1989. *Contingency, Irony, and Solidarity*. Cambridge: Cambridge University Press.

———. 1991. *Objectivity, Relativism, and Truth*. Cambridge: Cambridge University Press.

———. 1992a. The Pragmatist's Progress. In *Interpretation and Overinterpretation*, ed. Stefan Collini, 89–108. Cambridge: Cambridge University Press.

———. 1992b. A Pragmatist View of Rationality and Cultural Difference. *Philosophy East and West* 42: 581–96.

Rosch, Eleanor. 1988. Coherences and Categorization: A Historical View. In *The Development of Language and Language Researchers*, ed. Frank S. Kessell, 373–92. Hillsdale, N.J.: Lawrence Erlbaum.

Rosenmeyer, Thomas G. 1955. Gorgias, Aeschylus, and *Apate*. *American Journal of Philology* 76: 225–60.

Rowe, C. J. 1986. *Plato: PHAEDRUS*. Warminster: Aris and Phillips.

Rummel, Erika. 1979. Isocrates' Ideal of Rhetoric: Criteria of Evaluation. *Classical Journal* 75: 25–35.

Russo, Jospeh. 1983. The Poetics of the Ancient Greek Proverb. *Journal of Folklore Research* 20: 121–30.

Sandys, John. 1937. *The Odes of Pindar*. Cambridge, Mass.: Harvard University Press.

Schiappa, Edward. 1989. "Spheres of Argument" as *Topoi* for the Critical Study of Power/Knowledge. In *Spheres of Argument: Proceedings of the Sixth Biennial Conference on Argumentation*, ed. Bruce Gronbeck, 47–56. Annandale, Va.: Speech Communication Association.

———. 1990a. Did Plato Coin *Rhetorike? American Journal of Philology* 111: 457–70.

———. 1990b. Neo-Sophistic Rhetorical Criticism or the Historical Reconstruction of Sophistic Doctrines? *Philosophy and Rhetoric* 22: 192–217.

———. 1990c. History and Neo-Sophistic Criticism: A Reply to Poulakos. *Philosophy and Rhetoric* 23: 307–15.

———. 1991. *Protagoras and Logos: A Study in Greek Philosophy and Rhetoric.* Columbia: University of South Carolina Press.

———. 1993. Arguing About Definitions. *Argumentation* 7: 403–17.

———. 1995. Protagoras and the Language Game of History: A Response to Consigny. *Rhetoric Society Quarterly* 25: 220–23.

———. 1996. Some of My Best Friends Are Neosophists: A Reply to Consigny. *Rhetoric Review* 14: 272–79.

Schmalzriedt, Egidius. 1970. *Peri Physeos: zur Frühgeschichte der Buchtitel.* Munich: Wilhelm Fink.

Scholes, Robert. 1985. *Textual Power.* New Haven: Yale University Press.

Sealey, Raphael. 1976. *A History of the Greek City States 700–338 B.C.* Berkeley: University of California Press.

Segal, Charles P. 1962. Gorgias and the Psychology of the Logos. *Harvard Studies in Classical Philology* 66: 99–155.

Simons, Herbert W., ed. 1990. *The Rhetorical Turn.* Chicago: University of Chicago Press.

Sinclair, R. K. 1988. *Democracy and Participation in Athens.* Cambridge: Cambridge University Press.

Smeltzer, Mark A. 1996. Gorgias on Arrangement: A Search for Pragmatism Amidst the Art and Epistemology of Gorgias of Leontini. *Southern Communication Journal* 61: 156–65.

Smith, Bromley. 1921a. Corax and Probability. *Quarterly Journal of Speech* 7: 13–42.

———. 1921b. Gorgias: A Study in Oratorical Style. *Quarterly Journal of Speech* 7: 335–59.

Smith, Charles Forster, trans. 1919–23. *Thucydides.* 4 volumes. Cambridge, Mass.: Harvard University Press.

Smith, Mary M., Peter E. Morris, Philip Levy, and Andrew W. Ellis. 1987. *Cognition in Action.* Hillsdale, N.J.: Lawrence Erlbaum.

Snell, Bruno. 1953. *The Discovery of the Mind.* Trans. T. G. Rosenmeyer. Oxford: Basil Blackwell.

Solmsen, Friedrich. 1966. Review of Havelock, Preface to Plato. *American Journal of Philology* 87: 99–105.

———. 1975. *Intellectual Experiments of the Greek Enlightenment.* Princeton: Princeton University Press.

———. 1979. Review of Kassel, Aristoteles "Ars rhetorica." *Classical Philology* 74:68–72.

Sprague, Rosamond Kent, ed. 1972. *The Older Sophists.* Columbia: University of South Carolina Press.

Stadter, P. A. 1973. *The Speeches in Thucydides: A Collection of Original Studies with a Bibliography.* Chapel Hill: University of North Carolina Press.

Stam, James H. 1980. An Historical Perspective on "Linguistic Relativity." In *Psychology of Language and Thought,* ed. R. W. Rieber, 239–62. New York: Plenum.

Starkie, W. J. M. 1911. *The Clouds of Aristophanes.* London: Macmillan.

Stone, I. F. 1988. *The Trial of Socrates.* New York: Little, Brown.

Storey, Ian C. 1993. The Dates of Aristophanes' *Clouds* II and Eupolis' *Baptai:* A Reply to E. C. Kopff. *American Journal of Philology* 114: 71–84.

Striker, Gisela. 1996. *Essays on Hellenistic Epistemology and Ethics.* Cambridge: Cambridge University Press.

Sutton, Jane. 1992. The Taming of *Polos/Polis:* Rhetoric as an Achievement Without Woman. *Southern Communication Journal* 57: 100–110.

Swartz, Omar. 1997. *Conducting Socially Responsible Research: Critical Theory, Neo-Pragmatism, and Rhetorical Inquiry.* Thousand Oaks, Calif.: Sage.

Swearingen, C. Jan. 1986. Literate Rhetors and Their Illiterate Audiences: The Orality of Early Literacy. *Pre/Text* 7: 145–62.

Tarán, Leonardo. 1965. *Parmenides.* Princeton: Princeton University Press.

Taylor, C. C. W. 1976. *Plato,* PROTAGORAS: *Translated with Notes.* Oxford: Clarendon Press.

Thomas, Carol G., and Edward Kent Webb. 1994. From Orality to Rhetoric: An Intellectual Transformation. In *Persuasion: Greek Rhetoric in Action,* ed. Ian Worthington, 3–25. London: Routledge.

Thomas, Rosalind. 1989. *Oral Tradition and Written Record in Classical Athens.* Cambridge: Cambridge University Press.

———. 1992. *Literacy and Orality in Ancient Greece.* Cambridge: Cambridge University Press.

Tompkins, D. P. 1969. Stylistic Characterization in Thucydides. Ph.D. diss., Yale University.

Thompson, W. H. 1871. *The* GORGIAS *of Plato.* London: Whittaker.

Timmerman, David M. 1993. Ancient Greek Origins of Argumentation Theory: Plato's Transformation of *Dialegesthai* to Dialectic. *Argumentation and Advocacy* 29: 116–23.

———. 1996. Epideictic Oratory. In *Encyclopedia of Rhetoric and Composition,* ed. Theresa Enos, 228–31. New York: Garland.

———. 1998. Isocrates' Competing Conceptualization of Philosophy. *Philosophy and Rhetoric* 31: 145–59.

Tod, Marcus N., ed. 1985 [1946–1948]. *Greek Historical Inscriptions.* New ed. Chicago: Ares Publishers.

Too, Yun Lee. 1995. *The Rhetoric of Identity in Isocrates.* Cambridge: Cambridge University Press.

Toulmin, Stephen. 1958. *The Uses of Argument.* Cambridge: Cambridge University Press.

———. 1988. The Recovery of Practical Philosophy. *The American Scholar* 57: 343–50.

Trevett, J. C. 1996. Aristotle's Knowledge of Athenian Oratory. *Classical Quarterly* 46: 371–79.

Turner, E. G. 1977. *Athenian Books in the Fifth and Fourth Centuries B.C.* 2d ed. London: H. K. Lewis.

Untersteiner, Mario. 1949–1962. *Sofisti: testimonianze e frammenti,* 4 vols. Firenze: La Nuova Italia.

Untersteiner, Mario. 1954. *The Sophists.* Trans. K. Freeman. Oxford: Basil Blackwell.

Usher, Stephen, trans. 1974. *Dionysius of Halicarnassus.* Cambridge, Mass.: Harvard University Press.

Van Hook, Larue. 1913. The Encomium on Helen, by Gorgias. *The Cl assical Weekly* 6: 122–23.

———. 1945. *Isocrates.* Vol. 3. Cambridge, Mass.: Harvard University Press.

Verdenius, W. J. 1964. *Parmenides: Some Comments on His Poem.* Amsterdam: Hakkert.

Verdenius, W. J. 1981. Gorgias' Doctrine of Deception. In *The Sophists and Their Legacy,* ed. G. B. Kerferd, 116–28. Wiesbaden: Steiner.

Verrall, A. W. 1880. Korax and Tisias. *Journal of Philology* 9: 197–210.

Versenyi, Lazlo. 1962. Protagoras' Man-Measure Fragment. *American Journal of Philology* 83: 178–84.

Vickers, Brian. 1988. *In Defence of Rhetoric.* Oxford: Clarendon.

Vitanza, Victor J. 1997. *Negation, Subjectivity, and the History of Rhetoric.* Albany: State University of New York Press.

Wagner, Russell H. 1922. The Rhetorical Theory of Isocrates. *Quarterly Journal of Speech* 8: 328–37.

Waithe, Mary Ellen, ed. 1987. *A History of Women Philosophers.* Dordrecht: Nijhoff.

Walz, Christianus. 1832–1836. *Rhetores Graeci.* 9 vols. Stuttgart: J. G. Cotta.

Wardy, Robert. 1996. *The Birth of Rhetoric: Gorgias, Plato and Their Successors.* London: Routledge.

Waters, K. H. 1985. *Herodotus the Historian: His Problems, Methods and Originality.* London: Croom Helm.

Weaver, Richard M. [1953] 1985. *The Ethics of Rhetoric.* Davis, Calif.: Hermagoras.

Welch, Kathleen E. 1990. *The Contemporary Reception of Classical Rhetoric.* Hillsdale, N.J.: Lawrence Erlbaum.

West, Cornel. 1989. *The American Evasion of Philosophy: A Genealogy of Pragmatism.* Madison: University of Wisconsin Press.

Whorf, Benjamin Lee. 1956. *Language, Thought, and Reality.* Cambridge, Mass.: MIT Press.

Wilcox, Stanley. 1942. The Scope of Early Rhetorical Instruction. *Harvard Studies in Classical Philology* 46: 121–55.

———. 1943a. Corax and the *Prolegomena. American Journal of Philology* 64: 1–23.

———. 1943b. Criticisms of Isocrates and His *Philosophia. Transactions and Proceedings of the American Philological Association* 74: 113–33.

Willard, Charles Arthur. 1989. *A Theory of Argumentation.* Tuscaloosa: University of Alabama Press.

Wood, Neal. 1988. *Cicero's Social and Political Thought.* Berkeley: University of California Press.

Wooten, Cecil W. 1987. *Hermogenes' "On Types of Style."* Chapel Hill: University of North Carolina Press.

Worthington, Ian. 1992. *A Historical Commentary on Dinarchus: Rhetoric and Conspiracy in Later Fourth-Century Athens.* Ann Arbor: University of Michigan Press.

———. 1996. Greek Oratory and the Oral/Literate Division. In *Voice into Text: Orality and Literacy in Ancient Greece,* ed. Ian Worthington, 165–77. Leiden: Brill.

Wright, W. C. 1921. *Philostratus and Eunapius.* Cambridge, Mass.: Harvard University Press.

Wyller, Egil A. 1991. Plato's Concept of Rhetoric in the *Phaedrus* and Its Tradition in Antiquity. *Symbolae Osloenses* 66: 50–60.

Ziolkowski, John E. 1981. *Thucydides and the Tradition of Funeral Speeches at Athens.* Salem, N.H.: Ayer.

Zucker, Friedrich. 1956. Der Stil des Gorgias nach seiner innerem Form. *Preussische Akademie der Wissenschaften Philosophisch-historische Klasse, Sitzungsberichte* 1: 3– 19.

Index